MAKING MEMORIES

Making Memories

Recipes, Cooking
Lessons, and Stories
from a
Home Economics Teacher

Verna Craig Shelton

Making Memories
Recipes, Cooking Lessons, and Stories from a Home Economics Teacher

iUniverse books may be ordered through booksellers or by contacting:

iUniverse
1663 Liberty Drive
Bloomington, IN 47403
www.iuniverse.com
1-800-Authors (1-800-288-4677)

ISBN: 978-1-4620-5790-0 (sc)
ISBN: 978-1-4620-5792-4 (hc)
ISBN: 978-1-4620-5791-7 (e)

Printed in the United States of America

iUniverse rev. date: 1/24/2012

For my parents, siblings, family, and friends,
and especially for those countless students
who filled my life with joy, satisfaction, and more.
God's blessing to you all—always.

MONDAY'S CHILD

A Mother Goose Nursery Rhyme

Monday's child is fair of face,
Tuesday's child is full of grace,
Wednesday's child is full of woe,
Thursday's child has far to go.
Friday's child is loving and giving,
Saturday's child works hard for a living,
But the child born on the Sabbath Day,
Is bonny and blithe, and good and gay.

ACKNOWLEDGMENTS

An expression of sincere gratitude and appreciation is sent to family and friends who allowed their recipes to be shared in Making Memories and gave their support and assistance.

A special thanks to Debbie at Ragú Photography for her photo editing skill, expertise, and time spent.

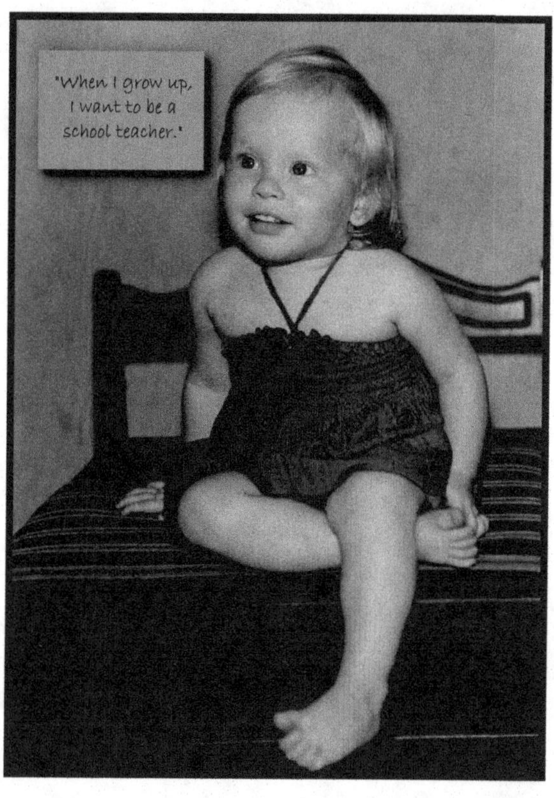

"The original photograph features a little girl sitting on her mother's dressing stool. She appears to be about two years old, too young to think about tomorrow or understand the complexity of the world today. Upon studying the photograph, you can't help but notice the look of wonder and amazement on the child's face, yet her eyes show determination. She sits with her little legs casually crossed, waiting for the future. The Xerox copy of the photograph is much larger, mounted on a black poster board; the caption reads, 'When I grow up, I want to be a school teacher.' This work of art was part of my family's celebration of my fortieth birthday. Afterward, it hung on the wall in my classroom as a clear reminder that teaching is what I have always wanted to do, a teacher is what I always wanted to be."

Excerpt from Teacher of the Year Essay
written by Mrs. Shelton

CONTENTS

MY STORY

I am a Friday's child–loving and giving, and no doubt that explains how I came upon the teaching profession. I've learned to like my middle name, freckles, and strawberry blonde hair although I was subjected to being called Peachtree by the older boys on the bus who, by the way, stole my apples and ruined my musical career when they broke my drumsticks. I was the second child, the second girl, to bless my parents. They married at a young age. Mother was only seventeen and a recent valedictorian, and Daddy a twenty-two-year-old middle child of a farming family. Mama and Daddy were both full-blooded Germans–neither could speak English when they started school. My sister Elaine, who likes to be called first-born, led the way for me. When I was two years old, we moved to the country and lived in a little three-room house with tarpaper siding that looked like brick. Our home featured both a front and a back porch. We had cold running water and a washhouse in the back yard where we took baths in a big aluminum tub in the summertime. Our outhouse was through a gate beside the washhouse in the pasture with the cows.

Me, my doll, and my dog sitting on the front porch of our three-room house.

Several years down the road, the third girl, Debbie, blessed our family and Mama and Daddy moved their bed into the living room. Still wanting a boy, and since their bed was in a separate room now, the fourth child became imminent. That's about the time we traded houses with my paternal grandparents who lived a couple of hundred yards away under some huge old oak trees. We moved just in time, too, as the fourth and last child, David, was born a few weeks later. Our new big house had hot and cold running water and a full bathroom. A breezeway connected the house to our two-car garage which boasted a hard, dirt floor. There was a circle driveway that Daddy once claimed Santa landed his airplane on while we had gone with him to get his hair cut on Christmas Eve. We had presents under the tree and tracks to prove his claim! Daddy moved the old washhouse into our backyard and put up a triple clothesline. I can still remember Mama's arm getting stuck in the wringer of our new washing machine–it scared us kids to death.

My family at Grandma Simon's house: Daddy is holding our bouncing baby boy, David. Elaine is beside Mama and Debbie is in front of her. I'm standing on the left by my Daddy. It must have been Grandma's birthday or Mother's Day since we came bearing flowers.

Not many people have a clear picture of their future, but it seems I did. Mama tells the story about me being in Vacation Bible School when I was about five years old. Evidently I told my teacher, the pastor's wife, that I wanted to be a school teacher when I grew up. Mama says that's all I ever wanted to be. For my fortieth birthday party, my siblings made gigantic blowups of all my grade school pictures. I wore the same pair of glasses from the fourth thru the eighth grade! Those pictures weren't very flattering, but the one of me on Mama's dressing stool at about age two stole my heart. They had it glued to a black poster board and written in white beside it was, "When I grow up I want to be a school teacher." After the party, I laminated the whole thing and it hung in my classroom where I could see it every day.

While some claim to remember events like cutting their first tooth, one of my most vivid and earliest memories is my Grandpa Simon helping me put the silverware in a white metal kitchen drawer at our big house. I recall learning to cook in that kitchen with its green linoleum countertop, metal cabinets, porcelain sink and drainboards, a freestanding gas range and tiny refrigerator, plus a kitchen table with six chairs, three doorways, and two windows. Surely this crowded little kitchen led me to my love of cooking. Now that I think about it, that kitchen played a significant role in my life.

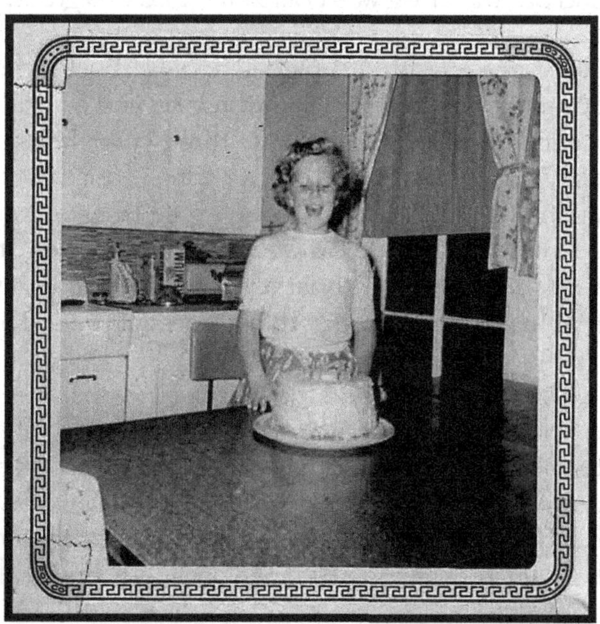

My first-born sister, Elaine, blows out her birthday candles in the kitchen of our big house. Notice those metal cabinets.

I joined 4-H at the age of nine and their foods show was a great venue for me to show off my budding cooking skills. I don't recall what my first entry was, but I do remember the first dress revue. I sewed a blue, black, and white plaid dress with a zipper, waistline, and set-in sleeves. Thank goodness Mama had already sewn all the flour sacks into dresses for Elaine and me when we were little–I got to choose store-bought fabrics for my endeavors. Making my own clothing was fun and challenging. My skills progressed quite nicely and I enjoyed cooking and sewing a lot more than playing doctor in the washhouse.

Mama went to work three days a week when Debbie started school and Grandma kept David. Good thing we got a phone at about that time because every afternoon we'd call Mama at the grocery store where she worked to get our instructions for cooking supper. We remained farm folks, with a huge garden, chicken house, hog pen, and cows. We shelled corn that Daddy grew, entered fryers in the county fair, and even processed our own meat. We travelled extensively as we attended church in Cypress every Sunday, bought our groceries in Tomball, and went to school in Waller. Add the occasional trips to shop at Sears and Penneys or to visit relatives on a Sunday afternoon and our travel log was complete. Life was great!

Just before I entered high school we built a new pink brick home—a 60s-style ranch with two bathrooms and an attic fan. It's almost in the identical spot where our little three-room house used to stand. It was planned to fit among the oak trees I remember helping Daddy plant when I was little-bitty. Today those trees are gigantic and awesomely beautiful. I don't know where time has gone; Grandma Simon used to say, "It seems like Christmas comes every two weeks!" It's not quite that fast for me yet, but things certainly seem to move right along.

I've already mentioned that my music career was shot. Well, I was never destined to be an athlete either, always being chosen last for any team. I even fell out of swings and crashed my new bike into the front porch. People my age or history buffs might be familiar with President Kennedy's Physical Fitness Program. At the end of its second year, half again as many students passed a physical fitness test as had a year earlier. I was not one of those students. I remember it well–being in the ninth grade and dead last to finish the 600 yard run, but the softball throw was my nemesis. My PE teacher sent me to the principal's office for insubordination. She thought I was just throwing the ball nine yards to make fun of her. I'm still waiting for someone to teach me how to throw a ball. That trip to the office did direct my life: Fessor (our affectionate name for the principal) never made me take physical education again. I got to work in the office instead–another step toward my inevitable career choice. I spent all my public school years in the same school district, taking homemaking every year in high school. I pretty much taught all my friends how to cook and sew. It still irks me that Donna, one of my best friends, won the Betty Crocker award though. She'll even admit she doesn't know how that happened. Maybe I was already developing some teaching skills.

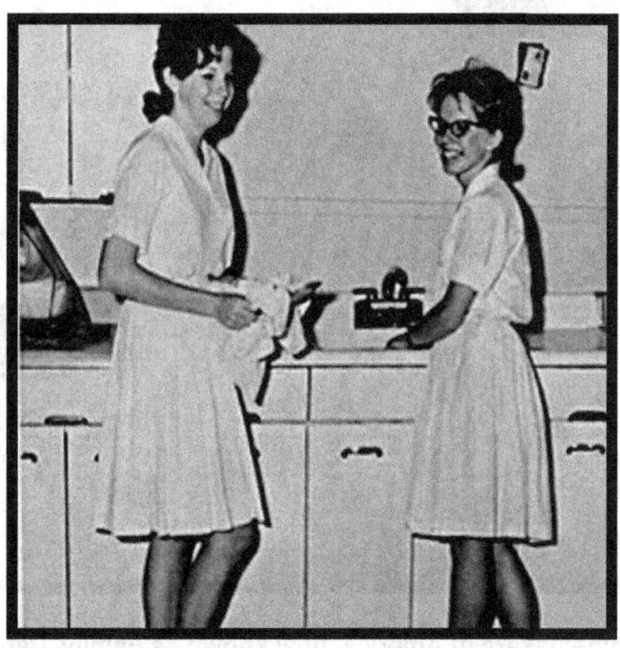

Best friend Donna and I are wearing our pep squad outfits in the homemaking kitchen one Friday. You've got to love the metal cabinets, porcelain sink, and linoleum countertops. They're just like the ones that were in my big house.

High school was a fairly idealogical time for me. Future Homemakers of America was my main heartthrob. Serving as president my senior year cemented my goal of becoming a teacher and helping youth find their place not only in school, but also in life. These pictures aren't the clearest, but show a glimpse of how it was.

Future Homemakers of America, now known as Family, Career, and Community Leaders of America, played a huge role in my life as a student–it provided my identity. This collage shows activities during my senior year as president of FHA: a tea for the faculty, monthly FHA meetings, school board dinner, eating food we prepared in the classroom, and modeling garments we made in our style show.

Following in Mama's footsteps, I graduated as valedictorian. It was easy to make 100s in homemaking and my friends were taking things like calculus and physics. I was privileged to attend college and began working to fulfill my dream of being a teacher. The only major that was ever on my radar screen was home economics. I'll never forget the thrill and fright of loading the truck with my belongings, including my cabinet sewing machine, and Mama and Daddy driving me to my college dorm at Lamar State College of Technology. After the two-hour drive, they left me to fend for myself. Two years later I transferred to Sam Houston State Teacher's College, a little closer to home and a little closer to the Aggie I was dating. My student teaching was conducted at an old rival school where Daddy was afraid our truck would get vandalized so he made me remove our hometown bulldog decals. I married the Aggie, finished my final semester, graduated cum laude, and began my teaching career at my alma mater, dear old Waller High School, replacing my high school homemaking teacher.

America experienced many dramatic changes during my youth. We really did practice tucking ourselves under our desk in case of a nuclear attack. Fallout shelters, the Bay of Pigs, the Berlin Wall, the Beatles, the first manned space flight for the US, the Kennedy assassination, civil rights demonstrations, and affordable televisions all bombarded our young psyches. My graduating class of 1967 was the first integrated class to leave our high school. A new generation of teaching was coming forth as schools across America faced total integration–a merging of different cultures. Coming back as a teacher four years later and facing racial tension required a totally unfamiliar mindset. I will forever be thankful to my mentor, Mrs. Fuller, a teacher who saw no color, for standing beside me as together we navigated through these trying times. She took this still wet-behind-the-ears teacher under her loving wing and helped me learn to fly. Without her, I'm not sure my career would have ever made it off the ground.

A couple of years later, I was in the family way and curious about maternity leave. Waller had no such policy when another pregnant teacher and I broached the subject. We were told to submit our leave request to the school board. Being from a stout Baptist community, the school board awarded us a year off with no pay and a guarantee of our same job back when we returned, telling us "women in our condition should not be in front of children." Never mind the fact that we were properly married before even a "twinkle of an eye" had entered our lives. This was 1971 folks! My how times have changed.

I have two beautiful daughters. The youngest, Jennie, is a marketing executive, a great cook, and is waiting for Mr. Right. My firstborn, Julie, another great cook, is a geophysicist, grows a garden, and cans food.

Julie and Jennie, my beautiful daughters, have grown up to be beautiful young women. This has always been one of my favorite pictures.

Julie and her husband have provided me with the absolute loves of my life. My grandson Peyton, who is eleven and almost as tall as I am, already wears a size eleven men's shoe and is way above average intelligence. He was just under the age of two when he pointed to the water collected on the outside of the morning room window and said, "condensation." My six year old granddaughter Lydia, who is learning to cook, can already roll and cut sugar cookies almost as good as her mom and I. Lydia started teaching at a very young age, informing Grampa that he would have to be her student because the teddy bears were being bad and wouldn't listen. She tells me I am a very good student and gives me stickers all the time. Last weekend she called to play school over the phone–she's only in kindergarten. Maybe she has teachers blood flowing through her veins just like me.

I've lived through the dreaded divorce, experienced being single again to its fullest, and am now married to Gary, the love of my life who takes care of me and loves me back even more. He is learning to be my sous chef. How awesome is that? He peels, chops, tastes, stirs, eats, and helps clean up the kitchen. Could I ask for anything more?

Mama's always said she doesn't know how I put up with students; she says she would probably have to strangle them. Although I came close to doing just that, I agree with a recent report that teaching is the third highest career when it comes to job satisfaction. Surely, part of that is because spring break and Christmas vacation are pretty much a guaranteed event every year. These, combined with summer vacation, help teachers maintain their sanity.

I spent a total of 44 years in the Waller Independent School District, 26 of those years teaching in the same classroom where I once studied home economics–with the metal drawers and cabinets, linoleum countertops, and porcelain sinks with built-in drainboards just like my big house and that metal drawer Grandpa Simon and I filled long ago.

When a bond issue finally passed to build a new high school, I was called upon to help plan it. Having a hand in orchestrating our new department put me in home economics heaven. The result was that my last six years were spent in a new, highly organized, efficient lab. So, doing the math reveals that I taught home economics for 32 years. I retired when I just didn't want to do it any more. Dear old compadres have asked me how I knew it was time to throw in the towel and hang up my lab coat. My answer is simple: you just know.

Since retiring, I've tried my hand at building a design business with sister Elaine and working as a home party consultant selling kitchen products, home decor, and even jewelry. As a result, I have a beautifully decorated home with cabinets and closets full of gorgeous dishes and more jewelry than any one person can possibly wear. Finally, I realized that I retired so I could write a cookbook. So, here it is. I hope you derive just a little bit of the joy I've experienced while writing Making Memories as you read and use it.

Enjoy reading my stories and preparing my recipes.

Xoxoxoxo,

Verna

Gary and I toast the beginning of our life together. Celebrations of life's events are a family tradition.

COOKBOOK SYNOPSIS

Back in my day, all home economics majors were required to spend a semester living in the home management house for three hours credit. My stay was in the old president's mansion that stood in the center of campus right beside the student union. While a resident there, I rotated between jobs: upstairs housekeeper, downstairs housekeeper, cook, assistant cook, outside gardener, inside gardener, etc. There were ten of us along with the professor whom we affectionately called Honey Annie. Tricking day lilies to open at night and smuggling eggs from the ag farm were skills added to my ever-increasing database. Life with nine young women plus a live-in teacher was challenging. As cook I planned three meals a day, did all the shopping, prepared the meals, stayed within a strict budget, and kept up with my other classes, too.

My favorite recipes from this era are identified as **Home Management Special**. What an education. As I think back, everyone should have to do this–life just might not be complete without experiencing a "Honey Annie" going over their open, metal bedspring with a white glove. She lowered my grade because her glove picked up a speck of rust. I was an overachiever, but that was out of my control!

~ XOXOXO ~

In the beginning, most students arrived in my class with a basic knowledge of measuring and cooking. After all, it was the early 70s—life was fairly simple with three meals a day and the family sitting down to eat supper together. It was easy to teach students to prepare the items I have identified as **Classroom Standard**. These recipes, the same recipes I prepared in those kitchens, taught the basics of measuring and simple cooking terms and techniques. Students set the table and sat down to eat their finished products, giving me a small sample to taste as a part of their grade. Arriving late to the next class was tolerated as long as it didn't happen too often, especially if they were accompanied by a sample of their finished product.

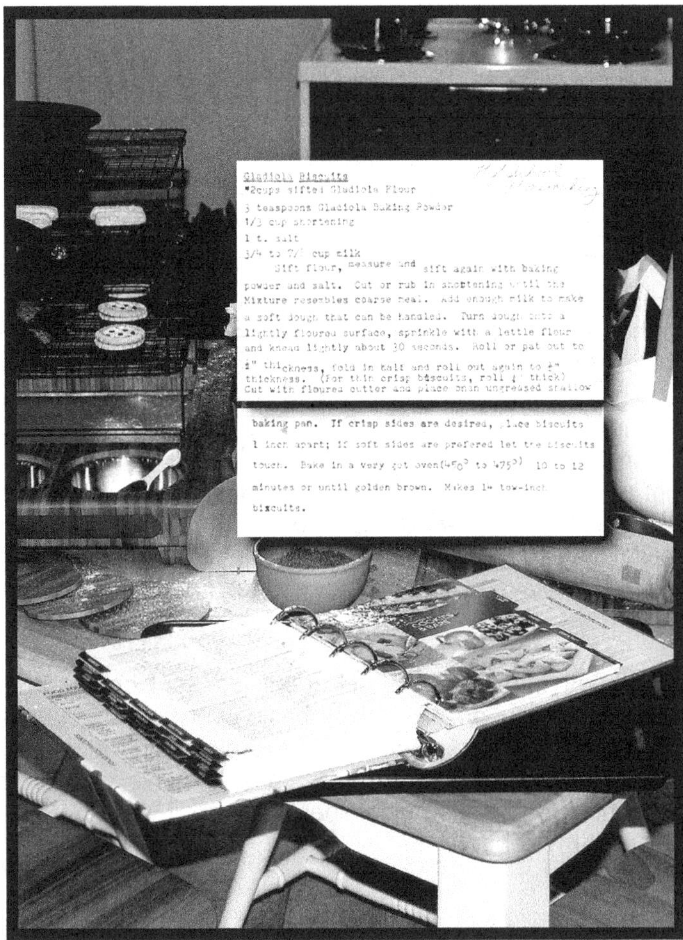

This biscuit recipe, with it's tattered corners and splotches, takes me back to a place where all is right with the world.

~ XOXOXO ~

My personal favorites that students chose to prepare are identified as **From the Food Lab**. These recipes are more adventuresome, including things like pie crust and yeast breads, and involve more technical skill–like the lost art of cutting up a chicken. Labs were planned one day and cooked the next. We had five kitchens and a single supply and food storage area. Ideally, there were four students per kitchen with each having specific tasks to accomplish. Exhibiting the true nature of a teacher–teach as much as possible, I required everyone to evaluate their learning and calculate the cost per serving of the dish prepared. Later, as fast foods, packaged mixes, and junk food ensconced themselves as staples in everyone's diet, nutrition became the main focus. Emphasis shifted to figuring the percentage of calories derived from fats, carbohydrates, and protein.

~ XOXOXO ~

As years went by and the class length grew shorter, the students' basic skills diminished and my classes grew larger. Recipes were simplified and students gobbled their food as they ran out the door and on to their next class. Today I wonder if basic cooking skills are even a part of the average person's repertoire. Considering the *throw a little of this in* attitude of television chefs, the teacher in me feels compelled to include bits and pieces of basic knowledge. I have included **lessons** and tips for preparing specific types of foods the inexperienced cook might need to know. Use your imagination and perhaps you can envision the classroom as we prepared for labs.

~ XOXOXO ~

Part of being a home economics teacher involved preparing and coordinating dinners, buffets, teas, (yes, teas, in the early years) and banquets. We had mother-daughter banquets, school board dinners, faculty lunches, fund-raising suppers, teacher appreciation breakfasts and luncheons, Veteran's Day receptions–the list goes on and on. Preparing dinners for 150 plus people is something I am sure those involved remember well. My two foot surgeries speak loud and clear, illustrating the work involved. School board dinners, a formal sit-down meal consisting of three to four courses with students serving as waiters and waitresses, were our favorite. Let's see–serve from the left, remove from the right, and never put your thumb in their plate. Recipes for all these events were diligently stored in a recipe box. Since catering became the norm and school board dinners had long since vanished when I retired, I brought that box home with me. You'll find the best of these recipes identified as **School Dinner Recipe**. Just remember we doubled, tripled, and even quadrupled them. Enjoy!

~ XOXOXO ~

It should be evident by now that I am a social animal that loves to entertain. My family has always had big get-togethers with friends and family: birthdays for young and old, baptisms, confirmations, fish fries, barbecues, 4th of July parties, Labor Day, Memorial Day, any day, Sunday dinners, more birthdays, anniversaries–get the picture? *We love to party!* The guest list was always extensive and everyone knew they would be welcomed with hugs, how are you's, and where have you beens. We danced on the concrete patio and carport. Everyone always brought their favorite beverage. And, as the saying goes, "A good time was had by all."

Whether hosting an event or just attending, food often takes center stage. While a home party consultant, I hosted many open houses and helped hosts plan their own home parties. Combine all these occasions with my teaching experiences and the result is an abundant collection of delicious, tried-and-true recipes. Since this is most likely the only cookbook I will ever write, all of my best recipes plus favorite recipes from family and close friends are included. These are an integral part of my life that I simply must share. Recipes from others are *identified by name or under Source* following the recipe. Unidentified recipes are my own favorites.

I have added historical food data and family secrets. Every recipe has been tested personally or the source speaks for itself, so use this cookbook without fear. If you are like me, you will try a recipe, examine the results, then tweak it a little. In all my years of teaching, there were very few recipes that turned out exactly the same. Sometimes it amazed me how different the results could be. So add your personal touch–your flair, along with your well-kept secrets, and make these recipes your own.

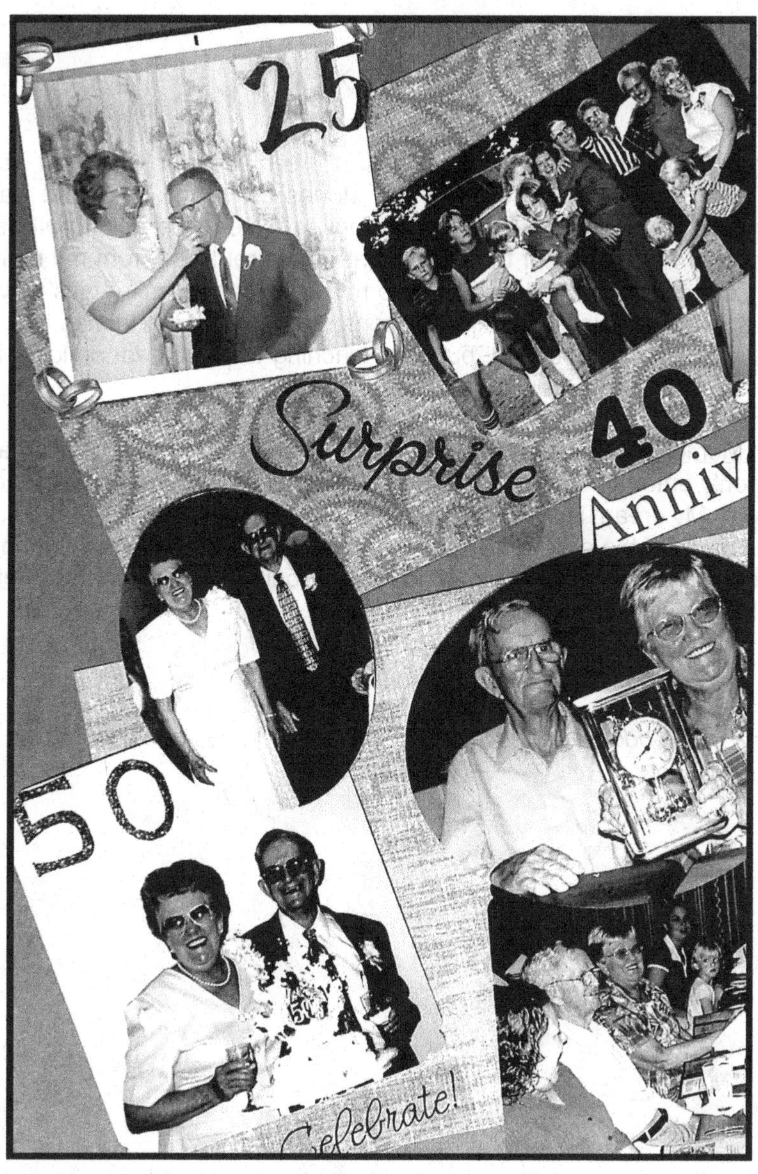

The big anniversary and birthday numbers always demand an extra-special celebration. We surprised Mama and Daddy with parties for their 25th and 40th anniversaries. Their 50th celebration was a big barbecue dinner complete with a dance. RV traveling friends of theirs came from far and wide. Their 60th anniversary was celebrated at our favorite German restaurant. Mama and Daddy were married 62 years.

~ XOXOXO ~

As I read cookbooks and magazines, I often wonder where a recipe originated. Personal recollections and stories are found in picture frames throughout. It has been a real mind-boggling experience getting all of this together and I am proud of the things that I have retrieved from my memory bank. Food is so intricately woven into my life experiences—that's why I've intermingled the recipes, cooking lessons, stories, and memories. It may seem a little discombobulated, but after teaching teenagers for so long, it's a wonder I am still sane–well, slightly sane.

Making Memories seems like it will always be a work in progress. Perhaps it will not only entertain and educate, but also inspire you to make memories of your own. My dream is that your pages will become as tattered, stained, and worn as many of the original recipes were. If you identify with something or a forgotten memory is jogged loose, immerse yourself in the moment: reflect, smile, laugh a little, enjoy.

"One of the oddest things in life, I think, is the things one remembers."
— Agatha Christie

BASIC SKILLS

There are some basic skills necessary for successful cooking and I spent many an hour teaching these to my students. One day I introduced a fundamentals of cooking lesson like this: "Did you hear about the farmer who was arrested and put in jail?" A wary student in the corner of the classroom replied, "No, Mrs. Craig, why was he arrested?" My answer, "He was caught beating the eggs and pulling the ears off the corn and..." elicited audible groans–one sly student suggested getting a straightjacket for me. Seriously, a working knowledge of cooking terms and skills involved is a must. I've even thrown in a few equivalent measurements and recipe ingredients. These will all work wonders for your cooking results. But first, just to clarify things, here is a list of accepted abbreviations used between these covers.

ABBREVIATIONS BETWEEN THESE COVERS

c. = cup
tsp. = teaspoon
T. = tablespoon
lb. = pound
oz. = ounce
pkg. = package
pt. = pint
qt. = quart
gal. = gallon
fl. = fluid

sq. = square
doz. = dozen
ea. = each
spk. = speck
f. g. = few grains
sm. = small
med. = medium
lg. = large
temp. = temperature

ACCURATE MEASURING

There are many measuring ideas and techniques out there. However, the procedures outlined here are used by home economists in test kitchens and I recommend that, for the best and most consistent results, they be followed.

EQUIPMENT

Use standard measuring cups and spoons, not coffee cups or soup spoons. While this may sound obvious, believe me, there are people out there who do not know the difference.

- Dry measuring cups usually have a handle of some sort and are packaged in a set of graduated sizes: ¼, ⅓, ½, and 1 cup. They have a flat top that can be leveled off. Dry measuring cups are also available with ⅔ and ¾ cups included in the set.
- Liquid measuring cups are generally clear with measurements marked on the sides of the cup. They come in sizes from 1 cup to 2 quarts or larger. They have space above the last measurement line so the liquid won't spill plus a spout for pouring.
- Measuring spoons are generally attached with a ring or magnets. They come in graduated sizes: ¼, ½, 1 teaspoon, and 1 tablespoon. The top surface of the spoon is flat so they can be leveled off. Diligent searching just might locate a set with an ⅛ teaspoon and ½ tablespoon included.
- A measuring spatula is a long, straight-sided spatula used for leveling dry measuring cups and measuring spoons when measuring dry ingredients. A dinner knife usually does not have a straight edge and should not be used for this task.

DRY MEASURING WITH CUPS

- Measure flour, sugar, cornmeal, etc., with these cups.
- Spoon the dry ingredients into the dry measuring cup.
- Level with spatula.
- When a recipe calls for *1 c. sifted flour*, either sift directly into the cup (without shaking the cup) or sift on to wax paper and spoon into the cup and level. If the recipe does not specify sifting, measure without sifting. When a recipe calls for *1 c. flour, sifted*, measure a cup of flour by spooning into dry measuring cup and leveling; then sift the entire amount. Sifting adds air, so there is less of the ingredient if it is sifted before measuring. Many recipes also call for sifting the dry ingredients together, in which case you would simply place them in the sifter and sift together after measuring.

DRY MEASURING WITH SPOONS

- Dip the spoon into ingredient.
- Level with spatula.
- Many ingredient containers, such as baking soda, baking powder, and spices, have a built-in straight edge for leveling.
- ⅛ is half of ¼, so if an ⅛ teaspoon measuring spoon is not available, use the ¼, fill and level; then use the rounded end of the spatula to scoop out half of the ingredient.

LIQUID MEASURING WITH CUPS

- Used for anything liquid that pours and seeks its own level.
- Follow these four steps to measure liquids:
  1. Use a liquid measuring cup.
  2. Place on a level surface and begin to fill.
  3. Bend down to view the measuring line at eye level.
  4. Look through the center of the cup and fill to specified level. The level on the side of the cup will be slightly higher, so look through the center of the cup for accuracy.

LIQUID MEASURING WITH SPOONS

- Pour the liquid into the measuring spoon until it forms a dome; add to recipe.
- Do not measure over the bowl of other ingredients. If the spoon is overfilled, the excess will be in the recipe and there is no way to determine how much was added.

INGREDIENTS PACKED INTO THE DRY MEASURING CUP

Use the back of a spoon to press into cup; level.

- Shortening
- Brown sugar
- Butter and margarine
- Peanut butter

INGREDIENTS LIGHTLY PRESSED INTO THE DRY MEASURING CUP

Fill cup and lightly press down with two fingers.

- Coconut
- Chopped nuts
- Cereals: dry oatmeal, Rice Krispies, cornflakes, etc.
- Bread or cracker crumbs

EQUIVALENTS

The first few days in the foods part of my high school homemaking class were spent copying information onto 4 x 6-inch recipe cards. It would be remiss of me to leave this out. Go ahead and pull out a pack of index cards and copy this information. After all, statistics prove that we remember much more of what we have written down. Reading over material after it has been written down vastly improves retention.

Dash = one shake of the container

Pinch = amount that can be grabbed with thumb and forefinger

Few grains = a sprinkle or just a few grains

3 tsp. = 1 T.

16 T. = 1 c.

2 c. = 1 pt.

2 pt. = 1 qt.

4 qt. = 1 gal.

1 c. = 8 fl. oz.

2 T. = 1 fl. oz.

1 pt. = 16 fl. oz.

1 qt. = 32 fl. oz.

1 gal. = 128 fl. oz. = approx. 16 servings tea or other beverage

16 oz. = 1 lb. (net weight)

1 stick butter or margarine = ½ cup = 8 T.

1 lb. butter or margarine = 2 c. = 4 sticks

1 lb. cheese = 4 c. cheese, grated

1 lb. flour = 4 c.

1 lb. sugar = 2 c.

1 lb. brown sugar = 2¼ c. (packed)

1 lb. powdered sugar = 4½ c. (sifted)

1 lb. shortening = 2½ c.

1 lb. cornmeal = 3 c.

1 can (14½ oz.) evaporated milk = 1⅔ c.

¼ lb. or 4 oz. chopped nuts = 1 c.

¼ lb. or 4 oz. marshmallows = 16 lg. marshmallows

28 finely crumbled salted crackers = 1 c. crumbs

14 finely crumbled graham cracker squares = 1 c. crumbs
20 coarsely crumbled small vanilla wafers = 1 c. crumbs
1 slice bread = 1 c. soft crumbs
1 med. lemon = 3 T. juice
1 sq. chocolate = 1 oz. = 3 T. cocoa plus 1 T. butter
6 oz. chocolate chips = about 1 c.
2 lg. eggs = 3 sm. eggs
1 c. cake flour = 1 c. minus 2 T. all purpose flour
1 c. uncooked rice = 3½ c. cooked rice = 7 servings
1 c. uncooked macaroni = 2¼ c. cooked macaroni
1 T. quick-cooking tapioca = 1 T. cornstarch = 2 T. flour
A dash = a few grains = a speck

We adjusted quantities of recipes quite often and it didn't take me long to realize that not all students had a handle on fractions. So, I became a part-time math professor. As students began to rely on calculators and allowed their brains to atrophy, I devised this list in the interest of time and preserving my personal sanity.

FRACTIONAL BREAKDOWN

(For the Mathematically Challenged)

½ T. = 1½ tsp.
2 T. = ⅛ c.
4 T. = ¼ c.
8 T. = ½ c.
12 T. = ¾ c.
5 T. + 1 tsp. = ⅓ c.
10 T. + 2 tsp. = ⅔ c.
6 T. = ¼ c. + 2 T. = ⅜ c.
10 T. = ½ c. + 2 T. = ⅝ c.
14 T. = ¾ c. + 2 T. = ⅞ c.

COOKING TERMS

Al dente: describes pasta that is cooked only until it offers a slight resistance to the bite–Italian translation: *to the tooth*
Bake: to cook in the oven
Baste: to moisten foods during cooking with pan drippings or special sauce
Beat: to combine ingredients using a rapid stroke
Blend: to combine two ingredients, each losing it's own properties
Braise: to brown foods, usually meat, then cook in flavored liquid
Brown: to cook until food turns brown in color, as in toast or in cooking meat or flour
Boil: to bring liquid to the point where bubbles constantly break the surface
Broil: to cook under direct heat as in the oven
Blanch: to immerse in rapidly boiling water and allow to cook slightly
Combine: to join or mix ingredients
Cream: to beat fat, especially butter, using an electric mixer; butter and sugar are creamed together to form a smooth, fluffy paste
Cut-in: to combine shortening with dry ingredients using a pastry blender or two knives
Deglaze: a cooking technique for removing and dissolving caramelized bits of food from a pan; add small amount of liquid to hot pan, cook and stir.
Dredge: to coat lightly with flour, cornmeal, or crumbs
Entrée: the main course of a meal
Fold: to combine a delicate substance, such as beaten egg whites, with another substance without breaking air bubbles; generally done by slowly moving a wire whisk down, across, up, and over
Garnish: to decorate food with edible flowers or small pieces of food: parsley
Grill: to cook over direct heat as on the pit, grill, or in a grill pan
Julienne: to cut or slice foods into match stick shaped pieces
Marinate: to cover food with liquid and let set to add flavor or tenderize
Mix: to combine ingredients, usually by stirring
Pare/Peel: to remove the outermost skin of a fruit or vegetable
Poach: to cook gently in hot liquid that is just below the boiling point
Sauté: to cook over direct heat in a small amount of fat, stirring often
Scald: to heat to just below the boiling point; when tiny bubbles appear at the edge of the saucepan
Simmer: to cook in liquid just below the boiling point
Steam: to cook foods above boiling liquid with a cover; use a steaming basket or a special pot.
Steep: to allow food to stand in hot liquid to extract flavor
Toss: to combine ingredients with a repeated lifting motion as in salad
Whip: to beat rapidly to incorporate air as in egg whites or heavy cream

IF WEBSTER ONLY KNEW...

Home Economics (hōm ek′ə näm′iks) *n.* the science and art of teaching career planning, job skills, resource management, time management, nutrition, food preparation, menu planning, parenting, substance abuse, child care and development, housing, interior design, healthy living, clothing and textiles, consumer education, decision making, problem solving, human relationships, family development, and anything else that touches the home and heart.

"You'll never know everything about anything, especially something you love." — Julia Child

APPETIZERS

Aunt Sue's Crab Dip

Jennie & Sue

2 pkg. (8 oz. ea.) cream cheese, softened
Pepper & garlic powder to taste
1 can (9 oz.) white crab meat, drained
Cocktail Sauce

Combine all ingredients and shape into a rectangle. Top with cocktail sauce. Place on serving platter and refrigerate.

Cocktail Sauce

½ c. ketchup
2 tsp. lemon juice
1 tsp. horseradish
4 dashes Worcestershire sauce
Pepper

Mix all ingredients together and pour over cheese. Serve with snack crackers or wheat thins. It's absolutely best with Triscuits.

Baked Crab Rangoon

1 can (6 oz.) white crabmeat, drained, flaked
4 oz. Neufchatel cheese, softened
¼ c. green onions, thinly sliced
¼ c. light mayonnaise
12 wonton wrappers

Preheat oven to 350°. Mix crabmeat, Neufchatel cheese, onions, and mayo. Spray 12 medium muffin cups with cooking spray. Gently place a wonton wrapper in each cup, allowing edges of wrappers to extend above sides of cups. Fill evenly with crabmeat mixture. Place on lower rack of oven. Bake 18–20 minutes or until edges are golden brown and filling is heated through. Serve warm. Garnish with additional chopped green onions, if desired. Yield: 12 servings, one wonton each

Artichoke Nibbles

1 sm. onion, chopped
1 garlic clove, minced
1 tsp. vegetable oil
2 jars (6½ oz. ea.) marinated artichoke hearts, drained & chopped
4 eggs
2 T. fresh parsley, minced
¼ tsp. salt
⅛ tsp. pepper
⅛ tsp. dried oregano
⅛ tsp. hot pepper sauce
2 c. (8 oz.) Cheddar cheese, shredded
⅓ c. crushed saltines (about 10 crackers)

In a small skillet, sauté onion and garlic in oil until tender. Stir in artichokes. Remove from the heat; set aside. In a large bowl, whisk the eggs, parsley, salt, pepper, oregano, and hot pepper sauce. Stir in the cheese, cracker crumbs, and artichoke mixture. Pour into a greased 11 x 7 x 2-inch baking dish. Bake, uncovered, at 325° for 25–30 minutes or until a knife inserted near the center comes out clean. Cool for 10–15 minutes before cutting into 1-inch squares. Serve warm.

CUTTING UP ONIONS WITHOUT CRYING

A friend of mine told me "real cooks don't cry" when chopping onions. Seriously, there are so many tales out there about how to keep from crying when cutting up an onion: hold a match stick between your teeth or breathe only through your mouth, wear goggles or stuff small carrots in your nose, peel onions under running cold water or chew gum. All of these might provide a little respite, but I have the absolute best tear-proof answer. *Do not cut the root end off of the onion until the very last.* First, remove the top and the outer layer. Lay the whole onion on its side and cut thin or thick slices, starting at the top. Stack 2 or 3 slices on top of each other; cut across one way; then cut across the other way. The result is small even-sized pieces. Cut as few or as many slices as needed and store the remainder. I love the Tupperware onion keeper–it keeps the smell of onion from invading your refrigerator plus the onion stays fresh longer. I guarantee that unless it is a really potent onion or there are bunches of onions to cut, leaving the root on will prevent tearing up and crying.

"Life is an onion and one cries while peeling it." – French Proverb

Black Tie Cream Cheese & Caviar

In Memory of Ann

1 pkg. (8 oz.) cream cheese, room temperature
1 med. onion, grated
¼ c. mayonnaise
Dash of Worcestershire sauce
1 T. lemon juice
Dash of Tabasco sauce
Salt & pepper to taste
1 jar (2 oz.) black lumpfish caviar
2 hard cooked eggs, chopped
Lemon wedges
Red onion slices, cut in half
Crackers, thin strips of toast, cocktail rye, or pumpernickel

Combine cream cheese, onion, mayonnaise, Worcestershire, lemon juice, Tabasco, salt, and pepper. Spread about 1-inch thick in center of your very best serving plate. With small spreader, gently frost cheese with caviar. Cover with waxed paper; refrigerate until serving time. Surround with chopped egg, onion slices, and lemon wedges. Place crackers/toast on a coordinating platter or in a cloth-lined basket. Serve.

Ann, a dear friend of ours, always brought the best out in each of us. She was the librarian at the high school. Ann passed away last year after a tremendous fight with liver disease. I miss her so much. Ann brought a caviar dish very similar to this to one of our get-togethers. The caviar added class and style to us plain ol' school teachers. Ann had such a keen wit and sense of humor, she really kept us on our toes.

"In my view, nineteen pounds of old books are at least nineteen times as delicious as one pound of fresh caviar." — Anne Fadiman

Cheese & Onion Canapés

School Dinner Recipe

½ c. mayonnaise or salad dressing
¼ c. grated Parmesan cheese
2 green onions, finely chopped
24 toast rounds

Combine all ingredients, except toast rounds, in small mixing bowl; mix well. Spread mixture on rounds; place in glass 3-quart (13 x 9-inch) baking dish. Microwave on reheat for 45–55 seconds or until just bubbly. Yield: about 24 canapés

NOTE: We made this canapé when the microwave was just becoming a standard in the kitchen. What a breakthrough in modern technology!

TESTING DISHES FOR USE IN THE MICROWAVE

I learned the hard way that not all dishes should be used in the microwave: the handles of a bowl got so hot my skin almost stuck to them. To test a dish to see if it is microwave safe follow these instructions.

- ✦ Fill a one-cup Pyrex measuring cup with water.
- ✦ Place in microwave beside the empty dish to be tested.
- ✦ Microwave for one minute.
- ✦ If the water is hot and the dish that is being tested is cool, the dish is safe to use for cooking in the microwave.
- ✦ If the water is warm and the dish that is being tested is warm, the dish is safe for short-term use in the microwave (less than a minute).
- ✦ If the water is cool and the dish being tested is hot, do not use that dish in the microwave.

The science behind this is based on the fact that the food, not the dish, should absorb the microwaves and thus be heated. Remember that when foods are heated for extended periods of time in the microwave, the hot food will transfer heat to the dish making it very hot to touch.

Brie in Pastry

1 sheet frozen puff pastry, thawed
¼ c. apricot jam
1 round (13.2 oz.) Brie or Camembert cheese
1 egg
1 T. water
2–3 apples
½ c. Sprite or 7-Up

Roll puff pastry into a 14-inch square. Spread jam into a 4½-inch circle in center of pastry; place cheese over jam. Fold pastry around cheese; trim excess dough. Pinch edges to seal. Place seam side down on ungreased baking sheet. Beat egg and water; brush over pastry. If desired, cut the trimmed pastry pieces into decorative shapes and place on top; brush with egg mixture. Bake at 400° for 20–25 minutes or until puffed and golden brown. Core and slice apples; dip in Sprite or 7-Up and drain well. Serve brie warm with the apple slices. Yield: 8–10 servings

Cheese Dip

Marilyn

1 lb. hamburger
1 lb. hot sausage
2 lb. Velveeta cheese
1 can (10 oz.) Ro-tel* tomatoes
1 can cream of mushroom soup

Brown the hamburger and sausage. Cut Velveeta in cubes. Combine all ingredients in crock pot; cook using low setting until melted.

Marilyn and my sister Debbie were both students in my class the first year I taught. Later Marilyn became one of my best friends–the one I give credit to for introducing me to cheese dip. Growing up on a farm and cooking what we grew never exposed me to things like Ro-tel tomatoes. There are so many versions of this cheese dip, but this is, by far, my favorite. I use hot tomatoes for adult groups and mild tomatoes and sausage when the occasion calls for it. I've been known to add sliced jalapeños and even a little jalapeño juice to heat it up a little more when necessary. Goes great with ice-cold long-necks!

*Ro-tel is a combination of diced tomatoes and green chilies and is also available in mild and hot versions. Substitute any similar brand.

Cheese Log

8 oz. cream cheese
8 oz. American cheese
½ c. pecans, finely chopped
Garlic powder & paprika

Crumble cream cheese and grate American cheese. Sprinkle with garlic; mix well. Add pecans and mix more. Roll into ball or log. Refrigerate. Roll in paprika and decorate just before serving.

Cheese Pennies

From the Food Lab

1 jar (5 oz.) pasteurized process sharp American cheese spread
¼ c. shortening
⅔ c. flour

Mix all ingredients with electric mixer on medium speed 20–30 seconds. Mold into 2 rolls, each 1-inch in diameter and 8-inches long. Wrap and chill 2 hours. Slice ¼-inch thick and place on an ungreased cookie sheet. Bake at 375° for 10–12 minutes or until light brown.

NOTE: Cheese Pennies is a classroom recipe, circa 1971. It was great for special occasions as one class could make the rolls and then later in the day, another could slice and bake them. As I remember, the cheese pennies are very flaky and delicious–they make everyone think they are difficult to prepare.

Chipotle Cheese Loaf

Jennie

2 lb. cream cheese, softened
1 can (16 oz.) chipotle peppers in adobo sauce
½ lb. Swiss cheese, thinly sliced
½ lb. Cheddar cheese, finely grated
4 oz. pimiento, diced
4 oz. mild green peppers, diced
½ lb. pecans, chopped

Puree chipotle peppers and strain out skins and seeds. Mix 1 tablespoon pepper puree and adobo sauce with softened cream cheese. Place in a pastry bag with a large tip. Line a loaf pan with plastic wrap. Place a layer of Swiss cheese in bottom of pan. Pipe a generous layer of cream cheese mix over, tapping to remove any air bubbles. Layer with green peppers, pimiento, shredded Cheddar cheese, and remaining adobo sauce; sprinkle with pecans. Repeat layering of all ingredients until used up, reserving ⅓ cup of cream cheese mixture. Finish with another layer of Swiss cheese. Cover and refrigerate for several hours. Unmold and remove plastic wrap. Spread a thin layer of cream cheese mix over loaf and sprinkle with additional pecans. Serve with sliced French bread or crackers.

NOTE: Read the entire recipe before beginning to get the whole picture and have enough ingredients to finish. Mini-loaf pans can be used for molds to make several loaves to share with family and friends. Delicious during the holiday season.

Crocked Cheese Spread

Mom

1 lb. cheese, grated
¼ c. scallions, chopped
3 T. parsley, chopped
2 tsp. Dijon mustard
¼ c. butter
2 tsp. sherry
Dash Worcestershire sauce
Salt
Hot sauce

Combine all ingredients, using the butter to soften. Serve with crackers.

Dipsy Devil Spread

School Dinner Recipe

1 jar (5 oz.) cream cheese with pimiento
1 can (2¼ oz.) deviled ham
2 T. parsley, snipped
1 T. onion, minced
¼ c. mayonnaise or salad dressing
4 drops Tabasco

Combine all ingredients in mixing bowl. Beat until creamy. Serve with crackers or bagel rounds.

NOTE: I'm going to have to go to the grocery store and see if they still make deviled ham. So many things have changed in my lifetime. I remember eating potted meat on crackers when we were kids. I guess that was the original appetizer for our family.

Crackers for the Golf Course

Doris

1 box (4 packs) wheat saltines
1 pkg. Hidden Valley Ranch Dip Mix
1 heaping tsp. crushed red pepper
1 c. canola oil

Find a container with a lid in which all 4 packs of the saltines will stand on edge without any extra space. They need to fit tight. The container should be just about as high as the crackers. Combine red pepper, dip mix, and oil. Drizzle evenly over all crackers and cover tightly. Turn the container over every 15 minutes for an hour, 4 turns in all. Crackers can be stored in same container.

SOURCE: Doris is a golfing lady. She says, "These crackers will not get soggy or stale. They're not going to last that long anyway–they're just too delicious." Doris makes these crackers for everyone. At first she told me to just get the ingredients and she would make them for me because mine wouldn't turn out as good as hers. Well, she's right. The first container I used was too big so things didn't work out quite right. I am still on the lookout for the perfect container. It is amazing–these crackers are not greasy, just delicious. For hotter crackers, just add more crushed red pepper. I used a really generous heaping teaspoonful.

"I've had a good day when I don't fall out of the cart." – Buddy Hackett

Golf: My Only Athletic Accomplishment

Coaching was such a hoot–especially enjoyable as I was on the course instead of in the classroom almost every Monday during the spring semester. I loved those tournaments!

It was the 90s and I became an avid golfer overnight. In fact, I loved it so much I volunteered to be the girl's golf coach–there was one girl golfer. The program grew and soon I had a full team–even received a stipend for coaching. That's what I'm talking about! I just loved hearing the girls call me Coach Craig. We placed in a few tournaments; one team member even ranked in the top 10 at district one year. For several years we had a class period for golf. We designed golf courses, putted in the hallways, chipped over the sidewalks, and hit range balls on the practice football field. You might be recalling my athletic history, but golf is a sport that agreed with me. I only had to go to the emergency room once.

Dr. Pepper Cheese Pecan Ball with Dried Beef

School Dinner Recipe

½ lb. processed American cheese, grated
1 pkg. (3 oz.) cream cheese
3–4 T. Dr. Pepper
2 tsp. lemon juice
Pinch of salt
¼ tsp. garlic, minced
⅛ tsp. crushed dried red pepper
½ c. pecans, chopped
1½ c. dried beef, chopped

Combine cheese, cream cheese, and Dr. Pepper; blend with electric mixer until light and fluffy. Add lemon juice, salt, garlic, red pepper, pecans, and ½ cup dried beef. Mix until well blended. Shape into 2 balls. Chill about 20 minutes. Roll each ball in the remaining chopped beef. Place in plastic wrap or Ziploc and chill thoroughly. Serve with cheese knife for spreading on party rye slices or crackers. Yield: 2 balls about 4-inches in diameter

My how the memories come flooding back. I remember making this for a school dinner early in my teaching career. The students measured the red pepper and began combining with the other ingredients–then they saw the little bugs. I loved it when a teaching moment presented itself: "Always check ingredients before adding them to your recipe. Paprika and red pepper are especially susceptible to bugs, so if they are not used often, store in the freezer." Don't worry, we threw that batch out and started over with a fresh can of red pepper.

FRESHER SPICES PROVIDE MORE FLAVOR

To make sure you're getting the most flavor from your spices, replace them after a certain amount of time. Here are some suggestions.

Ground spices (e.g. nutmeg, cinnamon)	3 years
Whole spices (e.g. cloves, peppercorns)	4 years
Herbs (e.g. parsley, basil)	1–3 years
Most seeds (e.g. celery, fennel)	4 years
Poppy and sesame seeds	2 years
Extracts (e.g. almond, lemon)	4 years
(Except vanilla which has an unlimited shelf life)	
Seasoning blends/mixes (e.g. taco, Season All)	2 years

Signs of aging for McCormick spices: a rectangular tin is at least 15 years old. "Baltimore, MD" on the spice indicates it is at least 15 years old.

SUBSTITUTIONS FOR HERBS AND SPICES

Fresh Basil	fresh mint (slightly less) or fresh cilantro
Chili Powder	½ tsp. dried oregano, ¼ tsp. dried cumin, and a dash of bottled hot sauce
Kosher Salt	fine table salt, substituting ½ to ¾ the amount called for
Fresh Cilantro	fresh flat-leaf parsley
Fresh Herbs	the dried version, substituting ½ the amount called for
Nutmeg	cinnamon, ginger or allspice (for sweet, not savory, recipes)

Easy Party Bruschetta

1½ c. tomatoes, chopped & seeded
⅔ c. red onion, finely chopped
2 T. jalapeño pepper, seeded & minced
2 garlic cloves, minced
½ tsp. dried basil
¼ tsp. salt
¼ tsp. pepper, coarsely ground
2 T. olive oil
1 T. cider vinegar
1 T. red wine vinegar
3 dashes hot pepper sauce
1 loaf (8 oz.) French bread, cut into ¼-inch slices
2 T. fresh-grated Parmesan cheese

Drain any liquid that accumulates on the tomatoes. In a small bowl, combine the first seven ingredients. In another bowl, whisk the oil, vinegars, and pepper sauce; stir into tomato mixture. Place bread slices on an ungreased baking sheet. Broil 3–4 inches from the heat for 1–2 minutes or until golden brown. With a slotted spoon, top each slice with tomato mixture. Sprinkle with Parmesan cheese. Arrange on serving platter; serve immediately.
Yield: 2½ dozen

"When men reach their sixties and retire, they go to pieces. Women go right on cooking." – Gail Sheehy

BROILING FOODS IN THE OVEN

The broil temperature setting on an oven is designed to be used with the oven door ajar–there is a stopping point built into the oven door when the door is opened a couple of inches. This allows the heat to escape and the broiling unit will remain on. If the door is closed, the broiling unit will cycle on and off, allowing food to bake instead of broil. Also, leaving the door ajar reminds you there is something in there about to burn if you forget about it.

Feta Cheese Ball

1 pkg. (8 oz.) cream cheese
1 pkg. (4 oz.) Feta cheese
¼ c. butter
⅓ c. ripe olives, chopped
2 T. green onion, finely chopped
¼ c. snipped parsley or toasted almonds, finely chopped
Assorted crackers

Crumble the Feta cheese; bring cheeses and butter to room temperature. Beat until combined. Stir in olives and onion. Shape into a ball and roll in parsley or almonds. Cover; chill 4 to 24 hours. Serve with crackers. Yield: approximately 16 servings or 2 cups

NOTE: This makes a really large cheese ball; dividing the recipe into two balls provides one for now and one for later. As usual, cheeses should be taken out of fridge a few hours before serving as room temperature brings out the very best flavor.

Grape & Rosemary Focaccia

1 lb. pizza dough
2 T. extra-virgin olive oil
Coarse sea salt, for sprinkling
1 garlic clove, minced
1 shallot, thinly sliced
1 T. fresh rosemary leaves
½ c. green grapes
½ c. red grapes

Preheat the oven to 400°. Roll the pizza dough into a rectangle on a sheet of parchment paper. Place on a baking sheet. Using a pastry brush, coat the top of the dough with olive oil and sprinkle lightly with coarse sea salt. Sprinkle the dough with the garlic, shallot, and rosemary. Arrange the grapes over the top of the dough, pushing down into the dough. Bake the focaccia until golden brown, about 25 minutes. Cut into slices and serve.

Fresh Fruit Salsa with Baked Ginger Chips

1 can (20 oz.) unsweetened crushed pineapple
2 med. peaches
2 med. kiwi
¼ c. Macadamia nuts, chopped
¼ c. brown sugar
¼ c. flaked coconut
8 flour tortillas (8 in.)
1 T. water
¼ c. sugar
1–2 tsp. ground ginger

Drain pineapple; reserve juice. Peel and chop the peaches and kiwi. In a large bowl, combine the pineapple, peaches, kiwi, nuts, brown sugar, coconut, and 3 tablespoons of the reserved juice. Cover and refrigerate for a couple of hours. To make the chips, lightly brush one side of each tortilla with water. Combine sugar and ginger; sprinkle over the moistened sides of tortilla. Cut each into six wedges. Place a single layer on ungreased baking sheets. Bake at 400° for 5–7 minutes or until golden brown and crisp. Cool on wire racks and serve with salsa. Yield: about 12 servings

NOTE: This combination of fruity salsa with crisp gingery chips is wonderful on a hot day. Serve this with pineapple iced tea, which can be made by simply adding the rest of the drained pineapple juice from this recipe to a pitcher of tea. The chips are so good, sometimes I double the amount made.

Garden Veggie Pizza

Jennie

1 pkg. (8 oz.) refrigerated crescent rolls
1 pkg. (8 oz.) cream cheese, softened
1 T. mayonnaise
1 garlic clove, pressed
1 tsp. dried dill weed
Pepper to taste
2 c. veggies, diced (broccoli, cauliflower, cucumber, red & green bell pepper, tomato, onions, mushrooms, carrots, & zucchini or yellow squash)

Preheat oven to 350°. Unroll crescent dough on a baking stone or pizza pan. Separate into 8 triangles and arrange in a circle with points in the center. Roll, joining seams together. Combine cream cheese, mayonnaise, garlic, and dill weed; add pepper to taste. Spread over rolled dough. Top with veggies and bake for 12–15 minutes. Cool and serve.

NOTE: Cut with pizza cutter and indulge. Delicious on a summer day and it is very figure friendly. Jennie doesn't use any salt when cooking; you'll find that this appetizer has a slightly sweet flavor without it.

Gouda Bites

1 tube (8 oz.) refrigerated reduced-fat crescent rolls
½ tsp. garlic powder
5 oz. Gouda cheese, cut into 24 cubes

Unroll crescent dough into one long rectangle; seal seams and perforations. Sprinkle with garlic powder. Cut into 24 pieces; lightly press onto the bottom and up the sides of ungreased miniature muffin cups. Bake at 375° for 3 minutes. Place a piece of cheese in each cup. Bake 8–10 minutes longer or until golden brown and cheese is melted. Serve warm. Yield: 2 dozen

VARIATION: Use Tuscan garlic seasoning, Italian seasoning, Cajun seasoning, or your favorite in place of garlic powder. Hang out around the oven while the bites are baking as they will disappear very shortly after coming out. Just one recipe won't be enough of these, so it's a good place to include information on adjusting the quantity of recipes. It's simple math and the practical application of fractions.

HALVING AND DOUBLING RECIPES

- **To half a recipe, divide each ingredient by 2.**
  When using fractions, invert and multiply.
  Example: ¾ c. milk divided by 2/1 = ¾ x ½ = ⅜ c. milk
- **To half an egg:**
  Beat the egg and then divide by filling one of the half shells with beaten egg. Use that part.
- **To double a recipe, multiply by 2.**
  When using fractions, multiply by 2/1.
  Example: ¾ c. milk multiplied by 2 = 3/4 x 2/1 = 6/4 = 1 2/4 =1½ c. milk

Hidden Valley Ranch Herb Cheese

16 oz. cream cheese, softened
4 oz. butter, softened
1 T. Dijon-style mustard
1 tsp. garlic, minced
1 pkg. Hidden Valley Ranch Buttermilk Recipe Salad Dressing & Seasoning Mix

Use electric mixer to blend all ingredients. Spoon into serving bowl, cover and refrigerate overnight (or up to 4 days). Remove 30 minutes before serving. Serves 8 or more

NOTE: Everyone makes ranch dip. Be different–serve this variation made with the same mix. It's got that gourmet touch.

In Two Winks Bruscetta

2 lg. garlic cloves
½ tsp. salt
3 c. Roma tomatoes, finely chopped & seeds removed or 1 can (28 oz.) petite diced tomatoes, well-drained
¼ c. prepared pesto
¼ c. Parmesan cheese, shredded
2 tsp. olive oil
½ tsp. sugar
¼ tsp. pepper
1 tub (8 oz.) cream cheese with herbs
1 baguette, sliced ¼-inch thick
Olive oil
Italian parsley leaves or fresh parsley, minced

In a medium bowl, mash garlic and salt into a paste. Add tomatoes, pesto, cheese, oil, sugar, and pepper; blend well. Place baguette slices on a baking sheet, brush lightly with olive oil, and toast until light brown. Spread cream cheese on each baguette slice; top with bruschetta mixture. Garnish with parsley. Serve immediately. Yield: 30–35 appetizers

"Cooking is an art, but you eat it too." – Marcella Hazan

Hummus

My Mama

3–4 sm. cloves garlic, peeled
⅓ c. lemon juice
½ c. olive oil
1 can (16 oz.) garbanzo beans
½ tsp. salt
½ c. Tahini (sesame paste)
Spicy Olive & Okra Topping

Blend garlic, lemon juice, and olive oil until pureed. Rinse beans 3 times; drain. Add beans and salt to blender and process until smooth. Add Tahini to thicken.

VARIATION: Try adding diced sun-dried tomatoes and basil or your favorite flavor combination. I look at the latest versions of hummus in the grocery store for ideas. It's a lot less expensive to make at home. This makes quite a bit, enough to divide and flavor differently. Also, try using other oils: toasted sesame, grape-seed, etc.

SOURCE: Look at the source of this recipe. I never would have thought that my mother would introduce me to hummus. She never ceases to amaze me.

Spicy Olive & Okra Topping

1 tsp. lemon zest
1 sm. garlic clove, minced
¼ tsp. crushed red pepper
2 tsp. extra virgin olive oil
1 c. mixed pitted olives, chopped
4 pickled okra, sliced thinly
1 tsp. fresh rosemary, chopped

Sauté first 3 ingredients in hot oil in a large skillet over medium heat for 1 minute. Add olives and sauté 3–5 minutes. Remove from heat and stir in okra and rosemary. Let stand 5 minutes. Place hummus in serving dish; top with warm olive mixture. Serve with pita bread or chips.

SOURCE: I spend a lot of time looking at magazines, especially since I have retired. If I see something I think I'd like to try, I just tear out the whole page. When I started this cookbook project I had a stack of these pages about 3 inches tall. As I culled through them, some didn't contain anything that even sounded good anymore. Others merited keeping to try later, and still others made it to the kitchen counter where I prepared and adapted them. This is one of those that I regret not trying a long time ago. It's absolutely delicious, especially when I use my daughter's home-canned hot pickled okra.

My college home economics teachers are quite a memorable group of women, but one stands out among the rest. Although I can't recall her name, she was a petite, elderly individual, precisely dressed, and the absolute "queen of lecture"–no slides, no pictures, no blackboard, just words. She embedded nutrition in my brain forever. Everything she ever said was on a test–I mean everything! After that first test, I began taking so many notes trees became an endangered species. I still have those spirals somewhere; I kept them on a shelf in the closet in my schoolroom but I never had to refer to them because, like I said, it all got embedded. A thought that passes through my head, still today, is this statement of hers: "Ladies, you know that parsley is not only an excellent source of Vitamin A and an instant breath freshener, but it also automatically grows on the grave of every good home economics teacher." I'm glad I will be dead when and if my grave is covered with parsley...it would be too disappointing not to have any.

Jalapeño Cheese Squares

Marilyn's Mother

1 lb. Cheddar cheese, grated
1 lb. Monterrey Jack cheese, grated
3 eggs, beaten
3 T. flour
1 can (14.5 oz.) evaporated milk
Jalapeño nacho slices

Line bottom of 9 x 13-inch casserole with nacho slices. Put grated cheeses on top. Mix eggs, flour, and milk; pour over cheese. Bake at 350° for 30 minutes until brown and bubbly. Cut in squares. Serve warm.

Marilyn and I would often drive to see her parents who lived on Caranchua Bay. Her mother was an awesome cook–this recipe proves it. We would have such fun eating her concoctions. These squares go especially good with ice cold Miller Lite–it takes the bite off the jalapeños. Marilyn's mother and daddy lived in a turn-of-the-century, huge, white, two-story home on a bluff about 100 yards from the bay. I would often wander down to the water, taking a lawn chair with me. The beach–theirs a finely crushed shell–always calls me by name. I'd take off my shoes and dabble my toes in the tiny waves watching them advance, recede, advance. I remember writing the best poetry at the water's edge. Too bad I didn't take a pen and paper with me, but then this book would be way too long.

Jalapeño Squares

Elaine

6 eggs, beaten
1 jar (12 oz.) jalapeños, sliced
2 c. Cheddar cheese, shredded

Drain liquid from jalapeños. Place in a greased 9-inch square pan; top with cheese and then add eggs. Do not stir. Bake at 350° until done and knife comes out clean–about 30 minutes. Let set for 10 minutes; cut in bite-size squares. Great for brunch.

NOTE: Remember, Elaine is the first-born of my siblings. This is a quick, easy version of the recipe that Marilyn's mother prepares. See which one becomes your favorite.

Mexi-Corn Dip

Janis

8 oz. cream cheese, softened
1 c. sour cream
¼–½ c. mayonnaise
1 can (11 oz.) Mexicorn*, drained
½ tomato, chopped
3 green onions, chopped
Jalapeño to taste, chopped
1–1½ c. Mexican cheese, grated

Combine all ingredients and refrigerate.

NOTE: When I asked my friend Janis to send me a few of her favorite recipes, what where the chances that she would send me a recipe that is already one of my favorites? That's exactly what happened. I guess that's why our friendship has endured–that and great minds think alike. Janis comments, "This dip is delicious and easy. It uses very few exact measurements, leaving room for your individuality. It's best when made a day ahead of time–a great timesaver when there's lots to do to get ready for that big family get-together."

*Mexicorn is a brand name of whole kernel corn that also contains green peppers and pimientos–any similar brand will substitute.

SOFTENING CREAM CHEESE, BUTTER, AND MARGARINE

It never fails that I forget or just don't have time to remove cream cheese, butter, and margarine from the fridge so it can soften for use in recipes. Softening is necessary to achieve the proper consistency and texture. To soften these items quickly, unwrap and place cream cheese on a plate; microwave for 15 seconds and allow to set a few minutes. Butter or margarine can be softened the same way, but for a few seconds less. The first time doing this, watch closely as not all microwaves are created equal and the time might need to be adjusted up or down. You definitely don't want melting to begin.

Pineapple Cheese Ball

2 pkg. (8 oz. ea.) cream cheese, softened
1 can (8 oz.) crushed pineapple, drained well
¼ c. green bell pepper, diced
2 T. onion, minced
1 T. jalapeño pepper, minced
Tabasco sauce to taste
1 tsp. seasoned salt
2 c. pecans, chopped & divided

Combine the cream cheese, crushed pineapple, bell pepper, onion, jalapeño, Tabasco sauce, seasoned salt, and 1 cup pecans in a bowl; mix well. Chill in the refrigerator. Pat into a ball and roll in the remaining 1 cup pecans, coating well. Place on a cheese board and serve with bite-size crackers.

NOTE: Here's a hint for shaping the cheese ball: place mixture in middle of plastic wrap and use the wrap to help mold it. Often times, I divide a cheese ball recipe into two balls, so if all is not needed, I have a fresh ball to use later. I really like this cheese ball because everyone asks what's in it–I just love creating curiosity with food. I was introduced to this recipe in Destin. That makes this cheese ball even better yet–it's from my favorite vacation spot and brings back great memories every time I prepare it.

Olive Cheese Balls

From the Food Lab

2 c. sharp natural Cheddar cheese, shredded
1¼ c. flour
½ c. butter, melted
36 sm. pimento-stuffed olives

Drain olives. Mix cheese and flour. Add butter and mix thoroughly. Mold 1 teaspoon dough around each olive and shape into ball. Place 2 inches apart on an ungreased baking sheet. Cover; chill at least 1 hour. Heat oven to 400°. Bake 15–20 minutes. Serve hot.

VARIATION: Use any of the olive combinations: jalapeño stuffed, almond stuffed, etc. If giant olives are used, allow a little bit longer for baking.

Olive-Nut Spread

1 pkg. (3 oz.) cream cheese, softened
½ c. walnuts, finely chopped
¼ c. pimiento-stuffed olives, chopped
2 T. milk

Stir together all ingredients until well mixed. Makes about 1 cup. Serve with crackers or toast rounds.

Red Pepper Hummus

1 can (15 oz.) navy beans
2 cloves garlic, chopped
½ c. roasted red bell peppers, drained & chopped
⅓ c. Tahini (sesame paste)
¼ c. fresh lemon juice
½ tsp. salt
¼ tsp. ground cumin
¼ tsp. ground coriander
¼ tsp. ground red pepper
2 T. olive oil
1 T. fresh cilantro, chopped

Rinse and drain beans. Process first 9 ingredients in a food processor or blender until smooth, stopping to scrape down sides. With processor running, pour oil through food chute in a slow, steady stream; process until smooth. Stir in cilantro; chill 1 hour. Garnish with additional cilantro leaves.

Pecan-Pepper Brie

½ c. pecans, chopped
1 jalapeño pepper, stemmed & seeded
¼ c. apricot preserves
1 loaf French baguette (16 oz.)
1 round (8 oz./4-inch) Brie cheese with rind, at room temperature
Olive oil spray
Fresh parsley, finely chopped

Preheat oven to 425°. Dice jalapeño and combine with preserves. Cut Brie in half horizontally. Place one half of Brie, cut side up, onto center of large round baking sheet. Spread half of the apricot mixture evenly over bottom half of Brie. Top with half of the pecans and remaining half of Brie, cut side up. Spread remaining apricot mixture over Brie; sprinkle with remaining pecans. Cut baguette diagonally into twenty-four ¼-inch slices. Arrange baguette slices around Brie; spray with oil and sprinkle with parsley. Bake 8–10 minutes or until baguette slices are golden brown and Brie begins to soften. Remove from oven; let stand 5 minutes before serving.

NOTE: This adapted version of a much more difficult recipe is an instant favorite. It is delicious and so easy. Just be careful not to cook too long or the Brie will melt all over the place.

Prosciutto-Wrapped Cantaloupe

Jennie

Fresh cantaloupe
Prosciutto, thinly sliced

Slice fresh cantaloupe and cut slices in half. Wrap with thin slices of prosciutto. Hold the prosciutto in place with toothpicks. Serve on a platter. Cantaloupe can be cut into smaller pieces if desired.

NOTE: Jennie states, "A fresh and easy delight before any meal, straight from Palm Springs." Jennie forgot to say to mix your favorite drink, grab your sunglasses and a magazine, and find some water to gaze upon.

Sausage-Stuffed Mushrooms

Jennie

1 lb. whole lg. mushrooms
2–3 slices honey wheat bread
1 lb. Jimmy Dean's hot sausage
1 white onion
1 clove fresh garlic
Cracked pepper
1 tsp. sugar
¾ c. Cheddar cheese, grated
¼ c. Parmesan cheese, shredded
Tony Chacere's*
1 egg
2 green onions, thinly sliced
½ c. Italian bread crumbs

Chop an onion and mince some fresh garlic. Coat a skillet with non-stick spray and brown the onion and garlic. Add the breakfast sausage and brown. Add pepper and some Tony Chacere's. Wash mushrooms and remove stems. Chop the stems and add to the browned sausage mixture. Make bread crumbs from the honey wheat bread; add this and the teaspoon of sugar to the sausage mixture. This should now taste sweet and hot with a cake-like texture. Add Cheddar and Parmesan cheeses and an egg to hold the mixture together. If mixture is sticky, add additional bread crumbs. Place the mixture into the mushroom caps and top with green onions, some more Parmesan cheese, and sprinkle Italian bread crumbs on top. Bake on 350° for 15–20 minutes until the mushrooms start to juice.

*Tony Chacere's is a Cajun seasoning mix with a definite heat to it. There are many other brands to substitute: Slap Ya MaMa, Mrs. G's, or use your favorite brand.

VARIATION: For meatballs, use the same recipe and instead of placing in the mushrooms, form into meatballs and coat with the Italian bread crumbs. Then cook in skillet with olive oil until golden brown.

NOTE: As a mother, I can vouch for Jennie's cooking expertise, and her recipes always turn out the same. I think she really feels her German blood when she gets going in the kitchen because she doesn't have exact measurements. She'll tell me, "Mom, you need a little more this or you put too much of that."

"Learn to cook–try new recipes, learn from your mistakes, be fearless, and above all have fun!" – Julia Child

Sausage Wonton Cups

½ lb. bulk Italian sausage
2 green onions, chopped
16 wonton wrappers
1 T. olive oil
1 c. (4 oz.) Pepper Jack cheese, shredded

In a small skillet, cook sausage over medium heat until no longer pink; drain. Stir in onions; set aside. Press wonton wrappers into greased miniature muffin cups; lightly brush with oil. Bake at 350° for 6–7 minutes or until golden brown. Spoon 1 rounded tablespoon of sausage mixture into each cup; top with 1 tablespoon of cheese. Bake 3–4 minutes longer or until cheese is melted. Serve immediately. Yield: 16 appetizers

Shrimp Cocktail

School Dinner Recipe

1 bottle (12 oz.) chili sauce
1–2 T. prepared horseradish
1 T. lemon juice
½ tsp. Worcestershire sauce
¼ tsp. salt
Dash of pepper
36 med. shrimp, shelled, cooked, & chilled

Mix chili sauce, horseradish, lemon juice, Worcestershire sauce, salt, and pepper. Refrigerate until chilled. To serve as individual appetizers, mix shrimp with sauce and serve in flat champagne or sherbet glasses. For a snazzier appearance, place shredded lettuce in glass, top with shrimp (artfully arranged) and place a dollop of sauce in center of shrimp. For a party tray, fill large bowl with crushed ice. Place a dish of sauce in center of the ice and arrange the shrimp on the ice around it. Serve with wooden picks for dipping or leave the tails on the shrimp. 6 servings

Spinach Dip

My Mama & Myrna

1 pkg. (10 oz.) frozen spinach
2–3 green onions, chopped
1 (6 oz.) can water chestnuts, drained & chopped
2 c. sour cream
1 c. Hellman's mayonnaise
1 box Knorr's Vegetable Soup & Dip Mix

Thaw, chop, and drain spinach well. Combine all ingredients. Cover; chill 2 hours to blend flavors. The longer it waits, the better. Stir well before serving. Serve in a round bread bowl with vegetables or chips.

VARIATION: Add 2 cups shredded Swiss cheese with spinach.

SOURCE: Myrna was the spouse of one of our math teachers. We met when they helped me chaperone a group of students on a trip to the state fair in Dallas. We became fast friends, clocking many hours together deep sea fishing and playing 42. I'll tell more about all that later.

Stuffed Jalapeño Peppers

Gladys

1 lg. can whole jalapeño peppers
2 cans (5 oz. each) tuna fish, packed in water
½ apple
Pecan pieces
Salad dressing
Creole seasoning to taste

Clean peppers by slicing in half lengthwise and removing seeds. Peel and dice apple. Drain tuna and mix with other ingredients. Use just enough salad dressing so tuna and other items stick together. Fill pepper halves.

SOURCE: My cousin Gladys brings these to almost every family get-together and they are a huge favorite. I never knew anything so simple could taste so good. Of course, these are absolutely best when chased by a swig of your favorite ice cold beverage.

Sugared Jalapeño Slices

Elaine

1 jar (28 oz.) sliced jalapeños
1½ c. sugar

Drain all the juice from the jar of peppers. Rinse with water a couple of times. Remove the sliced jalapeños from the jar, making sure they are well drained. Place a cup of peppers back into the jar, followed by a half cup of sugar. Continue to alternate the layers in equal measure until the peppers have been used up. Shake well. Shake the mixture twice a day (morning and night) for 5 days. At this point, the peppers can be divided into smaller jars for gifts or kept to enjoy. Delicious served over cream cheese with crackers or as a snack. Keep refrigerated.

NOTE: These candied jalapeño slices make a great spread when chopped and mixed with cream cheese.

Tex-Mex Dip
(a.k.a. Hot Tub Dip)

1 can (16 oz.) refried beans
¼ c. picante sauce
1½ c. prepared guacamole
½ c. sour cream
½ c. mayonnaise
4½ tsp. (½ pkg.) taco seasoning
1 c. (4 oz.) Cheddar cheese, shredded
1 can (2¼ oz.) sliced ripe olives, drained
2 green onions, chopped
1½ c. lettuce, shredded
1 c. tomatoes, diced
Tortilla chips

Combine beans and picante sauce. Spread onto a serving platter. Spread with guacamole. (4 mashed avocados mixed with 2 tablespoons lemon juice can be substituted for the guacamole.) Combine sour cream, mayonnaise, and taco seasoning; spread over guacamole. Sprinkle with cheese, olives, onions, lettuce, and tomatoes. Refrigerate until serving with tortilla chips. Yield: 12–14 servings

NOTE: It's Tex-Mex, so be brave–go ahead and add sliced jalapeños to the beans or sprinkle plenty on top; serve on the side for wimps. (Wondering about the hot tub? This was a favorite at after-school, off-campus get-togethers with teachers. Check our fun punch recipe later on to gain some insight.)

Thirds Creamy Jalapeño Dip

Jennie

1⅓ c. mayonnaise
⅓ c. buttermilk
⅓ c. jalapeño, chopped
⅓ c. green chilies, chopped
⅓ c. fresh cilantro leaves, chopped
1 pkg. (1 oz.) dry ranch dressing mix

Mix all ingredients but cilantro in blender or food processor; process until smooth. Add cilantro and blend again. Chill. Serve with tortilla chips or as a salad dressing.

NOTE: This is Jennie's rendition of a dip from one of her favorite Mexican restaurants. Sometimes she chops up an avocado, stirring it in just before serving. Jenn says this is also great on fish tacos. Don't forget to garnish with a sprig of that fresh cilantro–it's a cousin of parsley.

Texas Caviar

½ c. margarine
2 tsp. green onions, diced
1 clove garlic, minced
1 can green chiles, chopped
1 jar (5½ oz.) Old English sharp cheese spread
1 can (16 oz.) jalapeño black-eyed peas, drained & mashed

Melt margarine in heavy saucepan. Add garlic and onion. Cook slowly, about 15 minutes. Add green chiles, cheese, and mashed peas. Continue stirring until well blended. Serve warm.

NOTE: Reduce the fat content of this recipe by using less margarine. Just use enough to sauté the veggies and produce a smooth, creamy dip.

My coworker, Mrs. Fuller, and I would take our students to Little Rhein Steak House every time we had an FHA convention in San Antonio. We enjoyed exposing them to fine dining. Little Rhein served a black-eyed pea dish and I came home and created this version. It gets rave reviews on New Year's Eve. For the majority of our students, these trips were the first time they stayed in a hotel, and for some, the first time they ate in a sit-down restaurant other than our local Dairy Queen. Another favorite classy place we frequented was in Dallas, Baby Doe's Matchless Mining Company–a terrific dining experience. I like to think that we had a positive influence on our students' lives.

"Some people wanted champagne and caviar when they should have had beer and hot dogs." – Dwight D. Eisenhower

Tortilla Roll-Ups

Jennie

8–10 tortillas, 8-in. dia.
2 pkg. (8 oz. ea.) cream cheese
½ tsp. garlic powder
Black pepper
Tony Chacere's
Jar of Bacos fresh bacon bits
4–6 green onions, chopped
Raspberry-chipotle sauce

Mix the cream cheese, bacon bits, chopped onions, pepper, garlic, and Tony Chacere's. Spread mixture over tortillas. Roll and slice into pinwheels; secure each roll with a toothpick. Lay in a circle on a tray and serve with a dish of raspberry-chipotle sauce. If not in the mood for roll-ups, make a cheese ball. Lay out a piece of Saran wrap and roll the cream cheese mixture into a ball. Coat the ball with crushed pecans and some bacon bits. You can even add Cheddar cheese if desired. Serve with raspberry-chipotle sauce and wheat thins.

NOTE: Jennie shares, "A quick and easy appetizer if served as a rollup or as a cheese ball. Thanks to Sandy's quick tips in her Fort Davis kitchen, these are now my specialty–my *go-to* for any party or lazy Sunday."

VARIATION: These roll-ups really are a favorite of everyone. Sometimes I just use cream cheese and diced green chilies (drained) and serve with picante sauce. Other times, I'll add thin-sliced ham before rolling up–it depends on what's in the fridge. The toothpick makes this the perfect party food.

Tuna Dip

Elaine

2 cans (5 oz. ea.) tuna, drained
2 c. sour cream
1 pkg. onion soup mix
1 tsp. Tabasco sauce

Combine ingredients and refrigerate. Serve with chips. Yield: 3½ cups

NOTE: It's amazing, but hardly anyone recognizes this as tuna. It's that good!

BEVERAGES

Amaretto Freeze

Jennie

Ice cream, preferably Blue Bell Homemade Vanilla
Milk
Amaretto

Place several scoops of ice cream into the blender; cover with milk and add a jigger of amaretto. Blend and serve in tall glasses.

NOTE: A sure delight for the family circled around the fire during the winter.

Blueberry-Lemon Iced Tea

1 pkg. (16 oz.) frozen blueberries
½ c. fresh lemon juice
4 c. water
3 family size tea bags
¾ c. sugar

Bring the blueberries and lemon juice to a boil in a large saucepan over medium heat. Cook, stirring occasionally, 5 minutes. Remove from heat and pour through a fine wire mesh strainer into a bowl, using back of a spoon to squeeze out juice. Discard solids. Bring water to boil in same saucepan; add tea bags, cover, remove from heat, and let steep 5 minutes. Remove and discard tea bags. Stir in sugar and blueberry juice mixture. Pour into a pitcher; cover and chill 1 hour. Serve over ice. Yield: 5 cups

NOTE: This tea is delicious plus it looks like a fine wine when served. I use either a carafe or sangria pitcher–clear glass or crystal.

"I'm trying to eat better. And, I do feel wise after drinking tea. After eating vegetables, I just feel hungry." – Carrie Latet

Cranberry-Raspberry Punch

1 pkg. (16 oz.) frozen sweetened, sliced strawberries
2 liters ginger ale, chilled
2 liters club soda, chilled
1 qt. raspberry sherbet
1 can (12 oz.) frozen lemonade concentrate
1 can (12 oz.) frozen cranberry–raspberry juice concentrate

Place the strawberries and thawed lemonade and cranberry-raspberry concentrates in a blender; cover and process until smooth. Transfer to a punch bowl. Gently stir in ginger ale and club soda. Top with scoops of sherbet. Serve immediately. Yield: about 5 quarts

Grandpa's Margarita

Unearthed by Julie

1 part tequila
1 part triple sec
½ part lime juice
½ part Sprite

Mix and serve over crushed ice.

NOTE: Who would have thought the Grandpa would have a margarita recipe. I didn't find this one out until the girls were of drinking age. Guess that's why Grandma was always so happy. Julie adds, "This simple, delicious drink was one of Grandpa's favorite early evening drinks. We all remember him reaching up into that impossibly high cabinet to get his glass. It also made for one especially uproarious Thanksgiving afternoon!"

Concentrated Tea Syrup

½ c. loose tea leaves
3 c. boiling water
2½ c. sugar
1 tsp. soda

Add tea to boiling water; remove from heat. Cover and steep for 5 minutes. Strain; do not dilute. Stir in sugar and soda. Refrigerate. To use, pour ⅓ to ½ cup in a glass; dilute to taste with water. Will keep about a week.

NOTE: When serving a crowd, make tea syrup ahead and then simply mix a pitcher full as needed. Speaking of crowds, now is as good a place as any to talk about serving a buffet.

SERVING A BUFFET

The most effective way to serve a large number of people is to set up a buffet. Follow these tried and true guidelines for not only the most gorgeous buffet, but also the most effectively organized one, too.

- ✦ Use inverted dishes, boxes, or other objects to raise some dishes on your buffet to a different height. A wide variety of serving dishes, equipped with stands or pedestals are also available, but I am a believer in using what you already have.
- ✦ To add pizazz, cover the boxes or whatever used to elevate food with remnants of shiny, silky material or fabrics to match your theme. I once used my red satin pajamas for a Christmas table setting–no one knew and it was beautiful. Add seasonal trim helter-skelter to your table setting.
- ✦ Set up a self-service beverage bar to make your guests feel comfortable and at home, plus it's easier for you, too. (I did not teach this to my students. Now that I am retired though, I can buy beer at the local grocery store without any qualms at all.)
- ✦ A spot at a table is not needed for every guest, but if there is space, go ahead and set places with flatware, napkin, and beverage.
- ✦ If there is not space for everyone at a table, make sure everyone has a place to put their beverage: trays on an ottoman, end or casual tables, even a plant stand can be squeezed in–without the plant, of course.
- ✦ Serve foods that are easily eaten with a fork.
- ✦ If a food requires the use of both hands to serve, set it far enough back from the edge of the buffet table so guests can set their plate down in front of it to serve themselves.

ARRANGE THE BUFFET AS FOLLOWS:

- ✦ Position the centerpiece toward the back or one end of the table if not serving from all sides of the table. The centerpiece can be larger and taller on a buffet table.
- ✦ Plates are placed at the beginning of the line.
- ✦ Position foods in this order:
    - Main dishes with their accompaniments following
    - Vegetables
    - Salads
    - Bread and butter
- ✦ Place flatware and napkin–preferably wrapped in a neat package–at the end of the buffet line.

Serving a Buffet, continued

- ✦ The beverage is the last item on your buffet. Think about this arrangement. Guests have both hands free to fill their plates, then they get their eating utensils and beverage when their plates are full. It just makes good sense.
- ✦ Serve desserts from a separate table or counter. Guests should not have to handle dessert along with their dinner plate.

Thinking about table settings brings to mind my sister Elaine's talent for creating absolutely gorgeous floral arrangements from silk flowers. They were one of our best sellers when we had our design business. She created the bouquets that made our weddings special and she has played the role of teacher when it comes to decorating. Her skill and expertise in creating wall groupings and arranging things is unequaled. She can move one little item and make the whole grouping look right.

Iced Tea

From the Food Lab

½ c. tea leaves or 4 family size tea bags	**1 c. sugar**
	2 c. water

Put about an inch of water and the sugar in a gallon jar or pitcher. Bring the 2 cups water to boil. Add tea leaves or bags. *Do not boil.* Cover; let steep 3 to 4 minutes. Strain into jar. Add water to reach desired strength.

BREWING TEA

Iced tea machines and gallons of prepared tea are quick and easy, but nothing beats real, fresh-brewed iced tea. It's becoming a lost art. In fact, my friend Dianne brings her own tea everywhere she goes. When you get addicted to that fresh-brewed flavor, nothing else will do. Now, for a little chemistry: tea contains tannins which provide flavor; if allowed to boil or to steep too long, these tannins turn to tannic acid and become bitter. Also, the sugar provides a sweeter flavor when dissolved in hot tea. That's why it takes so much sugar to sweeten tea when dining at restaurants–sugar just doesn't dissolve in ice cold tea. Just one last thing: always put a small amount of cold water in the bottom of your glass pitcher or jar before adding the hot liquid or it just might crack.

Nancy's Iced Tea

Nancy

2 c. Lipton instant tea mix with lemon
2 qt. water
1 qt. ginger ale

Dissolve tea mix in water. Add ginger ale and stir. Keep refrigerated.

NOTE: Nancy says, "It's not my original recipe but I love it! I keep this in my refrigerator all the time."

Hot Buttered Rum

Julie

1 c. sugar
1 c. butter
1 c. brown sugar
2 c. vanilla ice cream
Rum
Water, boiling
Nutmeg

In 2-quart sauce pan, combine sugar, brown sugar, and butter. Cook over low heat until butter is melted, 6–8 minutes. In mixing bowl, combine cooked mixture with ice cream. Beat at medium speed, scraping bowl often until smooth, 1–2 minutes. Store in refrigerator up to 2 weeks, or in the freezer up to one month. To serve, combine a jigger of rum and boiling water to fill a tall mug two-thirds full; top with a scoop of rum mix and a sprinkle of nutmeg.

Hot Wassail Tea

School Dinner Recipe

1 can (6 oz.) frozen orange juice
1 can (6 oz.) frozen lemonade
1 qt. apple juice
1 c. sugar
1½ tsp. whole cloves
2 sticks cinnamon
1 tsp. ground ginger
5 c. boiling water
3 c. strong tea

Mix first 3 ingredients. Place over low heat. Add sugar and spices, stir in boiling water and tea. Heat, but do not boil. Yield: 25 to 30 cups

NOTE: To prepare in 30 cup electric coffee maker (percolator), dissolve the sugar in the first 3 ingredients over low heat. Pour into coffee maker, add 5 cups tap water (not boiling), and the tea. Place the spices in the basket. Brew as normal. Be sure to clean the spigot of the coffee maker good before using for coffee again. The residue from the orange juice or lemonade floating in coffee makes people wonder.

Instant Chocolate Mix

8 qt. size pkg. nonfat dry milk
2 lb. Nestle's Quik
1 lb. powdered sugar
16 oz. Coffee-mate

Mix all ingredients well. Store in airtight container. Use ⅓ cup mix for each cup hot chocolate.

NOTE: This mix is a lot less expensive than the packaged mixes, plus I think it tastes better. Fill quart jars with this mix to give as gifts during the holidays; include the instructions on a cute little tag.

Mocha-Latte Syrup

¾ c. sugar
½ c. cocoa
4 T. instant espresso
½ tsp. cinnamon
½ c. water
2 tsp. vanilla

Combine the sugar, cocoa, instant coffee, and cinnamon in a small saucepan; add water and stir until combined. Bring to a boil and continue boiling for 1 minute. Remove from heat; add vanilla. Refrigerate up to 2 weeks. To prepare, combine 1 tablespoon mocha-latte syrup with ¾ cup hot milk.

Mocha Punch

6 c. water
½ c. instant chocolate drink mix
½ c. sugar
¼ c. instant coffee granules
½ gal. vanilla ice cream
½ gal. chocolate ice cream
1 c. heavy whipping cream, whipped
Chocolate curls, optional

In a large saucepan, bring water to a boil. Remove from the heat. Add drink mix, sugar, and coffee; stir until dissolved. Cover and refrigerate for 4 hours or overnight. About 30 minutes before serving, pour chocolate mixture into a punch bowl. Add ice cream by scoopfuls; stir until partially melted. Garnish with dollops of whipped cream (or use the can of real whipped cream) and chocolate curls. Yield: 20–25 servings (about 5 quarts)

NOTE: For a smaller group, just mix about half of the ingredients at a time in a small punch bowl or a trifle bowl. I'm calling the chocolate curls optional, because they are not easy to make. Mine were bits and pieces, more like chocolate flakes. Janis and I recently had lunch together at a really neat café; then we walked most of it off while shopping antique stores. At least that was our story when we returned to the café later that afternoon for one of their renowned desserts. They were so beautiful and the owner told me the secret to making chocolate garnishes. I'm happy to share so those curls won't have to be optional.

CHOCOLATE CURLS AND GRATED CHOCOLATE

CHOCOLATE CURLS: Get the giant chocolate bars and then use a high-quality peeler to strip off pieces from the side edge. Chocolate should be at room temperature.

GRATED: Unwrap chocolate squares, leaving each square on paper wrapper. Microwave on medium for 10 seconds; then grate using the largest hole of cheese shredder. Use the wrapping paper to hold the chocolate and protect your fingers while grating. Adjust the microwave cooking time if softening more or less chocolate squares. It's hard to grate melted chocolate, so be careful.

Mock Champagne Cocktail

School Dinner Recipe

1 bottle (7 oz.) lemon-lime carbonated beverage, chilled
½ c. apple juice, chilled
3 thin slices lemon

Mix just before serving. Pour into chilled, stemmed glasses. Cut lemon slices halfway across center and hang over edge of glasses. Yield: 3 servings

NOTE: I wonder if a 7-ounce bottle of 7-Up is even available any more. Today I would simply pour half soda and half apple juice and call it done. I'm going to remember this recipe the next time I have guests who don't drink alcohol. This is less expensive than the sparkling grape juices now available. Cranberry or other flavored juices can also be used.

MeaLea

Rosemary

2 cans (48 oz. ea.) pineapple juice
1 can (12 oz.) orange juice concentrate
4 c. strong tea
1 can (6 oz.) lemonade concentrate
4 c. rum
Lemon-lime soda

Mix juices, tea, lemonade, and rum; freeze. To serve: fill glass halfway with frozen mixture and use any lemon-lime soda for top half. Stir.

Sparkling Cranberry Punch

2 qt. cranberry cocktail juice
1 qt. sparkling water
1 can (6 oz.) frozen pink lemonade concentrate

Chill the cranberry cocktail juice and sparkling water; thaw the lemonade. In a large punch bowl, combine cranberry cocktail and lemonade concentrate. Stir in sparkling water. Serve immediately. 25 servings (about ½ cup each)

MAKING AN ICE RING WITH FRUIT

This recipe is so easy, why not make an ice ring to jazz it up a little? Fill mold about one-third full with cranberry cocktail juice and arrange lemon slices–they will float. Freeze, checking to make sure the slices stay in place. When frozen, add enough additional chilled juice to cover lemons; freeze again. Finally, fill completely and freeze solid. If short on time, just pour either cranberry cocktail juice or sparkling water into ice trays and freeze. The greatest advantage of using ice rings or cubes made from punch ingredients is that the punch isn't diluted as the ice melts.

"Vegetables are the food of the earth; fruit seems more the food of the heavens." – Sepal Felicivant

Spiced Tea Mix

My Mentor, Mrs. Fuller

⅔ c. instant tea
2 c. orange Tang
2 pkg. lemon flavored Kool Aid
1⅔ c. sugar
½ T. cloves
½ T. allspice
1 tsp. cinnamon

Mix well and store in a tightly covered jar. Use 2 teaspoons to each cup of water, hot or cold.

No doubt, without Mrs. Fuller's wisdom and assistance I would not have made it through those first years of teaching as unscathed as I did. Her memory will always have a special spot in my heart. We had so much fun together. When we had dinners, which were quite often, I was responsible for the majority of the cooking since I taught the foods classes. Besides, I knew she had put in her fair share–she reminisced about how she used to have to take the girls out to the ag boys' chicken coop to catch the chickens...you can imagine the rest. (I'm sure you've heard of the phrase "running around like a chicken with it's head cut off.") A smile still comes to my face when I remember our basking in the limelight of these events. The two of us would sit down, prop up our feet, and direct cleanup. Inevitably, after almost every occasion, something we forgot to serve would be found in the fridge–whipped butter, hors d'oeuvres, the parsley. It got to be too funny! How was parsley going to grow on our graves if we left it in the fridge?

Strawberry Shooters

Granee J–Texan's Tailgating

Strawberries, fresh & biggest available
Vodka
Whipped cream in squirt can

Remove leaves and hollow out strawberries; place in a clean, empty egg carton. Fill with vodka; top with whipped cream. Pass around carefully, make a toast, and enjoy.

"Strawberries are the angels of the earth, innocent and sweet with green leafy wings reaching heavenward." – Terri Guillemets

Teacher's Fun Punch

2 sm. cans limeade
2 sm. cans lemonade (yellow)
1 lg. can orange juice
8 c. water
1 fifth (750 ml) light rum
4 c. club soda

Mix and chill. Serve with Hot Tub Dip, page 38.

While elementary students vividly imagine their teachers living in their classroom, sleeping under their desks, and surviving on the treats they distribute, high school students haven't got a clue that teachers have a life outside of the classroom. Don't tell them, but our after-school, off-campus get-togethers were a blast. We'd spend a bit of time commiserating with each other over this or that problem–usually an administrator–then we'd get down to the business of enjoying each others' company and letting go of accumulated stress. The hot tub in Marilyn's backyard helped with that task. Of course, a smidgeon of alcohol made this whole process much more enjoyable. Thanks to Christmas, spring breaks, and these get-togethers, most of us managed to stay fairly sane. Notice, I said "most of us." And our students thought spring break was for them.

Wassail

2 liters ginger ale
64 oz. apple cider
1 sm. bag red hots
3–4 cinnamon sticks
1–2 tsp. whole cloves

Bring all ingredients to a boil in a large pot. Reduce heat and simmer 10–15 minutes. Remove cloves and cinnamon sticks before serving.

"Some people like to paint pictures, or do gardening, or build a boat in the basement. Other people get a tremendous pleasure out of the kitchen, because cooking is just as creative and imaginative an activity as drawing, or wood carving, or music." – Julia Child

Tipsy Tea

Mrs. Martin

25 fresh mint leaves
2 qt. strong tea
1 qt. water
Sugar
2 c. dark rum
2 cans (6 oz. ea.) frozen lemonade concentrate, thawed & undiluted
Fresh mint sprigs

Bruise mint leaves by rubbing between palms of hands. Combine bruised mint, tea, water, rum, lemonade concentrate, and sugar (about 1 cup) to taste; stir until sugar dissolves. Chill until very cold. Strain; serve over ice. Garnish with sprigs of mint. Yield: about 1 gallon

SOURCE: This recipe is from Mrs. Martin, the one who makes the hush puppies included later. She is from England where she met and married Mr. Martin during WW II; she still sports a lovely English accent. The Martins attended our church and were fast friends with my in-laws and parents. I knew she loved tea, but I had no idea about this. I spoke with Mrs. Martin recently to obtain permission to print her recipes and she said, "I took this tea to my daughter's one hot summer afternoon. She called me the next day and told me not to make this tea anymore, saying, 'It knocked me on my butt!' So, I haven't made that tea in a long time."

White Sangria

1 c. unsweetened pineapple juice
¼ c. lemon juice
1 med. orange, sliced
1 med. lemon, sliced
1 med. tart apple, thinly sliced
1 bottle (750 ml.) Riesling or other sweet white wine
1 c. triple sec liqueur
1 c. lemon-lime soda, chilled
Ice cubes

In a large pitcher, combine the pineapple juice, lemon juice, and orange and lemon slices; mash gently with a wooden spoon until fruit is partially crushed. Add the apple slices, wine, and triple sec. Refrigerate for 2–4 hours. Just before serving, add soda. Serve over ice. Yield: 7 servings

NOTE: Fruity and sweet, this goes together in minutes. Guests will find it as welcome as a splash of sunshine. Plus, there's an added bonus–it doesn't leave a stain if spilled on table linens or carpets.

Notes

SOUPS

Baked Potato Soup

Elaine

2 pkg. (32 oz. ea.) frozen hash brown potatoes
2 boxes (32 oz. ea.) chicken broth
1 carrot, grated
2 pkg. white gravy mix
Sour cream
Cheddar cheese
Bacon crumbles
Green onions or chives, chopped

Cook potatoes in chicken broth with grated carrot until potatoes are done. Prepare gravy mixes and pour into potatoes. Serve with choice of toppings for each bowl of soup, just as you would for a baked potato. Delicious.

NOTE: Elaine adds, "Takes about 30 minutes to make. Real simple. Sometimes I use a ham bone to cook with soup."

Elaine brought me this soup after I had been in the hospital and it made me better right away just knowing that she cared. I think that's the whole chicken soup thing in a nutshell. It makes us feel better because someone is taking the time to help us, showing us that we matter. I have always depended on my first-born sister and she has never let me down.

Clam Chowder

School Dinner Recipe

4 med. potatoes
1 med. onion
¼ c. celery tops, chopped
1 T. butter
1 tsp. parsley, chopped
1 c. water
1 can (6.5 oz.) minced clams
3 c. milk

Pare and chop potatoes and onion. Add celery, butter, water, and parsley. Cook until tender; mash slightly. Add clams and milk. Heat, but do not boil. Serve with breadsticks or croutons. For richer chowder, use part cream in place of milk. For a low-fat version, use reduced-fat or skim milk.

Creamy Onion Soup

Friends Christmas Dinner

8 med. onions, thinly sliced
⅓ c. butter
2 T. all purpose flour
1 tsp. salt
½ tsp. pepper
8 c. (64 oz.) chicken broth
1 c. (8 oz.) sour cream
½ c. milk
12 slices French bread (1-in. thick), toasted
1 c. (4 oz.) Mozzarella cheese, shredded

In a large kettle or Dutch oven, sauté onions in butter until tender. Sprinkle with flour, salt, and pepper; cook and stir for 1 minute. Gradually add broth. Bring to a boil; cook and stir for 2 minutes. Reduce heat; simmer, uncovered, for 30 minutes. Combine sour cream and milk. Stir into soup; heat through (do not boil). Place a slice of toasted bread in each soup bowl; ladle soup over bread. Sprinkle with cheese. Yield: 12 servings

Catfish Court Bouillon

3 lb. catfish fillets, broiled or boiled
1 c. oil
1 c. flour
1 c. bell pepper, diced
1 c. white onion, diced
1 c. celery, diced
1–2 cloves garlic, minced
3 c. tomato sauce (to taste)
3–4 qt. water
2 T. parsley, finely chopped
½ c. green onion tops, chopped
1 T. Worcestershire sauce
2 tsp. salt
2½ tsp. red pepper
2½ tsp. black pepper
3 tsp. paprika

Cook fish prior to preparing court bouillon. Fish may be broiled with butter or olive oil, lemon juice, and paprika or it may be boiled for 20–30 minutes. Fish can be boiled in the same water added to the court bouillon later. In a cast iron skillet, make the roux with oil and flour, cooking over medium heat and stirring constantly until it darkens to the color of peanut butter. Add bell pepper, onion, celery, and garlic; stir around skillet to prevent roux from further darkening. Place roux mixture and all the remaining ingredients except catfish in stock pot; simmer for 25 minutes. Then add cooked fish and cover; simmer another 30 minutes, being sure to stir pot carefully from side to side every once in a while to keep fish from sticking or burning to bottom of pot. Turn off the heat, add a bay leaf, cover and allow to set for 15 minutes. Reheat if necessary and serve over cooked rice.

NOTE: Refer to lesson on making a roux, page 65, if not familiar with that process. I begin with 3 quarts water and add more to stretch servings, if needed. I adjusted the quantity and simplified the preparation of this recipe from Paw Paw's Seafood and Steak House in Lake Charles, Louisiana.

Writing this cookbook is bringing back so many memories, I can almost smell the court bouillon. It was the summer of 1988 and we were headed to Disney World and stopped at Paw Paw's. I think this may have been the beginning of my love affair with Louisiana and its French and Cajun foods. Years later I learned how to pronounce court bouillon: koŏr bē 'ôn. Court is French and means "short" and bouillon is a broth made by stewing meat, fish, or vegetables in water. Anyway, on the way home from Disney, we headed across Florida to the Gulf Coast. What a beautiful drive, marking the beginning of our attraction to the white sands of Destin. We luxuriously stayed a few extra days–couldn't get the girls out of the water. Destin seems like one of my home away from homes now and I simply have to have a regular fix of its white sand beaches, emerald green waters, and abundantly fresh seafood.

Crab Gumbo

Donna

¾ c. cooking oil
2 T. flour
3 sm. onions, chopped
2 buttons garlic, chopped fine
2 stalks celery, chopped
1 green bell pepper, chopped
1 lg. (28 oz.) can crushed tomatoes
1 can (6 oz.) tomato paste
2 qt. water
8–10 male blue crabs, dressed
Salt to taste
Chili powder to taste
3–4 c. fresh or frozen okra, cut into ½-inch pieces
Gumbo filé

Brown flour in oil; chop vegetables very fine and fry in flour and oil. Add tomatoes, paste, water, crabs, and salt. Cover and cook slowly 3–4 hours. Add chili powder the last hour of cooking. If desired, add okra the last hour of cooking, also. Add filé just before serving. Serve over cooked rice.

NOTE: Donna recalls, "Absolutely every summer, usually 4th of July, Granny would make a big pot of gumbo–the longer it cooked, the better it smelled. This gumbo has been passed down through the generations. I make it, my kids make it, but none is as good as Granny's with the crabs Granddaddy caught right off the end of their pier in Galveston." In 2008 Hurricane Ike washed away the beach house and the pier, but not the memories.

Chicken Cheese Chowder

3 chicken breasts, cut in ½" x 1" strips
3 T. butter
1 c. onion, chopped
½ c. celery slices
¼ c. bell pepper, chopped
1 lg. clove garlic, minced
½ tsp. salt
½ tsp. coarse black pepper
¼ tsp. thyme
1½ c. water
1 Miller Lite longneck, opened
2 med. red potatoes, cubed
½ c. Browned Flour
1 c. fresh broccoli, chopped
8 oz. Velveeta cheese, cubed

In a Dutch oven, sauté onion, celery, bell pepper, and garlic in butter. Remove with a slotted spoon and set aside. Sauté chicken and seasonings in remaining butter. Add sautéed veggies, potatoes, and water. Cook over medium-low heat until potatoes are done, about 20 minutes. Make a thin paste with the browned flour and part of the Miller Lite. Slowly stir into the chowder. Let simmer a few minutes; cook the broccoli in a covered glass container on High in the microwave for 2 minutes. Lower the heat on the chowder and add the broccoli and cheese. Cook until cheese melts. Serve with those frozen biscuits that look homemade.

NOTE: The term Dutch oven may be unfamiliar to some–it's a 6-quart large, deep pan with a cover. It can be used on top of the stove over low heat, serving the same purpose as cooking in an oven in most cases. This chowder surely isn't a German recipe because no one ever has to tell a German to open a beer. Of course, a true German will drink the remainder of the beer!

Browned Flour

Place the flour on a baking sheet and cook in a moderately hot oven, 375°–400°, stirring every few minutes until brown. Or place the flour in a cast iron skillet and stir over medium heat until brown. This gives the soup a great flavor and does not add the additional oil or calories a roux would contain.

"It is disgusting to note the increase in the quantity of coffee used by my subjects and the amount of money that goes out of the country in consequence. Everybody is using coffee. If possible, this must be prevented. My people must drink beer." – Frederick the Great, German Ruler

FOLLOWING A RECIPE

This is a good place to discuss the importance of following a recipe–or at least reading through it before beginning preparation. The first time I made this chowder, I got down to the part about making a thin paste and thought, "Where do I get the browned flour?" So before continuing with the recipe, I had to stop and brown some flour. These helpful tips will make you an informed, unstressed performer in the kitchen.

- ✦ Recipes were written and tested by professionals, so follow them until experienced enough to make changes.
- ✦ Read entire recipe before beginning.
- ✦ Assemble ingredients and equipment.
- ✦ Follow recipe steps closely.
- ✦ Complete pre-preparation steps before beginning recipe. For example: preheat the oven, grease the pan, chop the vegetables.
- ✦ Leaving out an ingredient is the most common mistake made, so review ingredient list to make sure you've added everything.
- ✦ The second most common mistake is using a tablespoon instead of a teaspoon. With 3 teaspoons in a tablespoon, that can be a big mistake. My students once experienced an even bigger mistake: They put ¼ cup salt in peanut butter cookies instead of ¼ teaspoon.
- ✦ Always set the timer for the least number of minutes when baking products. Check and cook additional time if needed. It's impossible to *uncook* foods.

"My mother didn't really cook. But she did make key lime pie, until the day the top of the evaporated milk container accidentally ended up in the pie and she decided cooking took too much concentration." – William Norwich

Grandma Simon's Homemade Soup

In Memory of My Grandma

1 soup bone
6 c. water
1 tsp. salt
¼ c. cabbage, chopped
¼ c. celery, chopped
¼ c. onion, chopped
½ c. carrots, chopped
1 c. potatoes, diced
½ c. rice
4 oz. wide egg noodles
¼ tsp. pepper

Cook soup bone in water with salt until done. Remove soup bone; cool and bone meat. Add remaining ingredients and cook until done.

This soup is one of those memories that comes complete with smells and visions. Grandma had big, flat bowls for soup and I could hardly wait to fill mine with this delicious soup. I have a vivid memory of being at Grandma's house with the wide front porch and big square kitchen. I can still see the layout perfectly: the entrance to the kitchen was the entrance to the house; the kitchen table was on the left and a door to the living room on the right. My uncles' bedroom was straight through the kitchen to the back. The refrigerator was tucked in between the table and the one-wall kitchen counter. The sink was in the center of the counter and you could look out the window and see the gate and this huge deep-pink crepe myrtle. The stove was at the end of the counter–right next to the bedroom wall. I have Grandma's old coffee jar that was always filled with cookies and she had a metal Premium Saltines box full of crackers. These were great with the soup, but we also ate the crackers with homemade ice cream. Don't ask me why, but it sure was good. We always spent time with Grandma during the summer and Mrs. Krahn would stop by to pick us up for Vacation Bible School–which was two weeks long back then. Our old church was just a couple of miles from Grandma's house.

"From morning till night, sounds drift from the kitchen, most of them familiar and comforting.... On days when warmth is the most important need of the human heart, the kitchen is the place you can find it; it dries the wet sock, it cools the hot little brain."
– E.B. White

I was so excited when I found this picture of Grandma posing in her kitchen. Check out the running water and Borax soap dispenser–it's just above the faucet and the water bucket that's sitting on a stool. Can you imagine carrying the old dish water outside to dump it? Maybe that's why our grandmas always had such pretty flowers. Much later Grandma had a kitchen counter with a sink and cabinets added–that's what I remember.

Green & Gold Soup

Rosemary

1 head garlic (the whole thing)
1 lb. Italian sausage
1 T. olive oil
6 Yukon Gold potatoes, chopped
1 qt. chicken broth
1 bunch kale, washed, stems removed & chopped
Salt & pepper

Preheat oven to 350°. Wrap garlic in foil and roast for 30 minutes. Brown sausage in soup pot. Remove, drain grease; add olive oil and potatoes. Brown potatoes for about 5 minutes. Add broth and bring to a boil. Reduce heat and cook until potatoes are tender (about 15 minutes). Remove 1–2 cups of the mixture and puree in a blender until smooth. Add kale to soup pot and cook about 10 minutes. Return puree to pot along with sausage. Squeeze roasted garlic out of skin and add to soup. Salt and pepper to taste.

NOTE: Rosemary made this soup as the first course for one of our formal dinners for our friends at Christmas. It's not only impressive, but also nutritious. There are so many other things that can be done with roasted garlic: add to mashed potatoes, combine with fresh cooked vegetables, substitute for fresh garlic in recipes, make roasted garlic butter, use in sauces and gravies, the list goes on.

RAPID BOILING

Rapid boiling will not cook food any faster. 212°, the temperature at which water boils, is as hot as it gets. Rapid boiling causes foods to break apart, but is very useful when cooking pasta to keep it from sticking together. So, those potatoes will not get done any faster by boiling; your soup will just get cloudy from potatoes falling apart and releasing starch. If not careful, rapid boiling will reduce the liquid and the food might burn. In other instances, like reducing a sauce or making jelly, rapid boiling is required to evaporate the liquid.

Hearty Chicken 'n Rice Soup

1 can (14 oz.) chicken broth
2 c. cold water
½ c. uncooked rice
½ c. celery slices
½ c. carrot slices
¾ lb. Velveeta cheese, cubed
1½ c. cooked chicken, chopped
1 can (4 oz.) sliced mushrooms, drained

Combine broth, water, rice, celery, and carrots. Cover and simmer 20–25 minutes or until vegetables and rice are tender. Add remaining ingredients; stir until cheese is melted. Yield: 5 servings, 1 cup each

Hearty Lentil Stew

1 c. lentils, picked through & rinsed
1 can (14 oz.) reduced-sodium chicken broth (1¾ c.)
1 T. vegetable oil
1 T. cumin seeds
2 shallots, thinly sliced
⅓ c. sweetened coconut, shredded
1 lg. (10 oz.) Yukon Gold potato peeled & cut into ¼-in. cubes
6 oz. baby spinach
¼ tsp. salt

In a 2-quart saucepan, combine lentils, broth, and 1 cup water. Heat to boiling on high. Cover and reduce heat to medium-low; simmer 15 minutes or until tender. Meanwhile, in deep 12-inch skillet, heat oil on medium until hot. Add cumin seeds and cook 15 to 30 seconds or until fragrant, stirring. Add shallots and coconut; cook 3 minutes or until golden brown, stirring occasionally. Stir in potatoes and cook 2 minutes. Carefully pour lentil mixture into skillet; stir to combine. Cover and cook 10 minutes. Stir in spinach and salt. Cook 2 minutes or until spinach is wilted, stirring.

"Worries go down better with soup." – Jewish Proverb

Potato Soup with Chicken

4 slices bacon
2 chicken breasts, chopped
1 c. onion, chopped
½ c. celery, chopped
32 oz. frozen hash browns
1 can (14 oz.) chicken broth
3 c. water
1 lg. can evaporated milk

Fry bacon; remove and crumble. Sauté onion, celery, and chicken in bacon fat. Use paper towel to absorb extra bacon fat. Combine all ingredients except the evaporated milk in soup pot, Dutch oven, or crock pot. Cook until potatoes are falling apart. Add evaporated milk when nearly done.

Sauerkraut Soup

Mom

10 c. water
1½–2 lb. ham or sausage
½ c. pearl barley
2 lg. carrots, diced
2 ribs celery, diced
1 c. onion, chopped
2 lg. potatoes, diced
3 tsp. dried parsley
1 can (1 lb.) sauerkraut, drained
Salt & pepper

Bring water to a boil in large kettle and add ham or sausage, which you have diced, and the barley. Simmer uncovered 25–30 minutes. Add vegetables and parsley and return to boiling; simmer 15 minutes longer. Add sauerkraut which has been drained and rinsed. Simmer, covered for 30–40 minutes, stirring occasionally. Salt and pepper to taste.

NOTE: This recipe is on a piece of note paper in Jennie's handwriting and she says it was her Grandma's recipe. I don't particularly remember it, but since it uses traditional German ingredients, it has to be good. Caraway seeds can be added for additional flavor.

Sausage, Peppers, & Onion Soup

3 T. extra-virgin olive oil
1½ lb. hot or sweet bulk Italian sausage
4 cloves garlic, finely chopped
3–4 Cubanelle peppers, seeded & thinly sliced
2 med. onions, thinly sliced
2 T. balsamic vinegar
2 c. chicken stock
2 cans (15 oz.) fire-roasted tomatoes, diced
¼ c. parsley leaves, finely chopped
½ c. fresh basil leaves, torn
½ c. Parmigiano-Reggiano, shredded

Heat oil in Dutch oven or soup pot, add sausage and brown a few minutes; then add garlic, peppers, onions, and cook until soft, 6–7 minutes more. Deglaze pan with a little vinegar, stir in stock and tomatoes and reduce heat to simmer, cook 5 minutes more; then stir in parsley and basil and serve with cheese on top.

Taco Soup

Elaine

1 lb. hamburger
2 cans corn (or 1 can corn & 1 can hominy)
2 cans pinto beans
2 cans Rotel tomatoes
1 pkg. taco seasoning
1 pkg. ranch dressing mix
Shredded cheese
Jalapeño slices
Sour cream
Avocado slices

Brown and drain the hamburger. Add the veggies, juice and all. Stir in taco seasoning and ranch dressing mix. Bring to a boil and simmer until ready to eat. It will be a little thick at first, but will get juicier as it cooks. Garnish each bowl with cheese, jalapeño, sour cream, and avocado.

Shrimp Gumbo

2 c. celery, chopped
4 c. onion, chopped
1 c. bell pepper, chopped
4 cloves garlic, minced
2 bunches green onions
2 T. salt
½ T. black pepper
½ T. crushed red pepper
1 gal. hot water
3–4 lb. med. gulf shrimp, headed
Roux for Gumbo

Place celery, onions, and bell peppers in gumbo pot. Chop green onions, separating the green ends from the white onion part. Add the white ends to the gumbo mixture. Save the green tops to add to gumbo just before serving. Prepare the roux and pour over vegetables when golden brown. Stir and let set a few minutes, allowing the hot roux to sauté the veggies. Add water and seasonings. Bring to a boil, stirring often as ingredients tend to stick to the bottom until it has cooked a little while. Reduce heat and cook slowly for at least 2 hours, preferably all day. Peel and devein shrimp and place in colander with ice, sprinkling with additional crushed red pepper as you go. Set the colander in a bowl and refrigerate until needed. Just before serving time, bring gumbo to a boil; remove ice from shrimp. Add shrimp to gumbo. Cook only until shrimp turn pink, 3–5 minutes. Stir in onion tops and serve in soup plates over cooked rice with Gumbo Filé and hot sauce. Serves 12–16, depending on their appetites and how long it has been since they had my gumbo.

Roux for Gumbo

2 c. cooking oil
2 c. flour

Measure flour into large bowl. Heat oil over medium heat in large iron skillet. When a few grains of flour sizzles when dropped in oil, stir flour in gradually. Lower heat. It is very important to keep **stirring constantly**. After all the flour has been combined with the oil, turn fire down very low and cook until golden brown, **stirring constantly**. When roux is golden brown, pour into gumbo pot into which the chopped vegetables have been placed. Roux will get too dark if it remains in the skillet in which it was prepared.

ROUX AND GUMBO MAKING 101

- ✦ When making a roux, stay right beside the cast iron skillet, stirring constantly, or it will burn. It's a slow process, but well worth the time and effort.
- ✦ Use a wire whip when first adding the flour to the hot oil; then when mixture is smooth, switch to a wooden spoon. I have a wooden roux spoon that has a flat edge instead of being curved on the end. This makes it easy to scrape all the flour from the bottom of the iron skillet and helps prevent burning. A large wooden spoon will also work. A long handle prevents getting popped with hot oil.
- ✦ Again for emphasis: Be sure to **stir constantly** when making the roux. I have thrown batches of roux away because I turned around to get a drink of water. Plan on the roux-making to take about 30 minutes.
- ✦ Chop the veggies before starting the roux. The roux really will burn if left in the hot skillet, so pour it over those chopped veggies immediately and stir it all together. An added benefit is that the hot roux actually sautés the veggies a little bit, adding even more flavor.
- ✦ I have an *old, dark penny* that I keep in the drawer by the stove. I lay this penny by the skillet when making roux and use it's color to determine when the roux is brown enough.
- ✦ Leave the green onion tops on the counter by the gumbo. I can't remember how many times I have forgotten to add them and they really add the *piece de resistance* when serving.
- ✦ Always serve gumbo with additional Louisiana Hot Sauce, Tabasco Sauce and Gumbo Filé. Filé is a spice made from dried and ground sassafras leaves. It is sprinkled sparingly over gumbo when serving, giving it a distinctive flavor. The Filé also adds heat to the gumbo. For a thicker gumbo and enhanced flavor, add a little Filé while cooking.
- ✦ In poorer times, I have been known to use kingfish balls or chunks of firm fish, like a large drum, instead of shrimp in my gumbo. In richer times, I add lump crab meat just before serving.
- ✦ Pay the extra dollars a pound to get fresh gulf shrimp, preferably not split down the back. Their flavor just can't compare with any other.
- ✦ Use the least expensive rice, with broken grains so the starch oozes out making it sticky, to serve with gumbo. It's just better with sticky rice!

The girls and I have our family Christmas on December 23: Christmas Eve's Eve. We always have gumbo with enough shrimp so every ladle is full. As if that isn't decadent enough, we also have steamed snow crab or Alaskan crab legs with melted butter. Of course, we have a good wine and lots of garlic bread, too. Our favorite dessert is Death by Chocolate. After we have sufficiently dined, or overdone our eating, we open presents. This giving is made special by taking turns, each person opening one present at a time and waiting for their turn before opening another. The grandkids are finally old enough to take turns, but still wind up finishing way ahead of the adults. If you've ever been through a whirlwind of bow-untying and paper-tearing and didn't see what anyone received, you might want to start this tradition. Our family loves it. Daddy used to be so cute when we went from young to old–he just couldn't wait. He'd be peaking when he thought no one was looking. We switch each year, oldest going first one year and the youngest first the next.

Julie, Lydia, and Verna enjoying Christmas dinner:
All you can eat shrimp gumbo and crab legs.
Notice Lydia is eating a Christmas sugar cookie.
Serving from the crab and gumbo pots is part of our tradition, too!

Split Pea Soup

1 lb. dry split peas
2½ qt. water
1 meaty ham bone
1½ c. onion, chopped
1 c. each diced celery, carrots & potatoes
1 tsp. dried parsley flakes
½ tsp. pepper
¼ tsp. garlic salt
¼ tsp. dried marjoram
Salt to taste
½ c. rice, optional

In a Dutch oven or soup kettle, place the peas, water, and ham bone; bring to a boil. Reduce heat; cover and simmer for 2 hours, stirring occasionally. Stir in the remaining ingredients. Bring to a boil. Reduce heat; cover and simmer for 30 minutes or until vegetables are tender. Remove ham bone; when cool enough to handle, remove meat from the bone. Chop ham and return to the soup; heat through. Add the rice for a thicker soup. Yield: 3 quarts

Vegetable-Meatball Soup

Elaine

7 c. water
1 can (28 oz.) stewed tomatoes
4 chicken bouillon cubes
1 med. onion, chopped
1 c. potatoes, diced
1 c. celery, diced
2 pkg. (10 oz. ea.) frozen mixed vegetables
1 T. sugar
1 bay leaf
½ tsp. basil
¼ tsp. dill seed
¼ tsp. pepper
⅛ tsp. garlic powder
1 T. salt
1 c. barley, if desired
1–2 lb. ground beef, formed into sm. balls

Combine all ingredients, except ground beef. Bring to a boil, then add meatballs. Bring to a boil again, reduce heat and simmer for 1 hour or until vegetables are tender. Great to prepare in a crock pot. Yield: 3 quarts

Elaine is the business person of our family. She typed up St. John's first church cookbook years ago when you typed on a real typewriter without a word processing program. Elaine still takes dictation, using the shorthand she learned in high school and business college. She's still working in the oil and gas industry, and yes, her boss still gives dictation the old-fashioned way.

Notes

SALADS

Aunt Geraldine's Potato Salad

Aunt Geraldine

5 pounds potatoes
1 T. salt
2 ribs celery, diced
1 c. green onion, chopped
½ bell pepper, diced
1 lg. (4 oz.) jar pimientos, chopped
1 c. or more Hellman's or Kraft mayonnaise

Scrub potatoes and boil in jackets with salt the night before. Drain. Next day, peel potatoes, and cut into small pieces. Add the remaining ingredients and enough mayonnaise to make a moist salad. Taste and adjust for salt. Let set out until serving time. Refrigerate leftover potato salad.

Aunt Geraldine's potato salad is truly "to die for." Others have tried to make it just like hers and always come up short. This time, I went back to Aunt Geraldine and got all the hidden details, like cooking the potatoes the day before. There have been discussions about whether she used Kraft or Hellman's mayonnaise, does it have celery, and are there any pickles? Well, this recipe is the end of discussion. Make it just like this for potato salad just like hers. I just got off the phone with Aunt Geraldine and she adds, "I like my potato salad where it's wet. I don't like it dry. You can make it like this or you make it the day before and put it in the refrigerator–it'll work that a way, too."

NOTE: When a person makes a really great food, there is no end to the discussion about how it is made. I guarantee, whether you use Hellman's or Kraft mayonnaise, put celery or not, include pimientos or not, this potato salad is absolutely delicious. Just don't venture out there and put any eggs or pickles in it. Definitely not any mustard!

FOOD SAFETY AND SANITATION

Potato salad always brings up the question of food safety. Some foods just naturally spoil more rapidly than others. Generally foods prepared using eggs, mayonnaise, chicken, and all types of poultry are more susceptible to rapid growth of harmful bacteria. Remember that any food can and will spoil if not handled properly. Google "food safety and sanitation" for extensive details about food safety for every step of the journey from the farm to the table. Here's a simple list of facts to remember that I always taught my students. Follow them and most instances of food-borne illness will be avoided.

- ✦ Proper hand-washing requires the use of warm/hot water and soap. Rub hands together, including wrists and lower arms while singing "Happy Birthday to You" twice. Rinse and dry with clean or paper towel.
- ✦ Store foods properly, maintaining correct refrigerator: 35°–38°, freezer: 0°–4°, and dry storage temperatures.
- ✦ Replace dish towels and cloths daily.
- ✦ Keep foods out of the *temperature danger zone.*
- ✦ The danger zone ranges from 44–135°. In simple terms, that's the temperature of foods left on the counter or stove.
- ✦ Throw away foods that have been in the danger zone for 2 hours or more.
- ✦ Keep hot foods hot and cold foods cold.
- ✦ Reheat foods, especially chicken and poultry, only once. So, if you have leftover turkey and dressing, refrigerate within 2 hours of serving time, and when serving again, heat only the amount that will be eaten.
- ✦ Do not allow hot foods to sit out to "cool down" before refrigerating.
- ✦ Transfer cooked foods to shallow dishes for storage in the refrigerator or freezer. They will cool down faster, preventing harmful bacterial growth.
- ✦ Pork, poultry, eggs, and ground meats should be cooked *well done* to destroy harmful bacteria.
- ✦ Avoid cross-contamination. You'll find these instructions again under food cutting tips. Reading them twice will help you remember. Cut fruits and veggies before cutting meat, fish, poultry, eggs, pork, or cheese, thus preventing *cross-contamination.* Meat products contain bacteria that can be transferred to other foods from the knife or cutting board used. Fruits and veggies are great hosts, allowing these bacteria to grow and multiply quickly. So, either use a separate knife and board, wash and dry board and knife throughly between foods, or just do like I said above–cut veggies and fruits first and meats last.

- Use hot, soapy water with a hot-water rinse when hand-washing dishes.
- The most dangerous food contaminants are virtually invisible and don't have any odor, so do not taste a questionable food. *IF IN DOUBT, THROW IT OUT!*
- Do not use dent, bulging, or rusted cans of foods.

Broccoli Slaw

12 oz. broccoli cole slaw
8 oz. frozen green peas
6 oz. poppyseed dressing
¾ c. honey roasted peanuts

Combine slaw, peas, and dressing up to 1 day ahead of time. Stir in peanuts just before serving.

SOURCE: I took Mama to the senior citizen dinner at church and wouldn't leave until I found out how to make this dish. It is so simple and so good.

Carrot & Raisin Salad

2 lb. carrots, shredded
1 can (20 oz.) crushed pineapple, drained
1 c. raisins
½ c. powdered sugar
1 c. mayonnaise

Mix carrots, pineapple, and raisins. Blend sugar with the mayonnaise and pour over carrot mixture. Mix well, cover, and chill at least 2 hours.

"Vegetables are a must on a diet. I suggest carrot cake, zucchini bread, and pumpkin pie." – Jim Davis

Caesar Salad Dressing

FIRST THINGS FIRST: I really don't like anchovies in person. They're such hairy little things–yuk! But I absolutely love Caesar Salad. Being the nutrition and food safety freak that I am, the raw egg yolks in Caesar dressing always worries me. This recipe fits my needs perfectly.

3 garlic cloves
4–5 anchovy fillets, packed in oil
2–3 splashes Tabasco sauce
1–2 lemons
2–3 splashes Worcestershire sauce
1 tsp. red wine vinegar
1 T. Dijon mustard
2 tsp. balsamic vinegar
1–3 tsp. cracked black pepper
1 c. mayonnaise

Mince the garlic and anchovy fillets or process by pulsing in a food processor. Add the remaining ingredients except the lemon. Stir together until smooth. Squeeze in about 2 teaspoons or so of lemon juice; mix it in and taste. You're looking for a very tangy taste. Keep adding lemon juice until the dressing has a nice twang. Chill dressing for a few hours to allow the flavors to bloom (and to give you time to forget about the hairy things). The anchovy and pepper will become more pronounced. Can be made ahead and kept in the fridge a few days. Yield: about 1½ cups

NOTE: Additional Instructions (for real): Throw the remainder of the anchovies away–far away–along with their can. Place in a heavy Ziploc bag before putting in the trash. If possible, make this dressing the day before trash pick up comes. If using a recipe that calls for egg yolks, coddle eggs at 190° for 4 minutes before adding.

Cherry Blossom Mold

From the Food Lab

2 c. boiling liquid (water or fruit syrup)
1 pkg. (6 oz.) cherry gelatin
2 c. dairy sour cream
2 c. dark sweet cherries, pitted
⅓ c. blanched almonds, slivered

Pour boiling water over gelatin in small mixing bowl, stirring until all gelatin is dissolved. Cool. Add sour cream and beat until smooth. Chill until slightly thickened, but not set. Stir in cherries and almonds. Pour into 6-cup ring mold or into 10 individual molds. Chill until firm. If desired, garnish salad with additional cherries.

NOTE: Canned, sweetened black cherries can be used, just be sure to drain them. We never had access to a store with fresh cherries and these work just fine.

MAKING A JELLO MOLD

Measure the amount of liquid the mold will hold and match that amount to the total amount of recipe ingredients. Lightly grease the mold with vegetable oil. When adding solids to gelatin, chill until Jello is the consistency of egg whites. Stir in fruit or other solid ingredients, place in mold, and refrigerate until gelatin is set. If you want ingredients *fixed* in place, follow the instructions for making ice rings included in the beverage section. When ready to remove gelatin from the mold, loosen the edges with a dinner knife, and dip the mold in slightly hot water for a few seconds. Place the serving plate on top of the mold and invert. Gently shake and it will pop right out. To use lettuce leaves as a base for the Jello mold, place them up-side-down on top of the mold, place the serving plate on top of the lettuce leaves and invert. Be careful not to use water that is too hot or the mold will start to melt.

I remember having Jello for dessert after supper quite often while growing up. Even though it was just made in a plain bowl, Jello was a special treat. Unless it was Monday and we had part of Mama's weekend cake or pie left, we had Jello or canned fruit for dessert–but we always had dessert. More importantly, we always all sat down and ate together.

MEAL TERMINOLOGY

My family has lunch and supper during the week and on Sunday, after church, we have dinner. That's how us country folks defined our mealtimes. Technically speaking, lunch and supper are the smaller meals of the day while dinner refers to the larger meal. So if your larger meal is at noontime, you have breakfast, dinner, and supper that day. If your larger meal is at night, you have breakfast, lunch, and dinner. Breakfast is perhaps the most important meal of the day since food from the previous day has been used up. Nutrients from breakfast are burned up quickly, so it kicks starts your metabolism and assists with maintaining proper body weight.

Chicken Salad for Sandwiches

Laurie

1 pkg. boneless skinless chicken breasts (about 1½ lb.)
2 celery stalks, diced
½ sm. onion, diced
½ c. Miracle Whip
½ c. mayonnaise
1 T. mustard
Croissant buns

In a skillet, cook chicken in a small amount of water until done; add salt and pepper to taste. Drain and cool. Finely chop chicken and combine with celery and onion. Add 3 m's to taste. Chill and serve on croissant buns.

SOURCE: Chicken salad is one of those foods that I absolutely love and often resist. I never used to make it until one of my hosts, Laurie, served chicken salad sandwiches at her party and gave me her recipe. Laurie says, "I'm sure you've had a great time working on your cookbook, and I'm flattered that you chose to include my chicken salad recipe. The recipe is one that my mom made growing up and I think it was a family recipe that came from her mother. My husband likes me to add diced grapes or pineapple along with pecans. We have never added egg to the recipe, although some people may like it. This is making me hungry...."

Chinese Chicken Salad

Granee J

1 chicken breast (6 oz.)
2 T. almonds, slivered
2 T. sesame seeds, toasted
½ head cabbage, sliced thinly
½ pkg. Top Ramen chicken flavored noodles, uncooked & broken into pieces

DRESSING
1½ T. sugar
¼ c. salad oil (do not double)
1 tsp. Accent
1 tsp. salt
½ tsp. black pepper
3 T. white vinegar
1 pkg. Ramen chicken seasoning

Bake, grill, or broil chicken and chop into chunks. Combine with sesame seeds, cabbage, and noodles. Mix dressing ingredients well and pour over salad. Chill for a couple of hours before serving.

NOTE: Granee J says, "I always double the recipe so there is enough to enjoy the next day–it's better then anyway." Substitute Chinese cabbage for an Oriental flair.

Chinese Cabbage Salad

Jennie

1 head Chinese or red cabbage, chopped fine
6–8 green onions, chopped
8 T. almonds, slivered
4 T. sunflower seeds
2 pkg. Top Ramen noodles (save seasoning packets)

DRESSING
½ c. vegetable oil
5 T. rice vinegar
2 seasoning pkg. from noodles
4 T. sugar
½ tsp. salt
1 tsp. pepper
2 tsp. Accent

Crunch the noodles up into a large bowl. Mix all ingredients into the noodles. Make dressing and combine with dry mixture. Toss well. Serves many.

VARIATION: Jennie says, "Add cucumber slices, 1 teaspoon of orange zest, and juice from about ¼ orange. Serve topped with my Orange Peel Chicken. What's good about this recipe? The second day." The chicken recipe is on page 165. Sounds like a great combination to me.

Destin Shrimp Salad

Created in June 2004, while staying at the Mainsail in Destin, Florida

Leftover boiled shrimp, peeled & chopped (save a few to arrange on salad)
2–3 ribs celery, chopped
Green onions, chopped
Lemon zest
Lime zest
⅓ c. Kraft mayonnaise
Coarse ground black pepper
Mrs. G's or other Cajun seasoning
1 avocado, sliced
3 Roma tomatoes, seeded & slivered
Romaine lettuce

Mix all but avocado, tomatoes, lettuce, and a few reserved shrimp together; serve over Romaine and top with Roma tomatoes, avocado slices, and the reserved shrimp. The proportions are not too important in this recipe...the important thing is to enjoy the shrimp and the beach. Oh, in order to have leftover boiled shrimp, buy at least a pound of headless shrimp per person for the shrimp boil held the night before.

REMOVING AN AVOCADO SEED

Rosemary taught me how to remove the seed from the avocado. Halve the avocado by slicing lengthwise around the seed. Twist halves apart and the seed will remain in one half. Hold the half with the seed in the palm of your hand and carefully whack the seed with a paring or utility knife. Twist the knife and the seed will pop out.

Cranberry Mold

2 pkg. (3 oz. ea.) cherry Jello
2 c. sour cream
1 can (16 oz.) cranberry sauce

Prepare gelatin using package instructions. Chill until thickened but not set. Beat in sour cream and cranberry sauce. Pour into prepared 2-quart mold and chill until firm.

Dressed Waldorf Salad

School Dinner Recipe

1 c. mayonnaise
1 c. sour cream
2 T. honey
3 c. apples, diced
2 c. celery, diced
1 c. walnuts, chopped
2 c. red grapes, seeded & halved
Lemon juice

Combine mayonnaise, sour cream, and honey for dressing. Combine apples, celery, walnuts, and grapes; fold in dressing. Garnish with unpeeled apple slices that have been dipped in lemon juice. Yield: 10 servings

NOTE: I just learned recently that apples can be kept from browning for up to a day if dipped in Sprite or 7-Up. That way you don't get the sour flavor from lemon juice. This works especially great for packing apple slices in lunches or when putting apple slices on a fruit tray.

"Always eat grapes downward–that is eat the best grapes first; in this way there will be none better left on the bunch, and each grape will seem good down to the last. If you eat the other way, you will not have a good grape in the lot." – Samuel Butler

French Dressing

From My High School Homemaking Class

1 c. vegetable oil
¼ c. white or cider vinegar
1½ tsp. salt
⅛ tsp. pepper
¼ tsp. paprika
¾ tsp. sugar
1 T. lemon juice
1½ tsp. Worcestershire sauce
2 garlic cloves, peeled

Shake oil, vinegar, and seasoning together. Remove garlic cloves. Store dressing tightly covered and shake before using.

I had to call one of my oldest friends, Donna, to see if she still had the recipes for homemade salad dressings we made in homemaking class. Neither of us could locate the one for cooked salad dressing, but Donna did have this recipe and one for mayonnaise. Mrs. Bienski made us write down all kinds of things on recipe cards–most of which I included at the beginning of this book. Donna's card with equivalents has my writing on one side and hers on the other; we were true friends. Thanks, Mrs. Bienski, for helping us learn to remember. All that writing paid off.

Fresh Tomato Salad

Mom

½ onion, sliced
½ bell pepper, sliced
2–3 tomatoes, sliced
1 T. sugar
Dash salt
1 T. vinegar

Combine sugar, salt, and vinegar. Pour over sliced vegetables and refrigerate.

NOTE: We had so many fresh vegetables grown by my father-in-law–Grandpa Norman; this was a delicious way to enjoy fresh homegrown tomatoes for lunch, dinner, or even an afternoon snack.

"A world without tomatoes is like a string quartet without violins."
– Laurie Colwin

Greek Spinach Salad

Jennie

8 oz. uncooked orzo
1 pkg. (6 oz.) fresh sm. baby spinach
4 oz. Feta cheese, crumbled
½–1 red onion, thinly sliced
4 stalks celery, sliced
½ c. Kalamati olives
⅓ c. olive oil
½ c. Balsamic vinegar
½ tsp. garlic powder
¼ tsp. white pepper

Cook orzo according to package directions; drain and cool. Combine spinach, Feta cheese, red onion slices, celery, and Kalamati olives with cooled orzo. Shake together the remaining ingredients in a jar and pour over salad just before serving. Toss gently.

NOTE: My daughter Jennie makes this all the time; it's everyone's special request. It's absolutely delicious and, though slightly limp, even better the next day. Orzo is a tiny pasta that resembles rice and is easily found in large grocery stores in either the pasta or foreign food section. Sometimes I use the seasoned Feta cheese–it just adds another layer of flavor. For an interesting side dish, leave out the spinach, and voila–orzo salad. Make early in the day, allowing time for flavors to meld. For crispy spinach, wait until just before serving to add it.

Hot German Potato Salad

6 med. potatoes, boiled in jackets
6 slices bacon
¾ c. onion, chopped
2 T. flour
1–2 T. sugar
1½ tsp. salt
½ tsp. celery seed
Dash of pepper
¾ c. water
⅓ c. vinegar

Peel potatoes and slice thin. Fry bacon slowly in skillet, then drain and crumble. Sauté onion in bacon fat until golden brown. Blend in flour, sugar, salt, celery seeds, and pepper. Cook over low heat. Stir in water and vinegar. Heat to boil, stirring constantly. Boil 1 minute. Carefully stir in potatoes and bacon bits. Remove from heat; cover and let stand until ready to serve. Yield: 6–8 servings

NOTE: This potato salad is delicious, with a sweet 'n sour taste. Add one tablespoon of sugar first, taste and adjust to your liking.

OLIVE OIL FACTS

- ✦ Olive oil's price is always climbing higher, so treat it as a flavor condiment–use sparingly and wisely.
- ✦ Olive oil's rich character makes it easy to use less than other oils and still get more flavor impact. That means fewer calories.
- ✦ Olive oil, with a high smoke point, is among the more stable oils for frying, plus its composition permits minimal absorption by foods being fried.
- ✦ Use olive oil where flavor is appreciated: on a salad or to brush on seafood before broiling.

BASIC TYPES OF OLIVE OILS USED BY U. S. CONSUMERS

Virgin: Oil obtained from fruit of the olive tree by methods that do not lead to deterioration of the oil. Certain standards must be met in processing with up to 3 percent acidity permitted. Use pure or virgin olive oil to brush on fish and meats for grilling. Except in dessert recipes, virgin olive oil can often be substituted for vegetable oil.

Extra-virgin: The finest virgin olive oil, with the widest variety of flavors and aroma and no more than 1 percent acidity. Use for salads, marinades, or for dressing pasta and cooked vegetables.

Light or extra-light (refined): Virgin olive oils with acid levels of more than 3 percent. Much of the color, taste, and odor are removed, satisfying America's taste for bland oils. (Bertolli)

Pure or 100 percent olive oil: Refined olive oil with virgin olive oil added to replace some of the natural olive oil taste removed in refining. A 1.5 percent acidity is allowed. These blends account for almost 70 percent of the olive oil sold in the United states.

IMPORTED OLIVE OILS

Italian olive oils are considered by many food experts as among the finest. The olive oils of northern Italy range from pale and delicate to heavy and robust. The golden-yellow oils from the South have a full-bodied, fruity taste. The intense green oils of the central area are almost spicy.

French olive oils (Borges) tend to be lighter in flavor and color. They are good for more subtle cooking uses, such as preparing fish or for making mayonnaise.

Greek oils tend to have the most distinctly olive flavor and full character.

Spanish olive oils (Pompeian) are more like the heavier Italian oils, but with less complex flavor.

Jennie's Pasta Salad

Jennie

1 lb. bow-tie pasta
3–4 Roma tomatoes
3 jars (6.5 oz. each) marinated artichoke hearts, drained & cut into sm. pieces
2 cans (2¼ oz. each) black olives, sliced
1 sm. red onion
1 green pepper
1 lb. Feta cheese, crumbled
½ c. olive oil
½ c. dry white wine
1 lemon, juiced
1 tsp. basil
Pepper and salt to taste

Cook pasta al dente, drain and rinse in cold water to cool and prevent further cooking. Chop tomatoes, removing extra juices. Drain olives. Slice onion very thin, cut in half and separate pieces. Chop bell pepper and combine all these ingredients with the Feta cheese. Combine remaining ingredients in a shaker or jar with tight-fitting lid. Pour over all. Toss very carefully. Refrigerate.

Jennie's Greek Spinach Salad and this one are recipes that I prepare often. I had quite a time getting her other favorites. She really is very organized and regimented–things just move at her own pace and her job demands too much of her. So when I told her that the deadline for me to include her recipes in my cookbook was quickly approaching, she replied, "Mom, what's my drop dead date to get you my recipes?" At the time she was in Palm Beach for a work conference. She must have put her recipes into some sort of written form while she sat by the pool sipping her umbrella drink, because it wasn't very long until I had her recipes.

"Eating an artichoke is like getting to know someone really well."
– Willi Hastings

Latin Slaw

½ c. Kraft Mayo Real Mayonnaise
¼ c. lime juice
1 tsp. hot pepper sauce
¼ tsp. salt
1 can (11 oz.) whole -kernel corn, drained
2 c. green cabbage, shredded
2 c. red cabbage, shredded
2 Serrano chilies, seeded & minced
8 slices bacon, cooked & crumbled
½ c. green onions, sliced

Combine mayo, lime juice, hot pepper sauce, and salt; set aside. Cook corn in large skillet on medium-high heat until golden brown, stirring frequently. Place in large bowl. Add cabbage, chilies, bacon, and onions; mix lightly. Add mayo mixture and toss lightly. Refrigerate until ready to serve. Yield: 12 servings, ½ cup each

NOTE: Latin slaw is great with fish tacos or pulled pork sandwiches.

Layered Lettuce Salad

1 head lettuce
1 c. celery, sliced
4 hard cooked eggs, sliced
1 pkg. (10 oz.) frozen green peas, thawed & uncooked
½ c. green pepper, diced
1 med. red onion, diced
8 slices bacon, cooked & crumbled
1 c. mayonnaise
1 tsp. sugar
4 oz. Cheddar cheese, shredded
Parsley

Wash and tear lettuce into bite-size pieces. Layer first 7 ingredients in order given in a 12" x 9" glass dish or a trifle bowl. Combine mayonnaise and sugar; spread evenly over top of salad. Sprinkle with cheese. Cover and refrigerate 8–12 hours. Garnish with parsley before serving. To serve, dig deep into bowl with a serving fork and spoon so everyone gets ingredients from every layer. Yield: 12 servings

SALAD FACTS

- ✦ Tear lettuce into bite-size pieces. Cutting with a knife causes lettuce to brown.
- ✦ Unless the salad ingredient can be cut with the side of your fork, it should be bite-size.
- ✦ To wash a head of Iceberg lettuce, hold the lettuce with the core down. Rap the core several times on the side of your sink; then grab the core with your fingertips and twist it out. Run cold water into the head of lettuce; invert and drain. Rinse and drain again.
- ✦ Store Iceberg lettuce with the core down so all water drains out. I love the Tupperware lettuce keeper. It has a little stand for the lettuce head to hold it above the bottom of the bowl. Rinsed lettuce can also be stored in your salad spinner, but drain the water first.
- ✦ Starch-based salads like pasta and potato salad are best after the flavors have had time to meld. Prepare them several hours before serving or even the day before.
- ✦ Arranged salads are easy to make and impressive. Think about the salads at expensive restaurants or in cookbook photos and get creative. Everyone will feel special.
- ✦ Add the dressing to green salads just before serving to prevent wilting.
- ✦ If counting calories, instead of using the fat-free dressings–which I find less than satisfying–put a tablespoon of dressing in a custard dish or other tiny bowl. When eating your salad, dip the tip of your fork in the dressing before spearing salad ingredients. Far less dressing will be eaten, and the dressing flavor is experienced with every bite.
- ✦ Always ask for the dressing served *on the side* when eating out to control the amount of dressing used.

Mama's Fruit Salad

My Mama

2 cans (11 oz. each) Mandarin orange slices
2 cans (13¼ oz.) pineapple tidbits
1 c. pecans
2–3 c. miniature marshmallows
1 pt. sour cream

Drain juice from oranges and pineapple. Place all ingredients in a large bowl. Stir in sour cream. Chill and serve.

Mayonnaise

From My High School Homemaking Class

1–2 tsp. sugar
½ tsp. dry mustard
¼ tsp. white peppercorns
1 tsp. salt
Few grains cayenne pepper
2 egg yolks
2 T. vinegar
2 c. vegetable oil

Add seasoning to yolks, beating until mixed. Add vinegar to yolk mixture, beating until thick. Add oil, a few teaspoons at a time, to yolk mixture, beating after each addition. Store dressing tightly covered in refrigerator.

NOTE: My classes made this using the blender. Follow the same instructions, blending instead of beating. Pour the oil, using a very slow drizzle, into the yolks while blending. I honestly don't know why anyone would want to make their own mayonnaise, but if the economy keeps on like it is, this might be a way to save a nickel or two.

Mexican Chef's Salad

Home Management Special

1 onion
4 tomatoes
1 head Iceberg lettuce
1 lb. ground beef
1 can (16 oz.) kidney beans, drained
¼ tsp. salt
1 bag Doritos*
4 oz. grated Cheddar cheese
8 oz. Thousand Island dressing
Hot sauce to taste
1 lg. avocado, sliced just before serving

Chop and combine onion, tomatoes, and lettuce. Brown beef and drain off fat. Add beans and salt or just toss in a half package taco seasoning for a little kick. Simmer 10 minutes. Pour half of the Doritos into a serving bowl and crunch the remaining half. Toss salad, meat combination, crunched Doritos, cheese, dressing, and hot sauce together just before serving. Garnish with avocado slices and serve with additional chips.

VARIATION: Fill individual salad bowls with lettuce and top with tomatoes, cheese, onions, crunched Doritos, and meat. Garnish with avocado slices and serve with Thousand Island dressing and hot sauce. *This recipe is an old one–it says to use a 39¢ bag of Doritos. I'm guessing that's about a $3.00 bag in today's market.

Mama's Cole Slaw

My Mama

1 pkg. shredded cabbage, angel-hair preferred
¼ c. sugar
¼ c. mayonnaise
¼ c. cider vinegar
1 tsp. celery seed

Combine sugar, mayo, vinegar, and celery seed. Stir into shredded cabbage and refrigerate until serving. Slaw gets better as it sits, so make it early in the day or even the day before.

NOTE: 5 years ago, Mama would have shredded the cabbage herself. We are all so spoiled by the modern food processing available.

Pasta Primavera

Teacher Bake-Off

6 oz. linguine or fettuccine
3 T. butter or margarine
2 c. broccoli flowerets
1 c. carrots, bias-sliced
1 med. onion, cut in thin wedges
1 clove garlic, minced
1 c. fresh or frozen pea pods
½ c. cashews or almonds
¼ c. dry white wine
1 tsp. dried thyme, crushed
¼ tsp. pepper
¼ c. Parmesan cheese, grated

Cook pasta. Drain well. Meanwhile, in a large skillet melt 2 tablespoons of the butter. Stir in broccoli, carrots, onion, and garlic. Cook and stir over medium-high heat about 3 minutes or until broccoli is crisp-tender. Stir in pea pods. Cook 2 minutes more. Stir in cooked linguine or fettuccine, remaining butter, the nuts, wine, thyme, and pepper. Cover and cook 1 minute more. Transfer to a warm serving plate. Sprinkle with Parmesan cheese. Yield: 8 servings

VARIATION: To make this dish a meal, prepare as above, except stir 1 cup cubed, fully cooked ham into vegetable mixture with the pea pods. Yield: 4 main-dish servings

"There is no love sincerer than the love of food."
— George Bernard Shaw

Pink Salad

1 can (20 oz.) crushed pineapple
1 can (14 oz.) Eagle Brand sweetened condensed milk
1 can (21 oz.) cherry pie filling
1 c. pecans, chopped
16 oz. Cool Whip

Drain all the juice from the pineapple and combine with everything but the Cool Whip. Stir in Cool Whip. Keep refrigerated.

NOTE: Sometimes I add a cup of coconut, depending on who will be indulging. A low-calorie/low-fat version can be made by using products of that nature. Always be sure to grab the canned fruits that are packed in natural juices to avoid added sugar. Julie makes this often and says, "Everybody loves pink stuff! My work friends insist I bring extra bowls to the holiday potlucks so they can hide it for later, not quite coconut cream pie, but close." I don't recall the origin of this recipe–it's been around for years. When I posted on Facebook that I am writing a cookbook, a friend of Julie's said to be sure to include the *pink stuff*–that's what we call it.

Red Potato Salad

5 lb. med. red potatoes, halved
5 hard-cooked eggs, chopped
1 rib celery, finely chopped
½ med. onion, finely chopped
1½ c. mayonnaise
¼ c. sweet pickle relish
3 T. sugar
2 T. dried parsley flakes
2 tsp. prepared mustard
1 tsp. salt
1 tsp. cider vinegar
⅛ tsp. pepper

Place potatoes in a large kettle; cover with water. Bring to a boil. Reduce heat; cover and cook for 20–25 minutes or until tender. Drain and cool. Cut potatoes into ¾-in. cubes. In a large bowl, combine the potatoes, eggs, celery, and onion. In a small bowl, combine the remaining ingredients. Pour over potato mixture and stir gently to coat. Cover and refrigerate for 6 hours or overnight. Yield: 16 servings (about ¾ cup each)

NOTE: I always mash hard-cooked eggs with an old wooden-handle, metal-tined fork that was Grandma Simon's. The tines are really skinny and sharp so it does a great job. A pastry blender can also be used for chopping eggs.

Shrimp Salad

Rosemary

1 c. boiled shrimp, cut in sm. pieces
1 c. cooked rice
¼ c. celery, chopped
¼ c. pimentos, chopped
¼ c. green peppers, chopped
¼ c. green onions, chopped
½ tsp. salt
¼ tsp. pepper
3 T. mayonnaise
2 T. French dressing

Combine all ingredients. Stir and chill for 30 minutes. Better the next day.

NOTE: Arriving on the same boat I must have ridden, Rosemary says, "I usually add extra shrimp."

Special Cole Slaw

Rosemary

1 pkg. (16 oz.) red/green cabbage, shredded
¾ c. sunflower seeds
1 c. almonds, sliced
¾ c. oil
½ c. sugar
⅓ c. white vinegar
2 pkg. Ramen noodles

Toast sunflower seeds and almonds. Combine cabbage, sunflower seeds, and almonds. In a separate bowl, blend oil, sugar, white vinegar, and noodle seasoning packages. Add dressing to slaw mixture 30 minutes before serving. Crunch Ramen noodles and add at the last minute before serving.

NOTE: Rosemary said, "I did not use all the dressing and I think I cut back on the nuts. Just make it look and taste right. And nuts are expensive, so why use too many at one time?" Now, that is a real practical cook.

"Jack Sprat could eat no fat.
His wife could eat no lean.
And so between them both, you see,
They licked the platter clean."
– Mother Goose

Strawberry Deluxe Cocktail

From the Food Lab

1 pkg. (3 oz.) strawberry Jello
1 c. boiling water
1 can (15 oz.) fruit cocktail
Cold water plus liquid from fruit cocktail to equal 1 c.

Drain fruit cocktail, reserving liquid. Place Jello in a mixing bowl. Add boiling water; stir until completely dissolved. Add cold water mixture. Chill until mixture resembles the consistency of unbeaten egg whites. Stir in fruit cocktail. Pour into a lightly greased mold or into individual cocktail glasses. Chill.

Strawberry Spinach Salad

¼ c. slivered almonds
2 T. sugar
1 c. fresh strawberries, sliced
1 pkg. (10 oz.) fresh spinach, torn
Vinaigrette Dressing

In a large skillet, cook and stir almonds and sugar over low heat until the sugar is dissolved and the almonds are coated. Spread on foil to cool; break apart. In a large salad bowl, combine spinach, strawberries, and cooled almonds.

Vinaigrette Dressing

2 T. canola oil
1 T. raspberry vinegar or red wine vinegar
1 green onion, finely chopped
1½ tsp. sugar
1½ tsp. Worcestershire sauce
1 tsp. poppy seeds
¼ tsp. salt
Dash paprika

In a jar with a tight-fitting lid, combine the dressing ingredients; shake well. Drizzle over salad; toss gently to coat. Serve the salad immediately. Yield: 10 servings

NOTE: Sometime I include mandarin orange slices and arrange the salad on individual chilled plates instead of tossing. You can also break up Ramen noodles and brown these in a tablespoon of butter; cool and sprinkle on top of salad just before serving. Make a super simple version of this salad by using the following ingredients: spinach, strawberries, blueberries, mandarin orange slices, and poppyseed dressing–quick and easy and always loved.

Sunshine Salad

School Dinner Recipe

1 c. boiling water
1 pkg. (3 oz.) lemon flavor gelatin
½ c. cold water
⅛ tsp. salt
1 can (8¾ oz.) crushed pineapple
½ c. carrots, shredded

Pour boiling water over gelatin in bowl, stirring until gelatin is dissolved. Stir in cold water, salt, and pineapple (with syrup). Chill until slightly thickened, but not set. Stir in carrots. Pour into 4-cup ring mold or into 6 individual molds. Chill until firm. Yield: 6 servings

Three Fruit Dressing

School Dinner Recipe

½ c. sugar
1½ T. cornstarch
½ c. unsweetened pineapple juice
2 T. lemon juice
2 T. orange juice
Lemon & orange zest

Mix sugar and cornstarch in small saucepan. Stir in pineapple juice. Cook, stirring constantly, until mixture thickens and boils. Boil and stir 1 minute. Remove from heat and stir in remaining ingredients. Cool. Serve as dip for fresh fruits or as dressing for fruit salad. Looks especially good drizzled over arranged fruit salad. Yield: 1¼ cups

Tomato Feta Salad

5 med. tomatoes, thinly sliced
1 med. red onion, thinly sliced
1 pkg. (6 oz.) crumbled Feta cheese, tomato & basil flavor
1 can (2¼ oz.) sliced ripe olives
½ c. olive oil
¼ c. red wine vinegar
1 T. dried oregano

Drain olives. On a serving platter, layer tomatoes and onion (separated into individual rings). Top with Feta cheese and olives. In a jar with a tight-fitting lid, combine the oil, vinegar, and oregano; shake well. Drizzle over salad. Serve with a slotted spoon.

NOTE: What better way to enjoy the summer crop of fresh tomatoes unless maybe in the the next recipe?

Tomato Mozzarella Salad

2 fresh tomatoes, sliced
1 sm. onion, sliced
4 oz. fresh Mozzarella
2 T. extra-virgin olive oil
2 T. white wine vinegar
Salt & pepper to taste
Fresh Basil Chiffonade

Layer the tomato and onion slices. Top with Mozzarella. Shake together the remaining ingredients and pour over salad. Garnish with fresh basil chiffonade.

NOTE: I just naturally prefer red onions, but white or sweet Vidalia are good, too. When cutting the basil chiffonade, push the chef's knife back and forth across the basil roll. A little practice will make perfect.

Basil Chiffonade

10–12 fresh basil leaves
Olive oil

To quickly chop a lot of basil and end up with attractive results, create basil chiffonade, which is just a fancy term for thin shredded strips. Before cutting basil chiffonade, sprinkle a few drops of olive oil on the leaves and gently rub to evenly coat the them. This will prevent them from darkening. Stack several basil leaves and roll them into a tight tube. Slice the leaves widthwise into narrow pieces to create long, extremely thin strips. If you'd like smaller pieces, simply chop the strips. This cutting method works well with other leafy herbs, such as sage, to quickly enhance the appearance of your dishes.

"It's difficult to think anything but pleasant thoughts while eating a homegrown tomato." – Lewis Grizzard

Tropical Seafood Salad

Good Housekeeping's "The Great Salad Contest" Winner, August 1984

2 oz. liquid shrimp boil
2 qt. water
2 lb. fresh shrimp, shelled & deveined
1 lb. scallops
1 pkg. (20 oz.) frozen green peas, thawed & drained
4 c. fresh or canned pineapple chunks, drained
2 papaya, sliced attractively
¾ c. salad dressing
3 oz. cream cheese, softened
¼ c. pineapple juice
8 lettuce leaf cups
2 kiwi fruit, sliced
½ c. coconut, toasted
8 maraschino cherries

Add shrimp boil to water and bring to a boil; add shrimp and cook until just pink. Remove and drain in colander, rinsing with cold water. Add several cubes of ice to help cool. Add scallops to boiling water and cook until translucent. Drain well, rinse with cold water, and combine with shrimp; add a few more cubes of ice. Set aside to cool. Prepare peas, pineapple, and papaya. Remove ice from seafood and toss with peas, pineapple, and papaya. Chill. With wire whip, combine salad dressing, cream cheese, and pineapple juice until smooth. Chill. To serve, place lettuce leaves on chilled salad plates. Fill with tossed salad and top with dressing. Garnish with kiwi slices, coconut, and cherries. Yield: 8 servings

If you have ever been in a long, boring meeting that seems to go on forever, then you can identify with teacher inservice of the 70s and 80s. We sat for hours, endlessly listening to someone who had not seen the inside of a classroom since they left college (which I would say was usually a long, long time ago). Topics included invaluable subjects such as "teaching the student" or "creating a lesson plan" and, needless to say, we found other things to occupy our mind. Being of a polite nature, I indiscreetly read a magazine camouflaged inside my notebook. Well, this recipe contest grabbed my attention–with the grand prize a trip to Hawaii. So, pretending to take notes, I composed this recipe. I figured it really fit the occasion. I just knew I was on my way to Hawaii when I got a letter from John Mack Carter, the editor-in-chief of the magazine. Unfortunately, no travel plans loomed on my horizon, but I did win 3rd place, an Out to Lunch picnic basket, and my recipe was published in their magazine.

Vermicelli Salad

Julie

10 oz. vermicelli
4 T. oil
3 T. lemon juice
1–2 T. seasoning salt
1 jar (4 oz.) pimentos, chopped
1 can (2¼ oz.) black olives, chopped
¾ c. celery, chopped
½ c. onion, chopped
Mayo to consistency

Cook vermicelli 2–3 minutes. When done, rinse with cold water. Add oil, lemon juice, and seasoning salt. Marinate over night. Add other ingredients and let sit before serving.

Notes

VEGETABLES & SIDE DISHES

Apple & Dill Roasted Cauliflower

Rosemary

1 cauliflower
½ lg. red onion
1 lg. apple
3 T. extra virgin olive oil
¾ tsp. kosher salt
¼ c. + 2 T. fresh dill weed, coarsely chopped

Preheat to 450°. Core and separate cauliflower. Cut onion into ¼-inch slices. Core and chop, but do not peel the apple. Toss cauliflower, onion, and apple with olive oil and salt; spread mixture on jelly roll pan in a single layer. Roast for 20–30 minutes, stirring a couple of times until cauliflower begins to brown on the edges. Continue to roast for about 10 more minutes, stirring once or twice until most of cauliflower is browning. Sprinkle with dill and serve piping hot.

NOTE: Rosemary adds: "I have used dill seeds when I could not find fresh."

"Training is everything. The peach was once a bitter almond; cauliflower is nothing but cabbage with a college education." – Mark Twain

Beets with Orange Sauce

Home Management Special

⅓ c. sugar
2 T. cornstarch
⅛ tsp. salt
1 c. orange juice
1 T. butter
3 c. cooked beets, diced

Combine dry ingredients; add orange juice and butter. Cook for 5 minutes in top of double boiler or over very low heat in a heavy saucepan. Add beets and let stand for several hours before serving. Reheat and serve piping hot. 6–8 servings

NOTE: It's obvious that we were trying to impress the teacher with this recipe. Actually, for beets, this is pretty good. Still, I bet that in most crowds, this recipe would feed more than 8 people. At least they're not pickled. When cooking fresh beets, cut off the greens of the beets leaving about 1 inch of the stem. Do not trim the root end off. This will keep the beet juice from leaching out during cooking.

I learned about beet juice the hard way. I was cooking fresh beets in preparation for canning. I must have been in junior high school because we still lived in the big house. I didn't know the part about leaving the stems and roots on the beets. I left the kitchen and when I came back it looked like a massacre had taken place: purple beet juice covered almost every square inch of the floor. The stove was like a pop-art painting done in purples, the stovetop and burners were filled with purple juice–never again. It wasn't until much later in life that purple became my favorite color.

Bohemian Cheese Noodles

From the Food Lab

8 oz. egg noodles
½ c. butter, melted
1 tsp. salt
¼ tsp. ground pepper
½ lb. creamed small-curd cottage cheese
¼ c. milk
1 T. parsley, chopped

Cook noodles in boiling, salted water until tender, yet firm, about 4–5 minutes. Drain. Add butter, salt, and pepper. Blend cottage cheese and milk until smooth. Use the blender to remove the curds/lumps and have smooth, creamy noodles. Pour over hot noodles, mix lightly and simmer in covered saucepan for 3–4 minutes. Turn into serving dish and sprinkle with chopped parsley. Yield: 4–6 servings

I have the Bohemian Cheese Noodles marked as a student specialty from 1971–72. That was my first year as a teacher. My younger sister, Debbie, was a senior and she was in my Homemaking III class. Debbie avoided calling me anything that whole year–couldn't call me Verna and didn't manage to bring herself to call me Mrs. Craig. I must say, she is an excellent cook, but I doubt I can take much credit for that. She has used true grit and hard work to get where she is today and I am so proud of her. She has always been one of my biggest fans, offering me support and encouragement when I needed it most. Look for the story about her group's Black Bottom Pie later.

Broccoli & Rice Casserole

Classroom Standard

1 pkg. (10 oz.) chopped, frozen broccoli
Scant ¼ c. water
¼ tsp. salt
1 c. rice, cooked
1 recipe Cheese Sauce
Paprika

Cook rice according to the *Perfectly Cooked Rice Every Time* lesson on page 116. Prepare cheese sauce following the Cheese Sauce recipe variation, page 317. After these are underway, bring the water and salt to a boil in a saucepan with a tight-fitting cover. Add broccoli; break apart with fork. Reduce heat and cook a couple of minutes until the broccoli turns bright green. Cover and reduce heat, cooking 2–3 minutes longer. Drain. Place cooked rice in a 9 x 13 x 2-inch casserole. Top with cooked broccoli and gently stir together. Slowly pour cheese sauce over the mixture. Lightly sprinkle with paprika and serve. Can be heated in oven for 10–15 minutes, if desired and time permits.

NOTE: Beginning classes were required to prepare this recipe. It was great for teaching so many basic skills: fail-safe rice cooking, making a smooth and creamy sauce, preserving nutrients in veggies–not to mention teamwork, time management, and multitasking. In addition, this lesson possessed the added benefit of introducing a food that most said they didn't like. After this lab, the majority admitted that broccoli was actually pretty good.

"Grams, can you cook some of those little green trees?" – Peyton

COOKING GREEN VEGETABLES

- ✦ Add vegetables to boiling water; cook until they turn bright green, 2–3 minutes; cover and cook until fork-tender, 2–3 additional minutes.
- ✦ Science FYI: Green vegetables release chlorophyll in the form of gas when heated and this chemical reaction turns them bright green in color. Leaving the cover off until this color change takes place maintains that bright green color.
- ✦ The instructions for cooking frozen broccoli apply to other frozen and any fresh, green vegetables. Larger pieces, like broccoli spears, will take a little bit longer to cook.
- ✦ Use a small amount of water, just enough to barely cover the bottom of the saucepan, thus leaving just a couple of drops of nutrient-rich water when the vegetables are done. Why feed all those vitamins to the Ninjas that live down the drain?
- ✦ If green vegetables are allowed to set for a while or to overcook, they wind up army-green in color and their flavor will be less desirable.
- ✦ Both fresh and frozen veggies can be microwaved in a covered dish. A 10-ounce package takes about 3 minutes. Stir after 2 minutes. Let set a few minutes before serving. Microwaved foods continue to cook after the bell dings. (Wow, all this school stuff and that's the first time I have mentioned a bell. Retirement allows the mind to forget many unpleasant things–like one's life being similar to that of a Pavlov dog!)
- ✦ For maximum flavor and nutrient retention, cook vegetables just until fork-tender–a fork will pierce the surface, but veggie still has a slightly crisp texture.

Can't Go Wrong Asparagus

Jennie

1 lb. fresh asparagus	**1 lemon**
Extra-virgin olive oil	**Fresh cracked pepper**

Wash asparagus and break off ends. Place in a pie dish with 2–3 teaspoons water; drizzle with olive oil. Squeeze lemon juice over asparagus and generously cover with cracked pepper. Place plastic wrap over all and microwave for 3 minutes. Add additional cracked pepper before serving.

"A fruit is a vegetable with looks and money. Plus, if you let fruit rot, it turns into wine, something Brussels sprouts never do." – P.J. O'Rourke

Candied Yams

School Dinner Recipe

2 lb. cooked sweet potatoes or substitute lg. can yams
½ c. brown sugar
3 T. butter or margarine
3 T. light cream or milk
½ t. salt

If using fresh sweet potatoes, cook or bake and cut into chunks. Drain canned sweet potatoes. In medium skillet, combine brown sugar, butter, cream, and salt; cook over medium heat, stirring constantly until smooth and bubbly. Add sweet potato chunks; stir gently until glazed and heated through. 4–6 servings

NOTE: This recipe can be baked in the oven until hot and bubbly and topped with marshmallows the last couple of minutes. We just never had the time.

Corn Casserole

Marilyn's Mother

1 med. onion, chopped
1 green pepper, chopped
½ c. margarine
2 cans (15 oz. each) cream-style corn
2 c. Minute Rice, dry
1 egg, beaten
1 tsp. sugar
1 sm. (2 oz.) jar pimiento
½ c. water
Salt
Pepper
Grated cheese

Sauté onion and pepper in margarine. Add all remaining ingredients except the cheese. Place in a greased 9 x 13 x 2-inch casserole dish. Bake for 30 minutes at 350°. When done, sprinkle with grated cheese.

VARIATION: Add chopped, cooked chicken for a delicious family dinner or pot luck dish.

"An onion can make people cry, but there has never been a vegetable invented to make them laugh." – Will Rogers

Cornbread Casserole

Julie & Mrs. Martin

1 can (15 oz.) whole kernel corn, undrained
1 c. butter, melted
1 can (15 oz.) cream-style corn
2 eggs
8 oz. sour cream
1 pkg. corn bread mix

Mix all ingredients. Bake in greased 9 x 13 x 2-inch dish at 350° for 45 minutes to 1 hour.

NOTE: In this day of fat-consciousness, use less butter. Julie submitted this recipe and says, "One of Grandma's dearest friends, Mrs. Martin, made this corn recipe for family gatherings. Even as a kid, I absolutely loved it and would eat an extra serving for dessert!"

Couscous & Tomatoes

Julie

1 can (14½ oz.) stewed tomatoes
¼ c. chopped onion
⅛–¼ tsp. ground red pepper
⅛ tsp. garlic powder
1 c. water
¼ tsp. salt
⅔ c. couscous
¼ c. ripe olives, pitted & sliced
¼ c. snipped parsley

In saucepan combine undrained stewed tomatoes, onion, pepper, garlic powder, water, and salt. Bring to boil. Stir in couscous. Cover, remove from heat and let stand 5 minutes. Stir in olives and parsley.

Cream de Sherry Mushrooms

Jennie

1 lb. fresh mushrooms, sliced
¼ c. butter
1–2 cloves fresh garlic, minced
Fresh cracked pepper
A bit of red wine
Cream de Sherry

Melt butter in a sauté pan and add mushrooms. Add some fresh minced garlic and fresh cracked pepper and a bit of red wine from your glass along with a couple of dashes of Cream de Sherry. Let mixture simmer until mushrooms are soft and perfect. It's like candy.

Easy, Crowd-Pleasing Potato Casserole

Myrna

1 pkg. (32 oz.) frozen hash browns, cubed, not shredded
1 can cream of mushroom soup
½ c. butter, softened, optional
1 c. sour cream
½ bunch green onions, thinly sliced
4–5 slices crisp fried bacon, crumbled
3 c. Cheddar cheese, shredded

Thaw the hash browns and combine with remaining ingredients, reserving a few green onions and bacon crumbles for garnish. Mix well. Cover with foil and bake at 350° for 45 minutes or so–until a knife inserted and held in the center for about 10 seconds is hot to the touch when removed. Remove the foil for the last 10 minutes of baking. Garnish with reserved green onions and crumbled bacon.

NOTE: Julie writes: "These yummy potatoes are always a hit. Myrna used to bring them to all of the get-togethers and I don't think she ever had any to take back home. Grandma made them with crushed corn flakes on top for extra crunch. No matter how it's made, this casserole is loved by all. Every summer I get at least one call from a friend who's trying to remember how to make it for their weekend barbecue."

SOURCE: I had forgotten that this recipe was Myrna's. Everyone should write a cookbook just to get things straight. I am a nut about the flavor of Velveeta cheese, so I use 1 pound of cubed Velveeta in place of the shredded cheese. It's sooo good. I have also used tater tots for this recipe. Use your hands or a large wooden spoon to break them into little pieces. If I am feeling fat, I will leave out the butter.

"Be a fearless cook! Try out new ideas and new recipes, but always buy the freshest and finest ingredients, whatever they may be. Furnish your kitchen with the most solid and workmanlike equipment you can find. Keep your knives ever sharp and–toujuours bon appetit!" – Julia Child

Egg Dumplings

1 tsp. salt
½ c. milk
1 egg, beaten
1½ c. sifted flour

Combine salt, milk, and beaten egg; stir into flour to form a smooth batter. Drop by teaspoons into boiling, salted water, soup or stewed chicken; cover tightly and cook 15 minutes. Do not lift the lid during this time. (These dumplings rely solely on the egg and steam for leavening, so *do not disturb* while cooking.)

SOURCE: I inherited my Grandma Simon's blue cookbook–The American Woman's Cook Book–that came with her Wizard stove from Western Auto. She got this gas range about the year I was born and the cookbook was tucked inside the oven. While almost anything you are looking for can be found in this book, (even beef tongue and braised heart) I was ecstatic when I came across a drop dumpling recipe that turned out almost like Grandma's. I've made slight adaptations to the original recipe, trying to bring the dumplings closer to how I remember Grandma's. I cook these dumplings quite often as they are much faster to make than Mama's rolled ones. I usually double the recipe so I can have left-overs. Be sure to sift the flour first so your dumplings will be light and fluffy–and don't over-stir them.

Come to find out, Mama has the same cookbook! About the beef tongue and braised heart: Mama really cooked both items for us to eat. Worse yet, on mornings after butchering a hog, we would find brains mixed in with our scrambled eggs. I will never forget the sight of those brains, soaking in water, in a bowl in the refrigerator. I also have to say that seeing that whole calf tongue sitting in a pot of some sort of juice on the back of the stove was quite repulsive. No doubt, living through the great depression had an impact on my parents. Count your blessings.

"No one who cooks, cooks alone. Even at her most solitary, a cook in the kitchen is surrounded by generations of cooks past, the advice and menus of cooks present, the wisdom of cookbook writers." – Laurie Colwin

Fresh Tomato Pie

Rosemary

1 deep dish (9 in.) frozen pie crust
6 lg. tomatoes
1 tsp. salt
1 c. Mozzarella cheese, shredded
1 c. Cheddar cheese, shredded
1 c. mayonnaise
1 bunch green onions, sliced
½ c. fresh basil, sliced
Extra basil for garnish

Bake pie crust according to directions. Peel and cut tomatoes in ¼-inch slices. Place tomatoes in a colander, sprinkle with 1 teaspoon of salt. Set aside to drain. Preheat oven to 350°. In a bowl, combine cheeses and mayonnaise. Place drained tomatoes in baked pie shell. Sprinkle evenly with green onions and basil. Spread mayonnaise mixture over the top. Bake 30–40 minutes or until cheeses are lightly brown. Garnish with basil.

This recipe is so Rosemary. It's delicious, different, and brings to mind a story she tells about cooking in her new home. You see, we have been friends for a very long time and our lives have mirrored each others in many ways. We grew up on farms (she a dairy farm), we taught high school (history is her forte), we both went through divorces after our children were grown (her's just a short time after mine), we both moved into new homes as independent single women. So, anyway, when Rosemary moved into her new home, she started cooking again, not just down-home, farm cooking, but more like gourmet cooking, and setting the dining table with seasonal and holiday decor–things were so different that her daughter asked her outright, "Who are you and what have you done with my mother?"

Eggplant Fritters

Mom

3 c. mashed, cooked eggplant (about 1 lg. eggplant)
1 pkg. (6 oz.) cornbread mix
1 egg, beaten
2 T. onions, diced
3 T. milk, or more

Peel and cook eggplant in salted water; drain and cool. Mix all ingredients, adding just enough milk to make a light consistency–a soft dough that will hold together. Drop by spoonful into hot fat. Fry 5–7 minutes until golden brown. Drain on paper towels.

Farmer's Delight

Maxine

1 can (15 oz.) whole kernel corn
1 can (15 oz.) cream-style corn
¾ c. sour cream
½ c. margarine
½ c. milk
1 egg, beaten
1 box Jiffy corn muffin mix
1 c. Cheddar cheese, grated

Mix cans of corn, sour cream, margarine, milk, and egg together. Add Jiffy mix and pour into greased baking dish. Sprinkle top with grated cheese. Bake at 350° for 40 minutes.

SOURCE: Maxine, an avid golfer friend, brought this casserole to one of our after-golf get-togethers. Naturally, I had to get the recipe. To turn this delicious casserole into a meal, brown and add 1 pound ground chuck or breakfast sausage and a few chopped jalapeños before baking. Serve with a side of picante sauce.

Golf being the only athletic endeavor that I have ever excelled at, I simply must relate this story to you. The first trophy I won was the "Worst Score" and that inspired me to try harder. It really was a cute trophy, though. Then, I won third place in the club championship. When I told my daughters about this, Jennie astutely asked, "How many players were there, three?" Completely burst my bubble–they could have let me bask in the glory for a little while, couldn't they? (How could they have known there were only 3 women playing in that tournament?) Sheer tenacity kept me working at the game, getting my handicap lower and lower until one day I broke 100. Then, I finally broke 90, shooting an 82! I won first place in the club championship several times and there were lots more than one player. Practice doesn't make perfect, but it sure does help. In golf, there is no perfect.

"Golf is a game in which you yell 4, shoot 6, and write down 5."
– Paul Harvey

Fettuccini Alfredo for Twelve

Friends Christmas Dinner

24 oz. fettuccine
1 c. + 2 T. cream at room temp.
2 c. Parmesan cheese, grated
6 T. butter, at room temp.
Nutmeg
Fresh cracked black pepper

Cook fettuccine in boiling, salted water until al dente. Drain and return to the pot. Add the cream, cheese, and butter; stir until well mixed. (Be sure the cream and butter are room temperature, as the pasta is not heated again after combining, and it should be served piping hot.) Place on individual serving plates, serving bowl, or platter. Top with nutmeg and cracked black pepper.

COOKING PASTA

- ✦ Always bring the water to a full, rolling boil before adding the pasta; after adding, stir until the water returns to a boil. Rapid boiling keeps the pasta from sticking together.
- ✦ Adding a couple of swirls of olive oil to the pot helps prevent sticking.
- ✦ Large amounts of water are required–follow the proportions on the package directions.
- ✦ *Al dente* is an Italian phrase for "to the tooth" which means to cook your pasta so it is firm but not hard. I usually let my students throw their spaghetti or fettuccine against the wall—if it stuck, then it was *al dente*. If it falls off, cook a little longer. Go ahead and try it. Oh yeah, don't forget to wipe the wall clean.
- ✦ Another way to determine doneness is to squeeze the pasta between your fingers and if it breaks easily, it is done. Be careful because the pasta will be hot.
- ✦ To figure out how much pasta is enough, allow 2 ounces raw pasta for each person if it is the main dish; use less (¾–1 ounce per person) if it will be served as a side dish. Two ounces of cooked pasta is a plate full.

"If you ate pasta and antipasta, would you still be hungry?"
– Author Unknown

Fried Green Tomatoes

Julie

2–3 lg. green tomatoes
1 egg, beaten
2–3 T. milk
1 c. flour
3 T. corn meal
½ T. baking powder
Salt & pepper to taste
Vegetable oil

Slice tomatoes ½-inch thick. Sprinkle generously with salt and let sit a few minutes. Mix milk and egg. Separately mix flour, corn meal, baking powder, salt, and pepper. Heat 1 inch of oil in iron skillet. Dip tomatoes in egg mixture and then dry mixture. Pan fry on medium until browned.

NOTE: A satisfying reward of motherhood is to have your daughter grow up and not only eat, but come up with her own recipe for fried green tomatoes. Guess it was all the fresh garden vegetables we had available when she was little.

Garlic Cheese Grits

4 c. water
1 tsp. salt
2 garlic cloves, pressed
1 c. grits, uncooked
½ c. butter
12 oz. (3 c.) Cheddar cheese, shredded
¼ tsp. white pepper
3 eggs, lightly beaten

Bring water, salt, and garlic to a boil in a large saucepan. Gradually stir in grits; return to a boil. Reduce heat and simmer, stirring occasionally, 15 minutes or until thickened. Add butter and cheese, stirring until cheese melts. Remove from heat; let stand 10 minutes. Stir in eggs and pour into a lightly greased baking dish. Bake at 350° for 1 hour or until set.

VARIATION: For spicy garlic cheese grits, add 1 teaspoon pepper, a few dashes of Worcestershire sauce, and several splashes of hot sauce along with the cheese and butter. Sprinkle with paprika before putting in the oven.

Garlic Mashed Potatoes

8–9 sm. new red potatoes
4 cloves garlic, pressed
½ tsp. salt
Water
¼ c. milk
1 T. butter

Wash and half new potatoes, leaving peelings intact. Add garlic and salt; barely cover with water. Cook until done. Drain; add milk and butter; mash. Leave potatoes slightly lumpy. Garnish with fresh parsley, if desired.

Glazed or Buttered Carrots

School Dinner Recipe

3 carrots
½ c. water
1 T. butter
Dash salt
Dash pepper

Peel and cut up carrots; place in saucepan with water. Bring to boil and lower heat to finish cooking. Add butter, salt, and pepper. Serve.

GLAZED VARIATION: Add ⅓ cup brown sugar, juice of half a lemon, and about ½ teaspoon lemon zest. Heat slowly, stirring occasionally, until nicely glazed, about 15 minutes.

I found this recipe on a strip of notebook paper marking the page for Swedish Meatballs. Joy, oh joy! I don't remember it, but I'm guessing we peeled and peeled and peeled carrots for that banquet. No doubt, we made fresh yeast rolls, too. I am officially turning into my mother because I am saying, "I can't believe all the things I have done. How did I ever do it?"

CARROT-TOLOGY

Cutting vegetables like carrots into long thin strips, with the grain, allows less nutrients to leak out than cutting into round coins. Vegetables cut into large pieces retain more nutrients. Also, cooking veggies only until fork-tender preserves nutrients. Carrots are high in vitamin A and really do help you see in the dark; they help prevent night blindness. These days, I like to use the mini-carrots that are available–no cutting or peeling required.

Fried Rice

2 T. cooking oil
2 beaten eggs
½ c. fully cooked ham, diced
¼ c. fresh mushrooms, diced
¼ c. green onions, thinly sliced
½–1 tsp. ginger root, grated
Dash ground red pepper
3 c. unsalted cooked rice, chilled
2 c. Chinese cabbage, sliced
½ c. frozen peas, thawed
2 T. soy sauce
1 T. water

In a large skillet, heat 1 tablespoon of the oil over medium heat. Add eggs and cook without stirring until set. Loosen eggs and invert skillet over cutting board to remove; cut into short, narrow strips. In the same skillet, heat the remaining oil over medium heat. Cook ham, mushrooms, onion, ginger root, and red pepper in hot oil for 3 minutes. Stir in cooked rice, cabbage, and egg strips; sprinkle with soy sauce and 1 tablespoon water. Cook for 3–5 minutes or until heated through, tossing gently to coat with soy sauce.
Yield: 4 servings

NOTE: As revealed in my story of growing up, we never ate anything out of the ordinary. Maybe that explains my love affair with Chinese food. I could eat fried rice every day and there is not any place close to me to get it. So, out of self-defense, I found a pretty good recipe to tide me over until my next Chinese restaurant fix. I should order some of those take-out boxes though, because eating straight out of that box is one of my favorite things to do.

Food triggers memories; it's funny how swamped one can become from just one little glimpse into the past. The night after I closed on the house I built "All By Myself," a friend of mine and I sat on the floor in the living room, ate fried rice from the box, and drank Freixenet champagne. I didn't really build that house all by myself–I was single, but had the encouragement, support, and assistance of so many like Roger, that dear friend with whom I shared the fried rice. Roger died from lung cancer several years ago. I remember all of the golf we shared and how he helped plan my deck with it's strategically placed bench; I still love to sit with my back to the brick wall and think about him every once in a while.

Grand Marnier Sweet Potatoes

Elaine

6 med. sweet potatoes, about 3 lb.
3 T. butter or margarine, melted
¾ c. sugar
3 T. Grand Marnier (orange liqueur) or orange juice
1 tsp. grated orange zest
¼ tsp. salt
¼ tsp. ground nutmeg
1 lg. egg, lightly beaten
½ can (14 oz.) sweetened condensed milk
1 c. brown sugar, firmly packed
1 c. pecans, chopped
⅓ c. all purpose flour
⅓ c. butter or margarine, melted
¼ tsp. ground nutmeg

Cook potatoes in enough boiling water to cover in a Dutch oven 30–40 minutes or until tender; drain. Let cool slightly. Peel potatoes and place in a large bowl. Add 3 tablespoons butter and mash. Add ¾ cup sugar and next six ingredients; mash again, or beat at medium speed with electric mixer until smooth. Spoon mixture into a lightly greased 2-quart casserole. Combine brown sugar and remaining 4 ingredients; sprinkle over sweet potato mixture. Bake, uncovered, at 425° for 30 minutes or until thoroughly heated, shielding with aluminum foil after 20 minutes to prevent excessive browning. Yield: 8 servings

NOTE: These are my absolute favorite sweet potatoes. Elaine always makes them for Thanksgiving, but this year I was given the opportunity, so I finally got the recipe. When cooking with liqueurs and wines, the less expensive varieties work just fine. Save brand names for sipping and for using in dishes where the alcohol is not cooked after adding. By the way, cooking alcohol reduces or removes its alcohol content, leaving only the flavor behind.

"My cooking is so bad my kids thought Thanksgiving was to commemorate Pearl Harbor." – Phyllis Diller

Granny's Cabbage

Julie

1 lg. onion
2 sm. heads cabbage
4–6 slices bacon
Vegetable oil
Salt, pepper, garlic powder
4 T. water
2 pkg. Sweet n' Low

Chop onion and slice cabbage as thin as possible. Cut bacon and fry in skillet. Remove bacon, discard grease. Return bacon to pan, add onion and cook until tender. Remove half of the bacon and onion. Add small amount of oil and half of the cabbage. Cook on medium. Drizzle with oil, sprinkle with salt, pepper, and garlic. Stir. When starting to cook, add 2 tablespoons water. When almost translucent, add 1 package Sweet n' Low. Remove from pan and keep warm. Repeat with second half of ingredients.

NOTE: Julie adds, "This cabbage is soooo good. The secret is in the method. It took me several Christmas dinners to really see the secrets, but mine is still not as good as Granny's!"

Green Bean Bundles

Friends Christmas Dinner

1 lb. fresh green beans
2 yellow summer squash (1½" dia.)
1 garlic clove, minced
¼ tsp. dried tarragon, crushed
4 tsp. olive oil
¼ tsp. salt
¼ tsp. coarsely ground pepper

Trim stem end from beans, leaving tails, and arrange in eight bundles. Cut squash into ½-inch wide slices; hollow squash slices to within ¼-inch of edges. Insert beans through squash rings. Put bean bundles in a steamer basket. Place in a saucepan over 1 inch of water; bring to a boil. Cover and steam for 8–10 minutes or until crisp-tender. Meanwhile, in a small nonstick skillet, sauté garlic and tarragon in oil for 1 minute. Remove from the heat. Arrange bean bundles on a serving platter; drizzle with garlic mixture. Sprinkle with salt and pepper. Yield: 8 servings

Green Beans Deluxe

2 pkg. (9 oz. ea.) frozen French-style green beans
1 can (10½ oz.) cream of mushroom soup
1 can (3½ oz.) French-fried onions

Heat oven to 350°. Microwave frozen green beans until bright green and completely thawed, 2–3 minutes. Combine beans and soup; pour into greased 9 x 13 x 2-inch casserole dish. Bake 15 minutes. Remove from oven and sprinkle with French-fried onions. Bake 5 minutes more.
Yield: 6–8 servings

NOTE: A cookbook just wouldn't be complete without a green bean casserole recipe. You can substitute 2 cans, 16 oz. each, green beans, drained, for the frozen beans. Some people add cheese, but I don't. Use your imagination and see what can be done with this Thanksgiving staple.

Green Beans with Toasted Almonds

2 cans (16 oz.) French-style green beans
Fresh ground black pepper
2 T. bacon drippings
2–3 oz. slivered almonds

Drain beans and cook with pepper and bacon drippings for 8–10 minutes or microwave 3 minutes. Toast the almonds in a little butter and set aside. When ready to serve, sprinkle the toasted almonds over the hot beans. For a fancy touch, add a little shredded cheese before sprinkling with almonds. This is a good dish to serve with baked chicken and herbed rice. Yield: 6 servings

"Life expectancy would grow by leaps and bounds if green vegetables smelled as good as bacon." – Doug Larson

Hopping John

Marilyn's Mother

1 c. dried black-eyed peas
4 c. boiling water
¼–½ lb. ham, cubed
1 lg. onion, chopped
½ c. celery & leaves, chopped
1 sm. bay leaf
2½ tsp. salt
⅛ tsp. pepper
½ c. rice

Place peas in boiling water in saucepan. Cover and let stand for 2 hours. Do not drain. Brown cubed ham. Add onion and celery; sauté. Add to soaked peas along with bay leaf, salt, and pepper. Add 2 more cups boiling water. Simmer in covered saucepan until peas are nearly tender. Discard bay leaf. Add rice and simmer, covered, until rice is done.
Yield: 4–6 servings

NOTE: I always wondered what Hopping John was so I was delighted when, on one of our trips to the coast, Marilyn's mother had prepared it. She was such a jewel for sharing with me. It's a great Southern dish worth including. I start out with less salt since the ham adds some. More salt can always be added, if needed.

Macaroni & Cheese

Classroom Standard

8 oz. macaroni
2 qt. water
4 oz. Velveeta cheese, cubed
¼ c. milk
2 T. butter

Bring water to a full boil. Drop in macaroni and stir until water returns to a boil. Adjust heat so the macaroni continues to boil. Cook until macaroni is done. Drain. Return to saucepan and add remaining ingredients. Stir and cook over very low heat until all the cheese is melted.

Mac and cheese was an all-time classroom favorite. At home, it was often our entire meal. Julie and Jennie used much more cheese when they made it. Really, theirs should be called Cheese and Macaroni! This was, and still is, one of our favorite comfort foods.

COOKING DRIED PEAS AND BEANS

- ✦ Dried beans will increase in size 2½ times when cooked. 1 cup dried beans equals 2½ cups cooked beans.
- ✦ Do not add salt until the beans are tender and cooked completely. Adding salt earlier will prevent the beans from absorbing water. This is because a bean has an opening that is large enough for water molecules to enter it, but salt molecules are larger. Salt will plug the bean opening, preventing the water from entering, thus creating hard beans that never seem to cook right. (I really did teach food science.)
- ✦ Reducing the flatulence beans create: Soaking dried beans activates the beans to begin the germination process. Once wet, the beans release enzymes that begin to break down their complex sugars into more simple ones. It is the bean's complex sugars that cause gas along with indigestion. The overnight soak method reduces the complex sugars and the gas they produce.
- ✦ Never cook canned beans in their liquid. Rinse several times in water and drain before cooking, otherwise your flatulence will be great.
- ✦ There is no need to presoak dried black-eyed peas, split peas, peas, or any variety of lentils.
- ✦ If dried peas and beans were not soaked overnight, this technique will hasten their cooking: Rinse and bring beans to a boil. Turn off heat, cover and let set 1 hour. Continue cooking until done. The hot water quickens the absorption process, thus speeding up the cooking time.

"The rich would have to eat money if the poor did not provide food."
– Russian Proverb

Mrs. Martin's Hush Puppies

Mrs. Martin

1 c. onion, chopped
2 c. cornmeal
1 c. flour
¼ tsp. poultry seasoning
2 tsp. baking powder
2 eggs
Salt to taste
Boiling water

Combine all ingredients except water. Then, add about 1 cup boiling water and stir, adding more as necessary to make a very thick batter of soft consistency. Heat oil and dip spoon in hot grease before making each hush puppy. To shape hush puppies, scrape hot, dipped spoon sideways across batter, helping it to form a crescent shape. This is really an art form. Drop into hot oil and fry until golden brown, about 4–5 minutes. Dip spoon in hot grease again and form another hush puppy. Do not crowd hush puppies. They all need to be able to float on the surface. Keep trying–it may take several fish fries to get the hang of shaping these hush puppies. The results will finally be worth the effort. Use a large soup spoon or a small serving spoon that can withstand the hot oil for shaping the hush puppies.

Mr. and Mrs. Martin were very good friends of the family and they always came to our fish fries. Mrs. Martin would make the batter and then Mr. Martin (Everyone called him "Red"–his hair was a shade brighter than mine used to be.) would carefully shape each hush puppy. He was a true master at this and such a sweet man; he patiently helped me learn the technique. The Martin's did a lot of crappie fishing at the lake, so they had lots of fish to fry. They also travelled with my parents and in-laws in their RV rigs all over the United States making many great memories together. Mrs. Martin says, "I should have been a salesman for RV's, I loved traveling so much!"

Thinking about traveling brings to mind this quote for backseat drivers and drivers like my husband: "If you are a nervous person, and are likely to offer advice to the driver, you should decline an invitation to make a motor trip. On the other hand, if you are the driver, you should drive carefully, and not take risks that may result in accidents, or in frightening the other occupants of the car." – Searchlight Homemaking Guide, Copyright, 1937

Noodle Kugel

1 pkg. (1 lb.) egg noodles
½ c. butter, melted
8 eggs
2 c. sugar
2 c. (16 oz.) sour cream
2 c. (16 oz.) small-curd cottage cheese
9 whole cinnamon graham crackers, crushed
3 T. butter, melted

Cook noodles according to package directions; drain. Toss with butter; set aside. In a large mixing bowl, beat the eggs, sugar, sour cream, and cottage cheese until well blended. (Use a blender to hide the cottage cheese.) Stir in the noodles. Pour into a greased 13 x 9 x 2-inch baking dish. Combine the cracker crumbs and butter; sprinkle over the top. Bake, uncovered, at 350° for 50–55 minutes or until a thermometer reads 160°. May need to tent with foil if crumbs start getting too brown. Let stand for 10 minutes before cutting. Serve warm or cold. Yield: 12–15 servings

NOTE: As a seasoned German girl, I can guarantee this is absolutely delicious and oh, so German. I have to resist the temptation to eat it with butter bread.

Polynesian Mingle

1½ c. Minute Rice
1½ c. celery, chopped
¼ c. onion, minced
2 pkg. (10 oz.) frozen peas
4 chicken bouillon cubes
1 T. soy sauce
1 tsp. sugar
¼ tsp. salt
2 c. water

Preheat oven to 375°. Combine rice, celery, onion, and peas in a 2-quart casserole. Place water in saucepan and add bouillon cubes, soy sauce, sugar, and salt; bring to a boil. Pour over casserole mixture and stir well. Cover and bake for 30 minutes. Remove cover, stir again, and bake uncovered for an additional 15 minutes. Yield: 8 servings

One Gallon Dressing

1 loaf dried bread
2 recipes baked cornbread (without sugar)
2 lg. onions, finely chopped
2 c. celery, finely chopped
½ c. margarine
1 can cream of chicken soup
2 c. giblets, boiled & chopped
Broth from cooked giblets
Salt & pepper to taste

Crumble dried bread and cornbread in a large bowl or pan. Sauté the onions and celery in the margarine. Do not brown. Add soup and giblets. Mix all ingredients together and add enough broth to make a thick mixture. Bake in greased casserole dish, uncovered, for 1 hour at 350°.

NOTE: This is the best dressing in the world–at least, in my opinion it is. It is the recipe we have used for years at our church's famous Turkey Supper. We serve over 2,000 people each year, so it has to be good. My students used to bake 5 turkeys and make 5 batches of dressing for the supper. It was a great opportunity to learn how to roast and carve a turkey and make dressing, plus it was a great community service project. Mama uses this recipe for our family Thanksgiving, too, and we all love it. She used to make stuffing especially for Daddy because he didn't eat onions or celery until much later in life. David loves the stuffing, too. I guess it's a man-thing: like father, like son.

CARVING A TURKEY

To get the maximum servings from the turkey's breast and have beautiful slices to arrange on your serving platter, follow the procedure outlined below.

- ✦ Remove the drumsticks and thighs; cut the meat from the bones, slicing parallel to the bone.
- ✦ Make a horizontal cut just above the wing, cutting all the way to the body cavity.
- ✦ Insert your knife just to the side of the center of the breast bone and cut close to the body cavity all the way to your horizontal cut.
- ✦ Insert your knife in the horizontal cut and remove the entire half of the breast from the body of the turkey. Place on a cutting board.
- ✦ Remove the skin and slice across the grain, making ¼-inch thick slices.
- ✦ Place a wide spatula under the slices and transfer to serving platter.
- ✦ Repeat with the remaining side of the bird.

Potato Pancakes

4 lg. (3 lb.) potatoes, peeled
1 sm. onion
2 eggs
⅓ c. flour
2 tsp. salt
⅛ tsp. pepper
Cooking oil

Coarsely shred potatoes and onions into large bowl. Add eggs, flour, salt, and pepper. Mix well. Heat griddle or large frying pan; add small amount of oil. Drop ¼ cupfuls of potato mixture onto hot griddle. Flatten and cook each side until golden brown. Drain on paper towel. Makes about 16 pancakes. Serve with German sausage and applesauce.

We used to go to the Wurstfest in New Braunfels. They made the best potato pancakes and served them with applesauce. Combine that with sausage on a stick and some German mustard and you are in "Deutsch Heaven." One year I came home, started experimenting, and concocted this recipe, which I must say, is just about as good as theirs. Pair these with our grilled Family Sausage and you just might be in "Double Deutsch Heaven."

Rice Dressing

4 c. chicken broth, divided
1½ c. uncooked long-grain rice
2 c. onion, chopped
2 c. celery, chopped
½ c. butter
3 T. fresh parsley, minced
2 cans (4 oz. ea.) mushroom stems & pieces, drained
1½–2 tsp. poultry seasoning
¾ tsp. salt
½ tsp. pepper
Fresh thyme

In a saucepan, bring 3½ cups broth and the rice to a boil. Reduce heat; cover and simmer for 20 minutes or until tender. Meanwhile, in a skillet, sauté onion and celery in butter until tender. Stir in cooked rice, mushrooms, parsley, poultry seasoning, salt, pepper, and the remaining broth. Pour into a greased 9 x 13 x 2-inch baking dish. Bake, uncovered, at 350° for 30 minutes. Garnish with fresh thyme. Yield: 10–12 servings

A three-year-old gave this reaction to her Christmas dinner: "I don't like the turkey, but I like the bread he ate." – Author Unknown

Rice Pilaf

Julie

½ c. rice
2 T. melted butter
1 clove garlic, minced
Salt, pepper, marjoram
½ c. onions, diced
Soy sauce
Worcestershire sauce
Water
1 can (4 oz.) sliced mushrooms, drained

Melt butter and add rice and minced garlic; brown. Add spices while cooking; then add onions. Place 3–5 dashes Worcestershire sauce and 3 dashes soy sauce in a 1 cup measure and fill with water to 1 cup line. Add this and mushrooms to rice mixture. Bring to boil. Reduce heat, cover and cook 15–20 minutes.

PERFECTLY COOKED RICE EVERY TIME

- First of all, use a heavy saucepan with a close-fitting cover.
- Use a 2-to-1 ratio: 2 cups water for every 1 cup rice makes 3½ cups cooked rice.
- Depending on how the rice will be used, add ½ teaspoon salt for each cup of rice being cooked.
- Rice cooks by absorbing liquid and this is accomplished by steam. So, once a simmer is achieved, reduce heat, cover and cook without raising the lid for 20 minutes. Raising the lid allows steam to escape and the rice will not be done and/or it will run out of water–so resist the temptation to check on it.
- It may take a while to determine just the right burner setting to achieve perfection, but it sure beats trying to figure out where to store a rice cooker.
- For fluffy, separate rice grains, use long grain rice–a more expensive variety like Uncle Ben's.
- For sticky rice, use a less expensive variety that has broken grains, too. I prefer sticky rice when serving with chili and gumbos or cooking jambalaya.

NOTE: If combining rice with cream soups or other ingredients that also contain salt, be aware of how much additional salt is added as dish may become too salty. Be aware that Velveeta and other cheeses also contain salt.

Risotto

From the Food Lab

1 c. fresh mushrooms, sliced
⅔ c. long grain rice
⅓ c. green pepper, chopped
2 T. margarine or butter
1 c. chicken broth
½ c. water
¼ c. dry sherry
⅛ tsp. pepper
2 T. Parmesan cheese, grated
Fresh rosemary or parsley

In a medium saucepan, cook mushrooms, rice, and green pepper in margarine until green pepper is tender. Remove from heat. Stir in broth, water, sherry, and pepper. Bring to boiling; reduce heat. Cover and simmer about 15 minutes or until tender. Remove from heat. Let stand, covered, for 5 minutes. Fluff with a fork. Sprinkle with Parmesan cheese. Serves 4. Garnish with fresh rosemary or parsley sprigs.

NOTE: Obviously, we didn't use dry sherry in the food lab. While it's distinctive flavor will be missed, water can be used instead.

Skillet Green Beans with Tomatoes & Bacon

Rosemary

6 slices bacon, cut in sm. pieces
1 lg. onion, chopped
1 lb. snapped green beans
½ c. chicken broth
½ tsp. salt
¼ tsp. pepper
4 med. plum tomatoes, chopped

Cook bacon until crisp, set aside. Using bacon grease, sauté onions. Add beans, broth, salt, and pepper; bring to a boil. Reduce heat and simmer for 10 minutes or until beans are fork-tender. Stir in tomatoes, cook 3 minutes until tomatoes are heated throughout. Sprinkle with bacon.

"The only way to keep your health is to eat what you don't want, drink what you don't like, and do what you'd rather not." – Mark Twain

Sautéed Mushrooms

½ c. butter
1 lb. fresh mushrooms, whole or sliced
½ tsp. oregano, crushed
½ tsp. basil, crushed
¼ tsp. ground cumin
¼ tsp. pepper
Salt to taste

Melt butter in a large skillet. Add spices. Simmer a couple of minutes. Add mushrooms and stir, cooking until desired doneness is reached. Overcooking causes mushrooms to become tough and rubbery.

NOTE: When cooking with dried herbs, crush using a mortar and pestle or rub between fingers before adding. This helps to wake up the flavor.

ABOUT FRESH MUSHROOMS

- Do not rinse or soak fresh mushrooms in water. Use a soft dish cloth or towel to remove peat. Mushrooms will absorb water, loose flavor, and the appearance will not be great. (If fresh ground black pepper is used, no one will see any peat anyway.)
- Don't prepare mushrooms until ready to serve. They will overcook, turn dark, and be chewy.
- Use real butter or margarine. Reduced fat varieties contain undesirable liquid.
- Do not crowd the mushrooms in the pan when browning or sautéing.
- If fresh mushrooms are not available, use canned variety. Just drain juice and cook in butter mixture just until hot.
- Serve sautéed mushrooms over or with grilled steak.
- Never pick your own mushrooms from the yard or forest, they just might be poisonous!

"When I'm old and gray, I want to have a house by the sea. And paint. With a lot of wonderful chums, good music and booze around. And a damn good kitchen to cook in." – Ava Gardner

Scalloped Potatoes

School Dinner Recipe

2 T. butter
2 T. flour
2 c. milk
1½ tsp. salt
⅛ tsp. pepper
¼ c. onion, chopped
3½ c. potatoes, sliced
1 c. cheese, grated

Melt butter; blend in flour. Cook and stir 1 minute. Add milk and cook over low heat until thickened, stirring constantly. Add salt, pepper, and onion. Layer with potatoes and cheese in greased 10 x 6 x 1½-inch greased casserole. Bake, covered, at 350° for 30 minutes. Uncover; bake for 30 minutes longer. Yield: 6—8 servings

NOTE: This sounds delicious and I remember that everyone loved it, but looking back, I think I would sauté the onions in the butter and then add the flour. That's an extra step, but the flavor of sautéed onion would be worth it to me.

Spicy Potatoes

Jennie

10 red potatoes, with skin
1 med. onion
Olive oil
Fresh cracked pepper
2–3 cloves fresh garlic, minced
Tony Chacere's

Chop potatoes and onion. Cover a pizza pan with foil. Place chopped onions, garlic, and potatoes on the pan. Cover with fresh cracked pepper and Tony Chacere's. Drizzle with olive oil. Mix with your hands to thoroughly coat the potatoes. Bake on 325° for 30 minutes, until golden brown. Use a spatula half-way through to turn the potatoes so they cook on all sides.

VARIATION: Try replacing the Tony's with dill for an interesting twist.

"I was 32 when I started cooking; up until then, I just ate." – Julia Child

Stir-Fried Cabbage

1 sm. head cabbage
Olive oil
Salt
Pepper

Wash and shred or thinly cut cabbage, discarding the core. Over medium to medium-high, heat olive oil in a large skillet. Add about ½-inch layer of cabbage and sprinkle with salt and pepper. Continue with layers until skillet is holding all it can, hopefully, all the cabbage. Cover and cook for 3–4 minutes. Stir. Continue cooking, stirring ever so often, until cabbage reaches desired doneness. I like it to still be a little crunchy.

NOTE: This is one of those "sprinkle until it looks right" recipes. Use a cast iron skillet and increase your intake of iron for the day.

Yummy Baked Potatoes

Julie

Lg. baking potatoes
Butter
Course ground salt
Fresh ground pepper

Scrub potatoes well. Prick with a fork. Place on pieces of foil. Rub with butter. Salt and pepper well. Wrap in foil. Place on baking sheet. Bake at 350° for 80–90 minutes.

NOTE: Julie adds, "We love to make these on the weekends and sometimes top them with chopped brisket that we keep in the freezer for quick meals. My favorite part is the skin. Yum!"

BEEF

Beef Enchiladas

Julie

1 lb. ground meat
1 c. onion, chopped
1 pkg. taco seasoning
2 c. grated cheese
1 lb. Velveeta
1 can cream of mushroom soup
¾ c. evaporated milk
8 flour tortillas
1 can enchilada sauce

Brown meat and onion. Add taco seasoning and cook per package directions. Mix with grated cheese. Heat soup, Velveeta, and milk in saucepan to make cheese sauce. Pour some enchilada sauce in the bottom of a 9 x 13 x 2-inch baking dish. Dip tortillas in enchilada sauce. Fill with meat and place in pan. Cover with cheese sauce. Bake at 350° for 30 minutes.

Beer Braised Cutlets

Julie

1 lb. beef or venison cutlets, 2 inch pieces
Flour seasoned w/ salt & pepper
Oil
2–3 onions, sliced thin
2 cloves garlic, minced
1 tsp. thyme
Salt & pepper
1 can beer

Lightly flour and quickly pan fry cutlets in about ¼ inch of oil (does not have to be *done*). Remove from oil. Brown onions and garlic. Add seasoning. Layer onions/meat/onions in a baking dish. Add ½–¾ can of beer. Cover, bake at 350° for 30 minutes.

"Red meat is not bad for you. Now blue-green meat, that's bad for you!"
– Tommy Smothers

Cheese Enchiladas with Chili Sauce

Julie

CHILI SAUCE
1 lb. hamburger
1 onion, chopped & divided
2 cloves garlic, minced
1 tsp. cumin
1 T. chili powder
Salt & pepper to taste
¼ tsp. cayenne pepper
1 can (14.5 oz.) diced tomatoes
2 cans (8 oz.) tomato sauce
ENCHILADAS
10–12 lg. corn tortillas
1 lb. Velveeta
½ tsp. oregano
1 c. shredded cheese

Brown meat, onion, and garlic (reserving some onion for rolling with cheese). Drain any fat. Add spices, tomatoes, and tomato sauce. Cook. Lightly fry corn tortillas in oil in iron skillet to make pliable. Drain well on paper towels. Place small amount of chili sauce in the bottom of a greased glass baking dish. Cut Velveeta–slice and then cut in fourths. Place 6 pieces in the center of each tortilla, sprinkle with reserved diced onions. Roll and place seam side down in pan. Cover with chili sauce and sprinkle with cheese. Bake at 350° for 30 minutes or until cheese is fully melted.

Company Hungarian Roast

Mom & School Dinner Recipe

6 lb. lean sirloin roast (in one piece)
1 tsp. salt
¼ tsp. pepper
½ tsp. paprika
¾ lb. ready to eat Canadian-style bacon slices
2 pkg. (8 oz.) natural Swiss cheese slices
¼ c. salad oil

EARLY IN THE DAY: Cut roast crosswise to depth of about 1 inch from bottom into 10 slices. Sprinkle roast top and slices with salt, pepper, and paprika. In each cut place 3 bacon slices, side by side, then 1 slice Swiss cheese, trimmed at top corners. Now tie roast lengthwise securely. Set on rack in shallow roasting pan. Refrigerate.

ABOUT 2 HR. AND 15 MIN. BEFORE SERVING: Start heating oven to 450°. In small saucepan, heat salad oil and pour over top and sides of meat. Roast sirloin 30 minutes. Baste occasionally. Then cover with foil and roast 45 minutes longer for very rare and/or about 65 minutes for medium rare. Allow 2 hours at 350° for well done.

NOTE: This roast and Mom's Deluxe Roast Beef recipes are from the 70s and we made them for school board dinners.

SERVING MEALS

The tradition of sitting down to a family meal at home is fast losing its place in society. I remind you of this old adage: "The family that prays together stays together" and I suggest adding this: "The family that eats together stays together." At the very least, they know each other a little better. Yes, I know times have changed, but knowing how to serve a *sit-down* meal is a viable skill that should not be forgotten. I can make it really simple–all you have to do is carve out a little piece of time. Put dinner on the family calendar and text everyone to remind them.

Take time to set the table and gather round it with family and friends. Bring back those family values–spend some time together without technology interfering.

TABLE SETTING 101

First try to imagine my homemade flannel board with construction-paper images that had sandpaper glued to the back so they would cling to the board. Can't you just see my plate, fork, spoon, knife, and everything? Here's what I taught:

- ✦ The table cloth should extend 10–12 inches below the tabletop. All sides of the cloth should be even. If your table is like mine–old–the ready-made sizes don't fit. So just make sure that the two sides are the same length and both ends are even.
- ✦ First, place the dining chairs around the table, leaving them about halfway out. Everyone needs at least 24 inches of space at the table.
- ✦ The plate or charger is centered in front of each chair. Use the first joint of your thumb to get the flatware lined up the same distance (about an inch) from the edge of the table. Hook your thumb over the edge of the table and put the bottom of each item at the tip of it.
- ✦ To remember what goes where, follow this simple procedure:
  - Look at your hand and count each finger...1, 2, 3, 4, 5.
  - Spell out "right," counting the letters. R-I-G-H-T: 5 letters.
  - Spell out "left," counting the letters. L-E-F-T: 4 letters.
  - Now spell out the name of the item being placed on the table and count its letters.
  - If an item has five letters, it goes to the R-I-G-H-T of the plate.
  - If an item has four letters, it goes to the L-E-F-T of the plate.
    - K-N-I-F-E: <u>Always</u> on the right–next to the plate, with the blade facing the plate.
    - S-P-O-O-N: Place on the right, to the right of the knife.
    - D-R-I-N-K or G-L-A-S-S: Place on the right side, at the tip of the knife.
    - F-O-R-K: Place on the left, beside the plate.
- ✦ If more than one fork or spoon is used, place them in the order of use from the outside in. For example, if serving a salad before the meal, place the dinner fork next to the plate and place the salad fork on the outside—to the left of the dinner fork. If having soup and then ice cream for dessert, place the dessert spoon beside the knife and the soup spoon on the outside—to the right of the dessert spoon.
- ✦ The dessert fork or spoon can be placed European style: above the plate with the handle of the fork extending to the left; extend the handle of the spoon to the right.

- When using more than one beverage glass, place the first glass at the tip of the knife and place the second glass to the right and slightly closer to the edge of the table.
- A few things don't fit the R-I-G-H-T/L-E-F-T scenario.
- The napkin can be placed anywhere: rolled up or stuffed in the wine glass, folded and in the position of the dinner plate, or traditionally just to the left of the place setting, folded into a rectangular shape, with the fold of the napkin facing the plate. The only place the napkin should not be is under something since it is the first item to be used. (Restaurants and cafés do this all the time. It's an easy way to train wait staff to set the table quickly, but that doesn't make it correct.)
- The bread and butter plate is placed above the forks on the left. The butter knife is placed across the right side or across the top of the plate, if used.
- When salad is served as a separate course, place it in the position of the dinner plate. If it is served with the meal, place above the forks, or to the left of the forks when a bread and butter plate is used. A separate salad fork is not needed if the salad is served with the main course.
- Coffee cups and saucers are placed to the right of the spoons. If you want to get technical, place the handle of the cup to the right, parallel to the edge of the table.
- The centerpiece should be below eye level of guests when seated.
- If candles are used, they should be lit.
- When food is served in bowls or stemware, place on a liner plate. This plate provides a spot for the guest to put their eating utensil when not in use. For example: When serving shrimp cocktail in a stemmed glass, place the glass on a small plate. Diners can then put their fork on the plate and not break a cardinal rule: Never place a used eating utensil back on the table.
- The most common type of food service is *family style.* Place serving dishes on the table with the serving spoon or fork on the table beside them, on the right or left. Put food in front of someone and as out of the way of the beverage glasses as possible.
- Everyone helps themselves to the dish in front of them and passes it to the right, counterclockwise.
- If one food is served with another, place the accompaniment to the left of the food. For example, place the gravy to the left of the mashed potatoes.
- For seconds, pass food the closest route.
- After the meal, place flatware across the center of your plate with the handles extending to the right, making it easy for wait staff to remove your plate without dropping the flatware in your lap.

Table Setting 101, continued

- ✦ When finished, cloth napkins should be placed on the table, not on the plate.
- ✦ FORMAL DINING: Serve from the left and remove from the right. The school board dinners we served were formal events and students had a quick practice session just before the guests arrived. I wonder if anyone remembers that? I wonder how many became professional waiters?
- ✦ FYI: If you find yourself a guest for dinner at the White House and there is such an array of silverware that you are dumbfounded, here's two choices. First, remember how the table is set, with the first-used flatware farthest from the plate. Then decide if the course placed in front of you requires a fork or a spoon; work your way from the outside toward your plate. The second option, is to watch the First Lady (or the hostess). It's hard to go wrong doing that.
- ✦ This last point reigns from the home management house. After a meal, the proper statement is, "I have sufficiently dined." I tell it like it was!

Family Thanksgiving Dinner at Mama's

"One of the very nicest things about life is the way we must regularly stop whatever it is we are doing and devote our attention to eating."
– Luciano Pavarotti and William Wright

Continental Stroganoff

Home Management Special

2 lb. round steak, cut in thin strips
1 c. sliced onion
4 T. butter
2 cans condensed golden mushroom soup
1 c. sour cream
Hot buttered noodles

In skillet brown meat and cook onion in butter until tender. Stir in soup. Cook covered over low heat for 45 minutes or until meat is tender. Add sour cream 5 minutes before serving; heat through but do not bring to a boil. Serve over hot buttered noodles.

NOTE: Originally served in the home management house, we multiplied this recipe by 6 for school board dinners. Generally, allow ¼ pound of meat per person. For special events, we increased that amount so we could serve ample portions.

> Digging in the old recipe box from school is fun—I had forgotten about this recipe, originally from the home management house. Today, I will use reduced or sodium-free soup and maybe even low-fat sour cream. My how times have changed, nutritionally speaking.

Crescent Packages

Julie

1 lb. ground beef
½ c. onion, chopped
1 tsp. oregano
1 T. chili powder
1 tsp. cumin
1 can nacho cheese soup or cheese dip
1 c. milk
1 can crescent rolls
¼ c. shredded cheese

Brown meat with onions; add seasonings. Combine soup and milk. Spread evenly on bottom of greased 9 x 13 x 2-inch baking dish. Separate dough into 4 rectangles, seal seams, roll each to 8 x 4 inches and cut into 4 x 4-inch squares. Spoon ¼ of meat mixture into each square. Lift 4 corners, press and twist. Place in dish. Bake at 350° for 20–25 minutes until browned. Sprinkle with shredded cheese and bake 5 minutes to melt. To serve, spoon soup over top of bundles.

Daddy's Mopping and Barbecue Sauce

In Memory of My Daddy

Let me just start this whole thing by saying that my daddy was the absolute "Barbecue King." Although many have tried, including me, no one will ever top Daddy's pork ribs...or his beef brisket...or his chicken...or his sausage. In fact, anything he put on the pit was the best.

Mopping Sauce

3 gal. water
4 lg. onions
6 cans (8 oz. ea.) tomato sauce
Salt & pepper to taste
2 T. sugar
4 cloves garlic, crushed
6 lemons, sliced or juiced
1 qt. vinegar
4 lg. T. chili powder
1 lb. butter (3 lb. for chicken)
1 bottle (10 oz.) Worcestershire Sauce

Mix everything together and boil until onions are transparent. Keep hot to mop meat. Mama always made the sauce and then filled a small old pot for Daddy to put on the pit. Daddy made his mop with a rag and a stick and mopped the meat before and after turning. He would yell, "Honey, I need more mopping sauce" when the little pot ran dry. He turned the meat often, adjusting the heat–coals and air vents–to keep it just right. All he ever used to turn the meat was another rag–usually torn from an old undershirt (wife beater, of course) or work shirt. This is enough mopping sauce for 8–10 briskets or the equivalent. Briskets have to cook slowly, at least 6 hours on the pit–not a smoker. Ribs (oh, the ribs–I can almost taste them now) cook slowly, mopping often, stacking them as they approach doneness. Chickens cook at least 2–3 hours–chicken halves that is. Be sure to add the extra butter to the mopping sauce to keep chicken moist and cook over a slower fire.

INSIDER INFORMATION: Daddy usually added links of sausage to the pit so they would be ready just as family and friends arrived. He would tease our appetites with little bites each time he opened the pit. When cutting the meat, he would offer pieces of *rotten* barbecue to anyone who stood close by to watch. Needless to say, he always had an audience. When Daddy determined he had all the mopping sauce he would need for the meat on the pit, Mama would make barbecue sauce from the mopping sauce that was left.

NOTE: When selecting a brisket, try bending it in half. The farther it bends, the less fat it contains. When carving brisket, separate the two muscles and carve each piece individually, cutting across the grain.

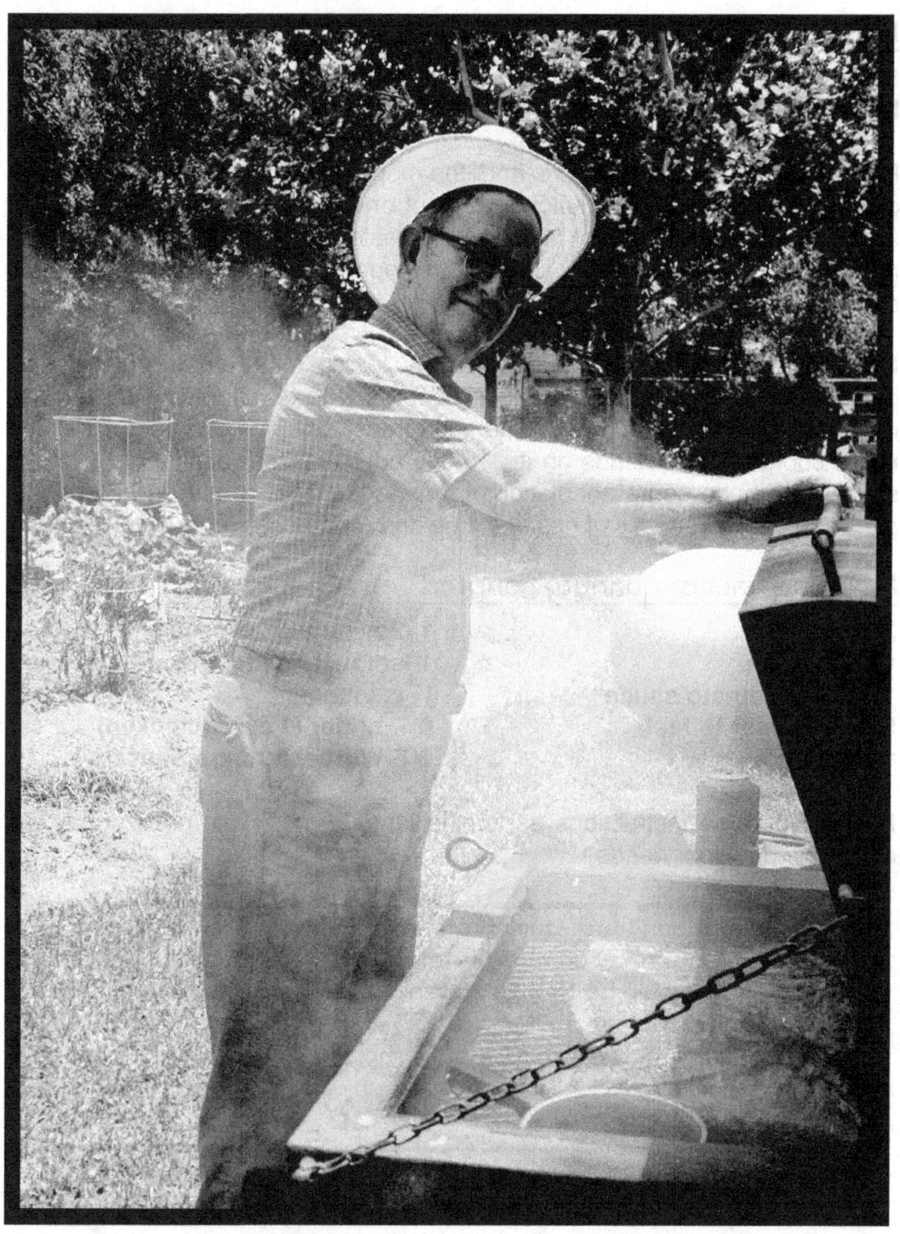

MY DADDY: THE ABSOLUTE "BARBECUE KING"

Can't you just smell the wonderful aroma of love?
I miss you so much, Daddy!

Barbecue Sauce

Mopping Sauce
Ketchup
Brown sugar

Remove the onions and lemons from the mopping sauce. Use about 1 quart of remaining sauce. Add ketchup…about one big bottle, and some brown sugar…about ⅓ cup. Cook and stir and taste. Adjust until you get it just right, sweet but tangy. Sorry, but there were never any precise measurements.

NOTE: Since I watched Daddy barbecue for so many years and special occasions, I have a pretty good idea about how to do all this. Daddy gave me his little barrel pit before he died and I treasure it. My only regret is that I never cooked him any ribs on it. I have adjusted the quantity of mopping sauce and made some adaptations—most added by Mama—to fit the little pit. I can cook two racks of ribs at a time and always use a rag to turn them.

Mopping Sauce–quantity adapted

2 qt. water
1 med. onion
1 sm. can tomato sauce
Salt & pepper to taste
1 tsp. sugar
1 clove garlic, crushed
1 lemon, sliced or juiced
½ c. vinegar
6 T. butter (1 c. for chicken)
6 T. Worcestershire Sauce

Follow the same instructions as for the large batch. (This portion may be more suited to your needs.)

Just the other day I was at my brother's house and he was cooking a quick version of barbecue ribs–his tailgating recipe. His wife decided his special rub would be enough and said she wasn't going to make the mopping sauce. Colton, their 4 year old grandson, said: "Granee, you have to have mopping sauce to cook barbecue. That's how you do it!" So, you see, it is very much a tradition that's passed from one generation to the next.

"Grilling, broiling, barbecuing–whatever you want to call it–is an art, not just a matter of building a pyre and throwing on a piece of meat as a sacrifice to the gods of the stomach." – James Beard

Crispy Chicken Fried Steak

Rosemary

Round steak, cut into pieces
Flour
Salt & pepper
1 c. water
⅛ tsp. baking soda
Oil

Mix flour, salt, and pepper. Mix water and soda. Dip steaks in wet mixture and then dredge in flour. Heat oil to 360°. Fry steak.

Deluxe Roast Beef

Mom & School Dinner Recipe

2 tip roasts (8 lb. total)
4 cans cream of mushroom soup
2 bottles (10 oz. ea.) A-1 Sauce
2 pkg. Lipton Onion Soup Mix
Mushroom Gravy

Cover roasts with A-1 sauce. Sprinkle with soup mix. Cover with soup. Bake at 350° for 1½–3 hours, or thermometer reading of 140°—170°.

Mushroom Gravy

3 cans cream of mushroom soup
8 oz. mushrooms, sliced
Roast juice
12 drops brown bouquet sauce

Combine all ingredients; cook and stir until bubbly and hot.

NOTE: In today's nutrition conscious world, this recipe is high in sodium. So, select sodium-free soup. An even lower sodium gravy can be made starting with a medium white sauce.

Reduced-Sodium Mushroom Gravy

½ c. butter
½ c. flour
3 c. low-fat or skim milk
8 oz. fresh mushrooms, sliced
1 c. roast juice or more

Melt butter and stir in flour. Cook over medium heat, stirring constantly until light brown. Add the milk all at once, stirring constantly until it begins to thicken. Lower heat; add mushrooms and some roast juice. Continue adding roast juice to reach desired consistency. Serve immediately.

I think I was married for over seven years before we had a Sunday dinner at home–we always went to one mother's house or the other after church. When I think back, that was a long time, but we were a very closely connected family and extended family has always played a huge part in our lives. My friend Estelle tells of an even longer stint of Sunday Roast, with her family dining together every Sunday from 1969 through 1995 when her mother died. The roast would go in the oven before they left for church and they'd prepare the fixings when they got home. She says, "Thru divorce, deaths, and our children marrying or going away to college, we had roast on Sunday. The kids complained until they went away...then they would write how they missed opening the back door and the aroma of Sunday dinner embracing them." Maybe we all need to take a step back in time and take time to smell the roast together. Here are Estelle's handwritten instructions for her family's Sunday Roast.

Sunday Roast

Estelle

Any size or cut of roast will work. Cut off as much fat as possible. Salt and pepper and flour. Brown in skillet on top of stove. Transfer to large roasting pan. Add one whole onion and bell pepper, garlic pods stuck in meat, and sprinkle Worcestershire over meat. Add flour and water to brown drippings in skillet and pour over meat. Make sure to put enough water in roaster, place in 350° oven, and go to church. When you get home from church–about 2 hours later, add whole potatoes and whole carrots. Bake another hour or until tender. You may have to add more water. Blend onion and bell pepper in blender and add to gravy.

NOTE: Sounds delicious. I wonder how many Sundays it takes to know just how much water is enough? I wonder if the kids ever knew the gravy had onions and bell peppers hiding in it?

"Roast Beef, Medium, is not only a food. It is a philosophy. Seated at Life's Dining Table, with the menu of Morals before you, your eye wanders a bit over the entrees, the hors d'oeuvres, and the things a la though you know that Roast Beef, Medium, is safe and sane, and sure." – Edna Ferber

Enchilada Lasagna

1½ lb. ground beef
1 med. onion, chopped
1 garlic clove, minced
1 can (14½ oz.) stewed tomatoes, undrained
1 can (10 oz.) enchilada sauce
1–2 tsp. ground cumin
1½ c. cottage cheese
3 c. Mexican cheese blend, shredded
8 flour tortillas (8 in.)
1 c. Cheddar cheese, shredded

In a large skillet, cook the beef, onion, and garlic over medium heat until meat is no longer pink; drain. Stir in the tomatoes, enchilada sauce, and cumin. Bring to a boil. Reduce heat; simmer uncovered for 20 minutes. In a small bowl, combine egg and cottage cheese; set aside. Cut the tortillas in half. Spread a third of the meat sauce into a greased 9 x 13 x 2-inch baking dish. Layer with half of the cheese blend, tortillas, cottage cheese mixture, and remaining meat sauce. Repeat layers. Sprinkle with Cheddar cheese. Cover and bake at 350° for 20 minutes. Test with a dinner knife inserted in center for 10 seconds to determine if piping hot–knife blade will be very hot to the touch when removed. Uncover; bake 10 minutes longer or until bubbly. Let stand for 15 minutes before cutting.

NOTE: An 8 ounce can of tomato sauce plus ¼ cup picante sauce can be substituted for the enchilada sauce. For an added kick, add sliced or chopped jalapeños to each layer. Sometimes I use Velveeta cheese instead of the cottage cheese and egg.

Fried T-Bone or Rib-Eye Steak

As My Mama Taught Me

4–6 T-bone Steaks, ⅜-in. thick
Salt & pepper
Flour
Shortening or vegetable oil

Season both sides of the steaks with salt and pepper. Fill the iron skillet with ½ inch of oil and place over medium to medium-high heat. Oil is hot enough for frying when a few grains of flour sizzle when dropped in it. Put some flour on a dinner plate and dredge the steaks through it, coating both sides. Lay in hot oil and cook for 4–5 minutes or until golden brown; turn and cook other side. Drain on paper towels and serve with ketchup.

We raised our own calves and had them processed according to Mama and Daddy's instructions. Steaks were thin and frying was the norm. I wouldn't dream of doing this now, but that's the way it was—we grew up on fried steaks. After visiting Germany, I think our fried steaks are really a take on schnitzel, except we had bones in ours. What can I say, we're 100% German! We always had mashed potatoes and gravy along with a vegetable from our garden, usually green beans, corn, or squash—maybe some fried okra in the summer. If we had rice, we still had to cook potatoes for Daddy. Mama claims that his mama spoiled him. I wish he were still living...I would love to spoil him some more.

Filet Mignon with Rum Glaze

4 filet mignons, 8 oz. ea.
2 dried ancho chiles
3 c. chicken broth
2 shallots, minced
2 cloves garlic, minced
3 T. butter
¾ c. dark rum
2 T. molasses
Salt & freshly ground black pepper to taste

Bring about 2 cups water to a boil and pour over the ancho chiles in a bowl; soak for 1 hour and drain. Process the ancho chiles in a food processor until puréed, adding a small amount of chicken broth to smooth paste. Sauté the shallots and garlic in the butter in a saucepan over medium-high heat until tender crisp. Add the rum and bring to a boil. Cook until reduced to ¼ cup. Add 3 cups chicken broth and bring to a boil. Reduce the heat to low. Whisk in the puréed ancho chiles, molasses, salt, and pepper. Simmer until reduced to 2 cups. Pour half the glaze into a bowl. Keep the remaining glaze hot in the saucepan. Add the steaks to the glaze in the bowl, turning to coat well. Grill the steaks until done to taste, basting occasionally with glaze remaining in the bowl. Discard any leftover basting glaze. Remove the steaks to serving plates and sprinkle with salt and pepper. Drizzle with the hot glaze. Serves 4.

NOTE:. The ancho chilies are a key ingredient and it really is worth the extra effort to process them. However, 2 tablespoons ancho chili puree can be substituted.

"Fifteen men on a dead man's chest / YO HO HO and a bottle of rum / Drink and the devil have done for the rest / YO HO HO and a bottle of rum."
– Robert Louis Stevenson

Green Pepper Meatloaf Rings

Rosemary

4 lg. green peppers, cut into 8 wide rings
1–2 lb. hamburger
1 pkg. meatloaf seasoning
2 eggs
½ med. onion, chopped
Leftover green peppers, chopped
1 can (8 oz.) tomato sauce
6–8 strips bacon
Ketchup

Mix all but pepper rings, bacon, and ketchup together. Stuff rings and place on grill pan with slotted drainer. Cut and place bacon strips on top of rings. Swirl ketchup on top of rings. Bake at 350° for 1 hour. Increase temperature to 375° the last 10 minutes.

Janis & Verna's Homemade Pizza

Janis & Verna

Yeast Bread for Crust

1 cake or pkg. yeast
¼ c. warm water
1 c. milk
1½ T. shortening
1 T. sugar
1 tsp. sugar
3 c. flour

Soften yeast in warm water. Scald milk, add shortening, salt, and sugar. Cool to lukewarm. Combine yeast with milk mixture in a large warm bowl. Add enough flour to make a stiff dough; mix thoroughly and turn out on floured board. Knead 5–10 minutes. Keep dough soft. Place in a greased bowl, brush the top with shortening, cover with waxed paper and towel. Allow to rise in a warm place to double in size. Punch down with fist, turn and allow to rise again. Grease your hands to make dough easy to handle. Turn out on board and spread in greased pans to form thin crust. Makes two to three crusts, depending on size of pans used.

"Cooking Rule: If at first you don't succeed, order pizza." – Anonymous

Hamburger Topping for Pizza

1 lb. ground meat
1 med. onion, minced
½ tsp. salt
¼ tsp. pepper
¼ tsp. garlic powder
1 tsp. basil
1 tsp. oregano
3–4 cans (8 oz. ea.) tomato sauce
3 c. Cheddar cheese, grated

Brown meat in large frying pan, drain off any grease. Add onion and cook on medium heat until done. Add seasonings. (Flavor is improved if covered and cooked slowly while dough is rising. A small amount of water can be added if necessary.) Place meat mixture on dough, cover with tomato sauce and top with cheese. Bake 20–25 minutes at 375°. Crust should be golden brown.

OPTIONAL: Before adding cheese, put bell pepper rings, sliced ripe and green olives, pepperoni or sausage, thinly sliced cooked shrimp or sliced mushrooms on pizza. Mozzarella cheese may be used along with Cheddar.

Janis and I always made pizza at her house, stayed up late, and then had cold pizza for breakfast. We never had pizza pans, so we used jelly roll pans and cookie sheets. Since we processed our own beef, I usually brought the hamburger meat. I will never forget the time I got in real trouble doing this. Daddy, being a meat and potato eater, thought it was a waste of our good beef to put it on pizza. Instead of asking for a package of meat to take that night, I just put one under some things on the front seat of the truck. Well, Daddy (not knowing I was going to Janis' house) put the truck in the garage and discovered the hamburger meat I was heisting...to make a long story short: no pizza that night. I got to stay home and eat fried steak instead. I learned my lesson.

"You better cut the pizza in four slices because I'm not hungry enough to eat six." – Yogi Berra

Janis and I pose for a yearbook picture in the homemaking department living room. We both earned our State Future Homemakers of America Degree–an arduous task involving both homemaking and community service projects.

How did we stay so skinny eating all that pizza?

Calzones

Prepare crust as for pizza, on a round pan, making it a little thicker so it will hold all the filling. Spoon sauce and meat on half of circle to within 1 inch of edge. Sprinkle with vegetables and cheese. Moisten edges of dough with water. Fold dough in half over filling. Seal edge by pressing with tines of fork. Prick top. Brush top with milk. If desired, sprinkle with grated Parmesan cheese. Bake in a 375° oven for 30–35 minutes or until crust is lightly browned.

We went on a family vacation to Washington, DC, years ago and while there we ate in this little Italian restaurant close to DuPont Circle. It was a long, narrow place with a street-front bay window filled with antipasto. In all, it reminded me of a place the Godfather would eat–I could just see him suddenly flip his table on its side and hide behind it to avoid gunfire. Anyway, I developed a love for calzones after eating one there and started making our pizza into calzones. So delicious–it's such fun to conjure up old memories with food.

Lasagna

Julie

1 lb. ground meat
1 c. onion, chopped
2 cloves garlic, minced
1 can (15 oz.) tomatoes, chopped
1 can (8 oz.) tomato sauce
1 can (6 oz.) tomato paste
1 tsp. oregano
2 tsp. basil
½ tsp. each salt & pepper
6 lasagna noodles
1 egg, beaten
2 c. Ricotta cheese
½ c. Parmesan cheese, grated
1 T. dried parsley flakes
1 pkg. frozen spinach, chopped
Zest of ½ lemon
1 pkg. (8 oz.) sliced Mozzarella cheese

For meat sauce, in large saucepan, cook meat, onion, and garlic. Drain any fat. Stir in tomatoes, sauce, paste, oregano, basil, salt, and pepper. Bring to boil. Reduce heat, cover and simmer. Cook noodles and drain. For filling, combine egg, Ricotta, ¼ cup of the Parmesan, parsley flakes, spinach, and lemon zest. Place a small amount of sauce in bottom of 9 x 13 x 2-inch baking pan. Layer half of the noodles, spread with half of the meat sauce, half of the filling, and half of the Mozzarella. Repeat. Sprinkle top with remaining Parmesan and bake at 375° for 30–35 minutes. Let stand 10 minutes before cutting. Allow 10–15 additional minutes of baking time if using a loaf pan.

Lone Star Chili

2 T. vegetable oil
2 lb. stewing beef, cubed (½ in. or smaller)
1 c. onion, chopped
1 green bell pepper, chopped
1 clove garlic, minced
1 can (12 oz.) tomato paste
2 pickled jalapeño peppers, rinsed, seeded, & chopped
2½ c. water
1½ T. chili powder
½ tsp. crushed red pepper
½ tsp. salt
½ tsp. dried oregano
½ tsp. cumin
1 can (15½ oz.) pinto beans

In a large heavy pan, heat oil and brown beef cubes on all sides. Add onions, bell peppers, and garlic; sauté with beef for about 5 minutes. Add all the remaining ingredients except beans and simmer the chili for 1½ hours or until the meat is tender. Add beans and simmer ½ hour longer.

NOTE: Since this is the "Lone Star" recipe, drink a couple of Lone Star beers while cooking and remember to stir the chili often–maybe even substitute some Lone Star for the water. Of course, serve the chili with chopped onions, grated cheese, sliced jalapeños, Tabasco sauce, and crackers or cornbread. Sometimes I serve chili over rice instead of having crackers or cornbread.

Manicotti

Julie

1 lb. ground meat
2 cloves garlic, minced
1 c. onion, chopped
Olive oil
1 can (14.5 oz.) tomatoes, chopped
1 can (8 oz.) tomato sauce
1 can (6 oz.) tomato paste
1 tsp. oregano
2 tsp. basil
½ tsp. each salt & pepper
2 c. Mozzarella, shredded
8 manicotti shells, cooked
White Sauce for Manicotti
Dry white wine
Parmesan cheese

FILLING

2 c. Ricotta cheese
2 eggs, beaten
½ c. Parmesan cheese, grated
Zest of ½ lemon
1 pkg. frozen spinach, chopped
2 T. dried parsley

Brown meat and season with salt, pepper, garlic, oregano, and basil. (Just let your imagination flow for the amounts.) Drain any fat. Sauté onion and garlic in 1 teaspoon olive oil. Add meat to onions. Combine filling ingredients and add some of meat/onion mixture. To make sauce, add tomatoes, sauce, paste, oregano, basil, salt, and pepper to remaining meat mixture and stir. Bring to boil. Reduce heat, cover and simmer. Cook noodles and drain. Stuff with filling. Place small amount of sauce in bottom of 9 x 13 x 2-inch baking pan and place manicotti on top. Cover with meat sauce, add white sauce and drizzle with wine. Bake covered at 350° for 35 minutes. Uncover, sprinkle top with additional Parmesan and bake at 375° for 5 minutes. Let stand 10 minutes before serving.

White Sauce for Manicotti

¼ c. green onions, sliced
1 clove garlic, minced
2 T. butter
2 T. flour
Zest of ¼ lemon
1⅓ c. milk
3 oz. Swiss cheese
⅓ c. dry white wine

Sauté onion and garlic in butter. Add flour and cook. Add lemon zest. Add milk all at once and stir. Cook until bubbly and thick. Add cheese and wine. Stir until cheese melts.

Oven Porcupines

Debbie

1 lb. ground beef
½ c. uncooked rice
½ c. water
⅓ c. onion, grated
½ tsp. celery salt
1 tsp. salt
⅛ tsp. garlic powder
⅛ tsp. pepper
SAUCE
1 can (15 oz.) tomato sauce
1 c. water
2 tsp. Worcestershire sauce

Heat oven to 350°. Mix meat, rice, water, onion, salts, garlic powder, and pepper. Shape mixture by rounded spoonfuls into balls. Place meatballs in ungreased 8 x 8 x 2-inch baking dish. Stir together sauce ingredients; pour over meatballs. Cover with aluminum foil; bake 45 minutes. Uncover; bake 15 minutes.

Pizza Crust, Brown 'n Serve

From the Food Lab

3¼ c. all purpose flour
1 T. sugar
1½ tsp. salt
1 pkg. RapidRise Yeast
1 c. water
2 T. cooking oil

Set aside 1 cup flour. In large bowl, mix remaining flour, sugar, salt, and yeast. Heat water and oil until hot to touch (125° to 130°); stir into dry mixture. Mix in only enough reserved flour to make stiff dough. On lightly floured surface, knead until smooth and elastic, about 5 minutes. Cover; let rest 10 minutes. Divide dough in half. Roll and stretch each half into 13-inch round. Place on 2 ungreased 12-inch pizza pans, pressing around edge to form standing rim of dough. Bake at 350° for 10 minutes. When cool, wrap tightly and store in refrigerator up to 6 days. To serve, unwrap and place on ungreased pizza pan. Cover with desired toppings. Bake at 425° for 15–20 minutes. Makes two 12-inch crusts.

SUBSTITUTION: To use regular active dry yeast, dissolve 1 package yeast in 1 cup warm water (105°–115°). Add to dry ingredients in bowl with oil. Continue as directed above.

NOTE: This is a really good-quality pizza dough and is relatively easy to make. It worked great for school labs since we could make the crust one day and top and bake it the second day. Try putting oil on your hands and press the dough into the pan instead of rolling. Regretfully, I never mastered throwing the dough in the air. Crusts can be frozen after baking.

Rib-Eye Steak with Black Olive Vinaigrette

STEAK
1 boneless rib-eye steak, 2-in. thick
1 T. olive oil
1 T. Herbes de Provence
1 tsp. salt
1 tsp. fresh ground black pepper

BLACK OLIVE VINAIGRETTE
½ c. black olives, pitted
3 T. red wine vinegar
2 tsp. Dijon mustard
1 garlic clove, crushed
½ tsp. salt
½ tsp. fresh ground black pepper
6 T. extra-virgin olive oil
6 T. vegetable oil
2 T. fresh flat-leaf parsley, chopped

FOR THE RIB-EYE: Preheat your grill pan on medium-high heat. Coat the beef with olive oil and sprinkle with the Herbs de Provence, salt, and pepper. Cook for 6–8 minutes a side until the meat is medium-rare, remove from heat, and allow to rest.

FOR THE BLACK OLIVE VINAIGRETTE: Combine the olives, red wine vinegar, mustard, garlic, salt, and pepper in a blender and blend until mixed. In a small pitcher combine the olive oil and vegetable oil. Drizzle the oil into the blender with the machine running. Transfer the vinaigrette to a serving dish. Stir in the parsley and serve with the rib-eye.

"We may live without poetry, music and art; we may live without conscience, and live without heart; we may live without friends; we may live without books; but civilized man cannot live without cooks."
– Edward Bulwer-Lytton (1831-1891)

Savory Cabbage Rolls

From the Food Lab

1 sm. head cabbage
¼ c. onions, chopped
3 T. green pepper, diced
½ lb. ground beef
⅔ c. Minute Rice
2 T. butter
½ c. hot water
1 can (8 oz.) tomato sauce
¾ tsp. salt
Dash of pepper
⅛ tsp. savory

Remove core and outer leaves of cabbage. Cook whole cabbage in boiling, salted water just to soften–about 8 minutes. Meanwhile, sauté onions, green pepper, beef, and rice in butter until meat is lightly browned, stirring constantly. Add hot water, tomato sauce, salt, pepper, and savory. Bring to a boil. Reduce heat and simmer 5 minutes. Drain cabbage and separate leaves. If inner leaves are difficult to separate, return cabbage to hot water and boil an additional 2–3 minutes. Using a slotted spoon, place 2–3 tablespoons beef mixture onto each cabbage leaf at core end. Roll leaves tightly and place in large heavy saucepan. Pour remaining juice over cabbage rolls. Cover and cook over moderate heat until cabbage is tender--about 45 minutes. Yield: 3–4 servings, about 14 rolls

This recipe hails from one of my food lab classes at Sam Houston. I remember we had stainless steel sinks and they could not have one drop of water or even a damp spot remaining anywhere or our grade would be lowered. I guess the best thing I learned from such rigidity is to dry the stainless sink and then wipe down with baby oil and a paper towel–do this every few weeks and the sink will stay beautiful for years.

S. O. S.

1 lb. hamburger
1 med. onion, chopped
Salt, pepper & garlic powder
1 can cream of mushroom soup

Brown meat and sauté onion together. Drain. Add seasonings. (Remember the soup is loaded with sodium, so go light on the salt or leave it out.) Add soup. Heat through. Serve over rice, noodles, or toast.

NOTE: The original S. O. S. is on a shingle–toast, that is. Get fancy and add an 8 ounce container of sour cream and serve over hot, buttered noodles: Poor Man's Stroganoff.

Schlumgullion

1 lb. hamburger
1 med. onion, chopped
½ tsp. salt
½ tsp. pepper
¼ tsp. garlic powder
1 tsp. basil, crushed
1 tsp. oregano, crushed
2–2½ c. water, maybe more
1 can (16 oz.) crushed tomatoes, with juice
1 can (16 oz.) whole kernel corn, drained
1 can (4 oz.) mushroom stems & pieces, drained
8 oz. elbow macaroni
8 oz. Velveeta cheese, cubed

Use a 10-inch skillet with a tight-fitting cover. Brown hamburger with onion. Drain fat, if any. Add seasonings and all remaining ingredients except cheese. Stir. Cover and cook over low heat until macaroni is tender and hopefully, the water will be gone–takes about 25 minutes. Experience will teach just how much water to use. Add the cheese and serve when it's melted.

NOTE: With a name like schlumgullion, measurements are really not needed–just shake, pour, whatever. We usually have this with garlic bread or toast. It's great because it's all in one pan, and if using a stainless steel pan, any leftovers can be refrigerated in it. Seems I always prepared this after a day of labs or other hard work. It's so easy to get started–then just sit down and put your feet up.

VARIATION: Use stewed and flavored tomatoes. I like to use hot or spicy ones.

"Man is what he eats." – German Proverb

Spaghetti with Homemade Meat Sauce

(a.k.a. Mrs. Craig's Spaghetti Sauce)

From the Food Lab

1 lb. ground beef
1 sm. onion, chopped
1 T. oregano, crushed
1½ tsp. basil, crushed
½ tsp. garlic powder
½ tsp. black pepper
1 tsp. salt
24 oz. tomato sauce
1 can (4 oz.) mushrooms, drained
12–16 oz. spaghetti

Brown meat and sauté onion. Drain any fat. Add the seasonings and cook a little longer. Add the tomato sauce, tomatoes, and mushrooms. Simmer over very low heat for several hours. Cook spaghetti, according to package directions, in large amount of water. Remember to make sure the water is boiling before adding the spaghetti and then stir until it returns to a boil. Allow 2 ounces of spaghetti per person. The sauce will serve 6 to 8 people depending on their appetites.

NOTE: The last lab of the year was usually a complete meal and my students loved to make spaghetti. We would spread this out over a two-day period. They would make the sauce the first day, refrigerate overnight and then cook spaghetti and serve the next day. I was so young and green at the time I never realized that I was also helping them prepare for the hectic life they would live in the future. When I worked full-time, I would prepare a huge pot of sauce and freeze in individual meals. I was the queen of Tupperware.

Back in the day when only girls were members of Future Homemakers of America, we would host a spaghetti supper to earn money for travel to the FHA state convention. I can't even begin to remember how many times we doubled this recipe, but we cooked the sauce in electric roasters. Notice, I said roasters! The morning classes would start the sauce and it would cook all day; my other classes would help by making garlic bread, salad, and desserts. Then, after school, we would invade the old school cafeteria kitchen and cook spaghetti in their huge pots. We would serve about 500 people. Remember, I said girls–I honestly don't remember how we lifted those heavy pots. One year, a ring was lost during the hustle and we actually found it in the trash nestled in a huge glob of stuck-together spaghetti. For all this effort, we would net about $200–$300 dollars–a lot of money back then.

Sicilian Meat Roll

Mom & School Dinner Recipe

2 eggs, beaten
¾ c. soft bread crumbs (1 slice)
½ c. tomato juice
2 T. parsley, snipped
½ tsp. dried oregano, crushed
¼ tsp each salt & pepper
1 clove garlic, pressed
2 lb. lean ground beef
8 thin slices boiled ham
6 oz. Mozzarella cheese, shredded (1½ c.)
3 slices Mozzarella cheese, halved diagonally

Combine eggs, crumbs, juice, parsley, oregano, salt, pepper, and garlic. Add beef; mix well. On foil, pat meat to a 12 x 10-inch rectangle. Arrange ham on top of meat, leaving a small margin around edges. Sprinkle shredded cheese over ham. Starting from short end, carefully roll up meat, using foil to lift; seal edges and ends. Place roll, seam side down in a 13 x 9 x 2-inch baking pan. Bake at 350° until done, 1¼ hours. (Center of roll will be pink due to ham.) Place cheese wedges over top of roll; return to oven until cheese melts, about 5 minutes. Let set a few minutes before slicing. Slice with sharp carving knife. Yield: 8 ample servings

NOTE: For variety, change up the fillings–pepperoni and Cheddar, German salami and Muenster cheese, or prosciutto and Romano cheese. Just a short testimony to the goodness of this recipe–Julie sent it to me when I asked her for recipes. She called it Special Meat Roll. Mom was a great cook and loved to share her recipes.

Stove-Top Pan Pizza

2 tsp. olive oil
1 pkg. (6 oz.) pizza dough
⅔ c. pizza sauce
½ c. pepperoni, sliced
1–2 c. Mozzarella or Cheddar cheese, shredded
¼ c. Parmesan cheese

Coat a cold 10" stainless steel sauté pan on bottom and sides with oil. On a lightly floured board, roll dough into an 11" circle. Place dough into skillet and pat dough ¼ inch up the side of the skillet. Spread sauce evenly over the dough. Arrange pepperoni on sauce and top with cheeses. Cover and cook at medium heat for 15 minutes. Remove pizza carefully from skillet. Cut and serve. This is so simple and easy to do and so much healthier than delivery.

The Craig's French Bread Pizzas

1 loaf French bread
Pepperoni
2 cans mushroom stems & pieces, well-drained
Sliced black olives (start with a can of whole pitted and when the kids are through eating & slicing, there might be enough left)
1 lb. ground chuck, browned with chopped onions and seasoned with Italian herbs
1 qt. jar of your favorite spaghetti sauce
Lots of Mozzarella & Cheddar cheese, shredded—at least 4 c.

Depending on your mood, slice the French bread horizontally and then into about 4 inch pieces or cut the loaf into 1-inch thick slices. Either way, place bread close together on a jelly roll pan so the ingredients don't have room to fall in between the pieces. Top with spaghetti sauce, then ground meat, pepperoni, mushrooms, and olives. Finally, pile on the cheese. Bake at 350° until heated through and the cheese is melted–probably about 25–30 minutes.

NOTE: One time we got on a low fat kick and boiled and drained the pepperoni to remove some of the fat. It works, but some flavor is sacrificed. When on vacation, line the pan with foil so it doesn't require a lot of cleanup. Speaking of vacation, I can almost hear the Gulf of Mexico's waves crashing on the warm white sand, can almost see the shimmer of the sun as it sets, can definitely smell the pizza.

Peyton's Pizza Rolls

My Grandson, Peyton

2 cans crescent rolls
8 oz. tomato sauce
6 oz. tomato paste
½ tsp. basil
½ tsp. oregano
¼ tsp. garlic powder
Pepperoni slices
Mozzarella cheese
Additional toppings as desired
Milk

On a cookie sheet, lay out dough by tearing off two rolls at a time, making a square and sealing seams. Mix tomato sauce, paste, and spices together; spoon onto half of each square, leaving a little area around the edge. Top with pepperoni and cheese. Brush milk on the outer edges, fold over, and seal. Bake at 350° for 15 minutes until golden brown. Check every five minutes to see how it is going. Yield: 8 rolls

Jennie shows Peyton how to make our pizza.

ANOTHER NOTE: Pizza is a popular dish around these parts. Consider the facts that we didn't have a pizza delivery place in the area until just a few years ago and my students always wanted to cook pizza–it makes sense that I have a plethora of pizza ideas. Pizza is a healthy meal: fresh veggies, wholesome milk products, lean meats–whole grain bread could even be used.

"Cooking is at once child's play and adult joy. And cooking done with care is an act of love." – Craig Claiborne

Quick Pizzas

Try these 10 minute recipes for after-school snacks and parties for kids

Tomato Cheese Pizzas

2 English muffins, split & toasted
4 slices American cheese
4 slices tomato
½ tsp. dried oregano

Place English muffins cut side up on a broiler pan. Top with cheese and tomato; sprinkle with oregano. Broil 4–6 inches from the heat for 2–3 minutes or until cheese is melted. Yield: 4 pizzas

NOTE: Ingredients can be assembled on bagels instead of English muffins.

Pineapple Ham Pizzas

2 English muffins, split & toasted
2 T. barbecue sauce
2 oz. sliced deli ham, julienned
1 snack-size cup (4 oz.) pineapple tidbits, drained
2 slices Swiss cheese, quartered

Place English muffins cut side up on a broiler pan. Spread with barbecue sauce; top with ham, pineapple, and cheese. Broil 4–6 inches from heat for 2–3 minutes or until cheese is melted. Yield: 4 pizzas

Swedish Meatballs

School Dinner Recipe

1 c. fine bread crumbs
1 c. milk
2 lb. ground beef
1 c. onions, finely chopped
2 eggs, slightly beaten
1½ tsp. salt
¼ tsp. pepper
1 tsp. nutmeg
½ c. butter or margarine
¼ c. flour
3 beef bouillon cubes
3 c. hot water
1½ c. milk
1½ c. light cream

Soften bread crumbs in the 1 cup milk. Add beef, onions, eggs, and seasonings; mix thoroughly. Shape into about 96 balls, about 1 inch in diameter. Heat butter in large skillet. Add meatballs, a few at a time, and brown on all sides. Remove meatballs and stir flour into the drippings; blend well. Dissolve bouillon cubes in hot water. Gradually add to flour mixture, stirring constantly until smooth. Add milk and cream. Cook over low heat, stirring constantly, about 3 minutes. Add meatballs to sauce. Simmer 10–15 minutes, stirring occasionally until sauce is of consistency desired. Makes 12 generous entrée servings–about 8 meatballs each, or 24 smorgasbord servings–4 meatballs each. Prepare 4 times for about 100 smorgasbord servings.

I almost cried when I came across this recipe! It was the main dish for the first Mother-Daughter Banquet my classes prepared. Although delicious, someone should have told me that making 8 meatballs each for over 200 people was a wee bit labor intensive. What a lesson to learn and I wasn't experienced enough to bake the meatballs in the oven. Of course, then they wouldn't have had the delicious flavor from frying in butter. I never realized how easy it is to burn butter until this endeavor. I can't miss a teaching opportunity, so I must explain that butter has a lower burning point than most fats, so cook over a lower heat and watch carefully when using it for sautéing or frying. So many memories...so happy to have my Swedish Meatball recipe back in my hands.

Western Chili Casserole

Home Management Special

1 lb. ground beef
1 c. onions, chopped
¼ c. celery, chopped
1 can (15 oz.) chili con carne with beans
¼ tsp. pepper
2 c. corn chips, slightly crushed
1 c. sharp processed cheese, shredded

Brown meat; add ¾ cup of onion and the celery. Cook until just tender. Drain off excess fat. Add chili and pepper; heat. Place layer of chips in ungreased 1½-quart casserole. Alternate layers of chili mixture, chips and cheese, reserving ½ cup chips and ¼ cup cheese for trim. Sprinkle center with reserved cheese and onion. Cover and bake at 350° for 10 minutes or until hot through. To serve, border casserole with reserved corn chips. Yield: 6 servings

"In general, mankind, since the improvement in cookery, eats twice as much as nature requires." – Benjamin Franklin

Wild Bill's Beef Cabernet

2 six-qt. Dutch ovens with covers
4 lb. beef chuck roast
2 oz. olive oil
Kosher or sea salt
1 med. yellow onion, chopped
4 garlic cloves, finely chopped
3 oz. soy sauce
1 oz. Worcestershire sauce
1 bottle dry red wine (Cabernet)
1 jar (25 oz.) spaghetti sauce
1 tsp. Italian seasoning
4 qt. water
1 lb. of your favorite pasta shape
1 tsp. salt
½ c. butter
6 oz. Parmesan cheese

Preheat Dutch oven over medium heat. Pour olive oil over roast and rub. Sprinkle on salt. Add roast to hot skillet and brown all around. Remove and set aside. Add onion and garlic to pan along with soy and Worcestershire sauces. Stir to deglaze. Add ⅔ bottle of wine and jar of spaghetti sauce to pan; stir together with 1 teaspoon Italian seasoning. Return roast to pan, bring to a boil, cover and reduce to a simmer for 4 hours (or place in a 275° oven). After 90 minutes, turn roast. After about 3 hours, cut roast into smaller pieces to allow it all to be in sauce. If more sauce is needed, add wine. After 4 hours, stir to break into pieces, much like pulled pork. Add salt, if needed. Keep warm.

PART TWO: In other Dutch oven, bring 4 quarts of water to a boil. Add salt and pasta; cook until almost done. Save 1 cup of pasta water; drain pasta. Add butter to pan. Mix about ⅓ cup of pasta water and half of the Parmesan cheese in with the melted butter and stir to blend. Return pasta to the pan and toss. Add a pinch of salt to taste and cover for about 5 minutes. Stir pasta and if sticky, add some additional reserved pasta water. To serve, place pasta in the center of a pasta dish or serving platter, top with meat and sauce that remains; sprinkle with remaining Parmesan cheese.

NOTE: This recipe gives the confidence a bonafide chef possesses. Buy an extra bottle of wine just in case all of it is needed for the roast.

"I cook with wine. Sometimes I even add it to the food." — W. C. Fields

CHICKEN

THAWING FROZEN MEATS

If the only thing that's keeping you from preparing dinner is a frozen chunk of meat, try one of these fail-proof techniques. Quick defrosting works best with small to medium-size pieces of meat such as steaks, chops, or chicken parts. Larger items should be thawed in the refrigerator over the course of a day or so.

IN A BOWL OF WATER: This quick-thaw method is the gentlest technique and takes from 15–30 minutes. Fill a large bowl with cold water. (Do not use hot water–it will encourage the growth of harmful bacteria as well as begin to cook the outside of the meat.) Place meat in a resealable plastic bag and submerge the bag fully in water. Make sure all the air is squeezed out of the bag and maybe even place something heavy on top of it to keep it submerged in the water. Let sit, changing the water with fresh cold water as it warms. Once the pieces are defrosted enough to be separated, pull them apart so the rest of the thawing goes quickly. Continue until meat is thawed.

IN THE MICROWAVE: Using the microwave to quick-thaw meat is fast, averaging from 5–10 minutes. It requires your attention or you'll risk moving into semi-cooked territory and your dinner will be stringy and tough. Consult the owner's manual of your microwave to find the setting for the type of meat being thawed and its weight. Check the progress often and remove it when it's close to being defrosted. Let stand a few minutes to complete defrosting. For best results, place thinner portions of meat in the center of the microwave; they'll be less likely to overcook.

Although it may be common practice in your family to place frozen meat on the kitchen counter in the morning to be thawed for dinner that night, it is not recommended. You risk the chance of the meat getting warm and bacteria multiplying.

"Blow in its ear." – Johnny Carson on the best way to thaw out a frozen turkey

Chicken & Rice

Marilyn's Mother

8–10 slices bacon
1 c. raw rice
1 fryer
Salt, pepper, & garlic powder
1 can cream of mushroom soup
1 can water

Line a 9 x 13 x 2-inch casserole pan with raw bacon strips. Pour the rice over this and sprinkle lightly with salt. Cut up fryer and lightly sprinkle with salt, pepper, and garlic powder. Arrange chicken pieces on top of rice. Mix soup and water together and pour over chicken. Cover with foil and bake for 2 hours at 350°. Remove the foil during the last 20 minutes of baking to allow browning.

CUTTING UP A CHICKEN

Cutting up a chicken can be a little tricky. Use a sharp knife and cutting board–more people have been injured with dull knives because you have to push harder and are more likely to slip and cut yourself. When cutting up a hen or roaster, the bones are stronger and the joints more firmly connected. I remember Daddy using a hammer to hit the back of the knife to cut up old hens. I demonstrated how to cut up a chicken in my advanced classes. The entire school knew when we had our chicken lab. First, the students complained to everyone that they were going to have to cut up a chicken. Second, the aroma of fried chicken filled the halls and wafted into every classroom. Nowadays, many stores don't even carry whole chickens. Today's chicken breasts might be healthy and easy to cook, but they sure don't give the flavor like a chicken with skin and bones does. For detailed visuals and instructions on the dying art of cutting up a chicken, google it. There are two different methods, family style which provides more servings, and cafe style, which provides larger pieces.

"People who count their chickens before they are hatched act very wisely, because chickens run about so absurdly that it is impossible to count them accurately." – Oscar Wilde

Chicken Chow Mein

Mom

1 fryer or 1½ lb. chicken breasts
¼ c. butter
2–3 c. celery, chopped
1 c. onion, chopped
1 can (14 oz.) bean sprouts, drained
1 T. soy sauce
2–3 c. chicken broth
1½ T. cornstarch + a little water
1 can (4 oz.) mushroom sauce (such as Dawn's mushroom sauce–must be sauce, not plain mushrooms)
Chow mein noodles or rice

Cook chicken, pick off bone and remove skin, or cut up breasts. Save broth. Sauté celery and onion in butter. Add bean sprouts, chicken, and mushroom sauce. Add soy sauce and 2–3 cups chicken broth. Bring to a boil and thicken with cornstarch that has been combined with a little water. Serve over chow mein noodles or over rice.

CORNSTARCH FOR THICKENING

- ✦ Recipes thickened with cornstarch have a brighter, more translucent appearance than those thickened with flour.
- ✦ To use cornstarch to thicken foods, dissolve the cornstarch in a small amount of a cold liquid before adding it to the hot mixture.
- ✦ To produce a nicely thickened sauce, gravy or pudding, cook and stir the mixture for a full 2 minutes after adding the cornstarch.
- ✦ Cornstarch has twice the thickening power of flour, so it's necessary to use only half as much. As a rule, use 1 tablespoon of cornstarch to thicken every 2 cups of liquid to a medium consistency.

"So when I do Chinese cooking, I mix everything together, then the kids have to eat their vegetables. They won't have the patience to pick them out."
– Martin Yan

Chicken Enchiladas

Myrna

12 med. corn tortillas
2 T. oil
8 oz. Cheddar cheese, grated
8 oz. Mozzarella cheese, grated
½ onion, chopped
¼ c. butter
¼ c. flour
1 can (14 oz.) chicken broth
8 oz. sour cream
Jalapeños or green chilies
2 c. cooked, boned chicken

Fry tortillas to soften. Fill with a little onion and a handful of each cheese. Roll and place seam down in greased 9 x 13 x 2-inch pan. Make sauce by melting butter, stirring in flour and cooking for a few minutes. Add broth and cook until thickened. Add sour cream, chicken, and peppers; pour over filled tortillas. Bake at 350° for 25 minutes. Add rest of cheese and bake 5 minutes longer.

When Myrna and I got together, we always had fun. With names of Myrna and Verna, we could ignore our husbands, pretending they were talking to the other one. We went offshore fishing a lot, always catching a mess of fish. We rubbed on gallons of sunscreen, suffered through rough waters, and even had to call the Coast Guard one time. The guys just had to fish one more rig even though storm clouds were gathering. The boat's steering went out, the waves got bigger and bigger, and wind was blowing us every which way. I held on to Myrna's legs as she stood on the seat–hanging onto the hardtop of their Grady White with one hand and trying to tune the radio with the other. We just knew our children would be left orphans. The Coast Guard was a mile away from us when the storm finally passed. That was the last time we went offshore fishing together, but we still played lots of 42 and this was one of our favorite dinner dishes. It was a pleasant diversion from fried, stuffed, broiled, or baked fish. Since we didn't go fishing anymore, we had to find something else to cook!

"They say you forget your troubles on a trout stream, but that's not quite it. What happens is that you begin to see where your troubles fit into the grand scheme of things, and suddenly they're just not such a big deal anymore."
– John Gierach

I just love the water, and can proudly claim that I have caught a fish almost as long as I am tall! After our experience in the gulf's rough waters, I only sail calm seas. This picture was snapped on a catamaran cruise off the coast of St. Lucia.

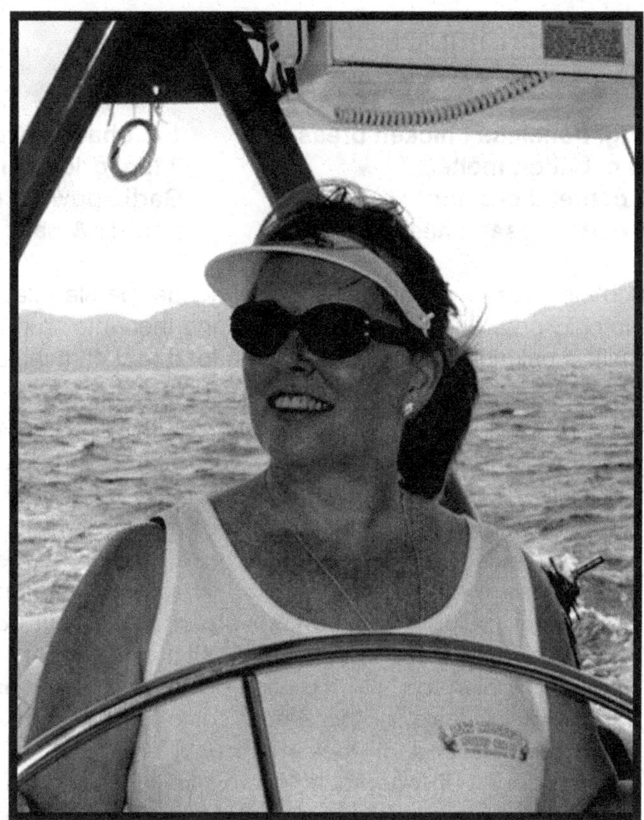

Chicken Crepes

Janis

1 doz. warm cooked crepes
1 can (10 ¾ oz.) condensed cream of chicken soup
1 c. sour cream
8 slices dried beef, chopped
2 c. cooked chicken, chopped or shredded
½ lb. fresh mushrooms, sliced
Butter flavored cooking spray
¼ tsp. seasoned salt

Prepare crepes following All Purpose Crepe Batter, page 328. Combine soup and sour cream in saucepan. Stir in chicken and dried beef. Heat but do not bring to boil. Fill crepes with chicken mixture; fold over. Keep warm. Sauté mushrooms in cooking spray, then sprinkle with seasoned salt. Spoon over filled crepes. Serve immediately.

Chicken Imperial

Janis

4 lg. boneless chicken breasts
½ c. butter, melted
2 c. bread crumbs
2 c. Parmesan cheese
1 c. shaved almonds
2 tsp. dried parsley flakes
Garlic powder (just a hint)
Pepper & salt

Combine bread crumbs, cheese, almonds, parsley flakes, and seasonings. Dip chicken breasts in melted butter and then into crumb mixture. Place in a shallow baking pan and bake at 350° for about 45 minutes, or until browned.

Growing up, Janis lived 2 sides of a country block away. (Translation: 2 miles) We were the only girls out our direction, so we became fast friends riding the bus back and forth to school. After school, we would each start out riding our bikes and meet in the middle–we'd talk, giggle, ride in circles–and finally head home in opposite directions. In the summer we would hop on our bikes, meeting up on the other side of the block. Our destination was about a two-hour ride, coasting down one glorious hill and grinding to a halt in sand about six inches deep; we kept pedalin' on to the only swimming pool anywhere around. Thankfully, Janis' mother would come gather us up, help us load our bikes in the bed of their old truck, and take us home in the late afternoon. It was such fun–picnic lunches, sun bathing, sharing secrets–we felt so grown-up. After high school, Janis married an Air Force man and they lived all over the country. When they finally settled closer to home, we went to cooking school together, wallpapered her kitchen, talked, giggled...did everything but rode in circles. Anyway, she made this chicken for dinner one night and I loved it. Who would have thought that a friendship forged out of the desperation of living on the same country block would endure a lifetime? Thinking back on the past often makes me wonder...what will our children and grandchildren remember?

"It takes a long time to grow an old friend." — John Leonard

Chicken Panini Florentine

1 pkg. (6 oz.) fresh baby spinach
2 tsp. extra-virgin olive oil
¼ c. butter, softened
8 slices sourdough bread
¼ c. creamy Italian dressing
8 slices Provolone cheese
½ lb. deli chicken, shaved
2 slices red onion, separated into rings

Sauté spinach in oil for 2 minutes until wilted. Begin heating the panini grill. Butter one side of each slice of bread. Spread the other side with salad dressing; layer 4 slices bread–buttered side down–with a cheese slice, chicken, spinach, onion, and top with second cheese slice. Cover with remaining bread, buttered side up. Cook in the panini grill and press until golden brown on both sides.

Chicken Pot Pie

Marilyn's Mother

4–5 chicken breasts or one fryer
1 c. chicken broth, reserved
1 can cream of celery soup
1 can (15 oz.) mixed vegetables, drained
1½ c. Bisquick
1½ c. milk
½ c. margarine

Boil chicken; debone and cut into small pieces. Layer chicken in 9 x 13 x 2-inch casserole dish. Mix broth and soup; pour over chicken. Sprinkle vegetables over chicken. Mix Bisquick and milk. Pour over chicken. Melt margarine and drizzle over entire mixture. Bake at 350° for one hour.

NOTE: Americans have so many options of packaged and ready-to-eat foods it can be mind boggling. Chicken pot pie is one of those foods that, when purchased, can be loaded with fat and calories. What better place to stress nutrition and reading the ingredients in prepared food packages than here, following a recipe prepared with wholesome ingredients? Take time to understand and use food labels to determine a food's suitability for yourself and your family.

"As a child my family's menu consisted of two choices: take it or leave it."
– Buddy Hackett

FOOD LABELS AND NUTRITION FACTS

Since we're talking about food packaging, it's a good time to address the information contained on food labels. First, it's put there for consumers to read. Second, we would be wise to understand what this information means to us. It seems every time I turn around someone else has a health condition that requires dietary adjustments. Learn about food labels and nutrition and maybe health issues caused by lifestyle can be avoided.

- ✦ Ingredients are always listed in order from the largest ingredient to the smallest.
- ✦ Choose foods with a short list of ingredients that you recognize. Stay away from highly processed foods with lots of additives.
- ✦ Always look at the serving size and the number of servings per container. The calories or fat content of a serving may seem low, but when you realize that a bag of chips contains 2½ servings, things change.
- ✦ % Daily Value is based upon a 2,000 calorie a day diet and indicates the daily recommended percentage of each food nutrient a particular food provides. Don't let yourself be confused by thinking that the percentages listed are the percentage of sugar or fat the food contains.
- ✦ *Net weight* is not the same as volume. When looking at cans and packages of foods, the net weight is the amount the food weighs, not the space it occupies. Keep this in mind when following ingredient lists on recipes.
- ✦ Nutrient density refers to the ratio of nutrients to calories. The best food choices, *nutrient dense* foods, contain many nutrients with few calories.
- ✦ Here is a breakdown of the sources of calories in your diet.
    - 1 gram protein = 4 calories
    - 1 gram carbohydrate = 4 calories
    - 1 gram fat = 9 calories
- ✦ To determine the number of calories from a particular nutrient, multiply the number of grams of that nutrient times the calories in a gram of that nutrient. For example, if a serving of potato chips contains 20 grams of fat, multiply 20 grams times 9 calories to find that those chips contain 180 calories from fat.
- ✦ Nutrition labels require the number of calories from fat to be listed. As shown above, fat is generous, providing more than twice the number of calories per gram as protein or carbohydrates.

- ✦ Eat a wide variety of foods, choosing those foods that are *nutrient dense*: whole grains, fresh fruits and vegetables, dried peas and beans, lean meats, and limited fats.
- ✦ To control caloric intake at home, use a smaller plate and do not have second helpings. Don't clean your children's plates by eating what they didn't. Watch how often you sample food while cooking, too.
- ✦ When eating out, share the entrée or ask for a to-go container before your food arrives. Remove half of the food (and the temptation to overeat) from your plate before starting to eat.
- ✦ Train yourself to check the milligrams of sodium present in packaged foods. A person only needs between 1500 and 2300 milligrams of sodium per day.

Chicken Spaghetti

Mom

1 (3½–4 lb.) hen or fryer
1 onion, chopped
1 green pepper, chopped
1 clove garlic, minced
½ c. butter
1 can cream of mushroom soup
1 can tomato soup
1 can (16 oz.) tomatoes, crushed
1 sm. jar (4 oz.) pimientos, chopped
16 oz. spaghetti
1 lb. Velveeta cheese, cubed

Cook hen until very tender. Remove meat and cool, reserving cooking liquid. Pull meat from bone and chop. Sauté onion, pepper, and garlic in butter. Add water to reserved liquid to make enough to cook spaghetti according to package directions and drain. (Reserve about a cup of liquid to add to casserole while cooking to add moisture and flavor.) Mix all ingredients well and dot cubes of cheese in and around mixture. Cook covered in 275° oven for 2 hours.

NOTE: Two cans of tomato soup may be substituted for the mushroom soup. Sliced mushrooms can be added if mushrooms are a favorite. I guess in this day and time, buying a roasted chicken at the deli and deboning it is a time-saving option, but the result wouldn't be quite the same.

"People who like to cook like to talk about food...without one cook giving another cook a tip or two, human life might have died out a long time ago."
– Laurie Colwin

Chicken Tetrazzini

1 fryer, cut up, or 6 whole chicken breasts
2 qt. water
1 tsp. salt
½ tsp. pepper
½ tsp. thyme
1 bay leaf
16 oz. spaghetti, broken
1 can cream of mushroom soup
½ c. pimientos, diced
2 T. Worcestershire sauce
¼ c. butter
1 c. celery, chopped
1 sm. onion, chopped
¼ tsp. thyme
8 oz. Velveeta cheese, cubed
½ c. Cheddar cheese, shredded
Salt & pepper to taste

Stew chicken in 2 quarts water, seasoned with salt, pepper, thyme, and bay leaf. Remove and cool, reserving cooking liquid. Cook spaghetti in stewing liquid until done, adding additional water if needed. While spaghetti is cooking, bone and chop chicken and sauté onion and celery in butter. Combine all ingredients but Cheddar cheese, salt, and pepper. Drain spaghetti and add to mixture. Taste for seasoning and adjust. Place in a greased 9 x 13 x 2-inch casserole dish. Bake 45 minutes at 350°. Sprinkle with Cheddar cheese about 5 minutes before done.

Dark Lemon Chicken

Julie

7–9 chicken tenders
Salt, black pepper, & garlic
1–2 T. oil
¼ c. lemon juice
Worcestershire sauce
½ c. water
¼ tsp. marjoram

Season chicken with salt, pepper, and garlic. Lightly brown in oil. Remove chicken and oil from pan. Add lemon juice, 3–5 dashes of Worcestershire sauce, and additional salt, pepper, and garlic to taste. Let simmer. Add water and reduce by half. Add marjoram. Replace chicken and cook. Serve over rice pilaf.

NOTE: Remember that Worcestershire sauce is high in sodium and that you will be reducing the liquid.

"There is one thing more exasperating than a wife who can cook and won't and that's a wife who can't cook and will." – Robert Frost

Gnocchi & Chicken with Mushroom-Marinara Cream Sauce

8 chicken strips
2 T. olive oil
2 tsp. basil
Salt & pepper
1 box (16 oz.) Gnocchi
2 cloves garlic, minced
1 can (14.5 oz.) diced tomatoes
1 can (4 oz.) sliced mushrooms, drained
1 can cream of mushroom soup, low sodium
Parmesan cheese, fresh grated

Brown chicken strips in olive oil, seasoning with basil, salt, and pepper. Prepare Gnocchi according to package instructions. Remove chicken and add garlic, tomatoes, mushrooms, and soup; simmer. Return chicken to sauce just before Gnocchi is done. Drain gnocchi; place in a large pasta bowl or serving platter and top with chicken strips and sauce. Serve with the fresh grated Parmesan.

NOTE: Badly in need of a grocery shopping trip, my pantry yielded few choices. The box of Gnocchi fanned the fires of my imagination and the result was this surprisingly quick and easy, delicious, and healthy dish. I recently read a list of moneysaving ideas for tough economic times and shopping your pantry first was one of them–guess I am right on target.

Mom's Fried Chicken

As Told to Me by Sister-in-Law, Sue

1 fryer
Salt & pepper
Flour
Grease/fat

Cut chicken up. Salt and pepper all sides of chicken pieces. Dredge in flour. Pour a small amount–less than ¼-inch deep–of grease or fat in a large cast iron skillet. Use just enough fat so that the chicken doesn't stick to the pan. Add all the chicken, putting the big pieces in first. Brown chicken pieces on all sides and then make sure the large pieces are on the bottom again. Cover and cook until done.

NOTE: I had to ask Sue how to make Mom's fried chicken. I always just ate it, taking its goodness for granted. Sue gave me the instructions and said, "My pieces of chicken are never recognizable, but it will all taste good." I can almost smell the chicken cooking just thinking about how good Mom's fried chicken was.

Grandma's Simmered Chicken

Recipe from My Mama's Grandmother

1 broiler chicken (3–4 lb.)
Salt & pepper
Flour
½ c. butter
2 c. water

Cut chicken in serving pieces; salt and pepper on each side. Melt butter in Dutch oven, 5-quart size. Put in 1 layer of chicken, sprinkle with flour; add another layer of chicken and flour. Brown chicken slightly. After most of chicken is slightly browned, add water and simmer covered until done. If gravy is not thick enough, make a paste of a little flour and water to thicken. Very good served with creamed potatoes or rice.

Herbed Cranberry Chicken

Friends Christmas Dinner

6 boneless chicken breast halves (4 oz. ea.)
1 T. salt-free herb seasoning
2 T. olive oil, divided
⅔ c. green onions, chopped
½ c. dried cranberries
½ c. reduced-sodium chicken broth
⅓ c. cranberry juice
4½ tsp. maple syrup
1 T. balsamic vinegar
⅓ c. pecans, chopped & toasted

Rub chicken with seasoning blend. In a large nonstick skillet, cook chicken in 1 tablespoon oil over medium heat for 4–5 minutes on each side or until juices run clear. Remove and keep warm. In the same skillet, sauté onions in remaining oil. Stir in the cranberries, broth, cranberry juice, syrup, and vinegar; bring to a boil. Reduce heat; cook and stir for 2 minutes. Return chicken to the pan; cook for 1 minute or until heated through. Sprinkle with pecans. Yield: 6 servings

"My doctor told me to stop having intimate dinners for four. Unless there are three other people." – Orson Welles

Hungarian Chicken

1 chicken (3 lb.)
Salt & pepper
6 T. butter, divided
2 T. sweet paprika
2 med. onions, thinly sliced
8 mushrooms
1 c. heavy cream
Mushroom caps for garnish

Cut chicken into serving pieces and sprinkle with salt and pepper. Then, heat 4 tablespoons of butter in a large skillet and place the chicken pieces skin side down in it. Cook chicken 15–20 minutes or until golden brown. Turn chicken, sprinkle with paprika and onions, then cover. After rinsing the mushrooms in cold water, drain them, slice and scatter them over onions. Cover again and continue to cook for 20 minutes. Spoon any excessive fat from skillet and discard. When chicken is cooked, transfer to warm serving dish, cover with aluminum foil and keep warm. Continue to simmer sauce in the skillet. Add cream, bringing sauce to boil while stirring. Then, turn off the heat and swirl in the remaining butter by rotating pan gently. Pour sauce over chicken and garnish with mushroom caps broiled or cooked in small amount of butter. Serve at once.

SOURCE: Just ask a Hungarian how he likes his chicken and chances are he'll include paprika in the recipe. Using paprika on chicken isn't too common in this country but in Hungary (where paprika is reputed to be the finest in the world) it has long been a favored spice. This traditional Hungarian Chicken entrée shows why. Edi, an exchange student from Hungary, taught us a lot about Hungarian cooking and even gave me a cookbook from her homeland, the Hortobágy region of Hungary. Nearly every meat recipe has paprika, noble-sweet paprika, or slightly hot paprika. She said, "When I go home–I know–I will keep these good eating habits and I will try to cook even the traditional foods healthier. It will be harder than here, because we don't have this variety of low-fat and fat-free foods, but I will try." She was a joy and such a learning experience for us all. Her Hungarian Chicken is still one of my favorite chicken dishes.

"Even were a cook to cook a fly, he would keep the breast for himself."
– Polish Proverb

King Ranch Chicken

School Dinner Recipe

1 cut-up fryer or 6 whole chicken breasts
2 qt. water
1 tsp. salt
½ tsp. pepper
½ tsp. thyme
4 T. butter or margarine
1 onion, finely chopped
1 bell pepper, seeded & finely chopped
1 can cream of mushroom soup
1 can cream of chicken soup
1 can (10 oz.) Ro-Tel tomatoes
1 tsp. chili powder
1½ tsp. oregano
1½ tsp. cumin
½ tsp. black pepper
1 pkg. 12 corn tortillas, cut into quarters
1 lb. Cheddar cheese, shredded

Cook the chicken in the 2 quarts water and salt. Remove and cool chicken, reserving liquid. Debone and cut chicken into bite-size pieces. Sauté the onion and bell pepper in butter. Combine all ingredients except the tortillas and shredded cheese. Layer in shallow greased baking dish in the following order:

Quartered tortillas
Soup/chicken mixture
Shredded cheese

Repeat twice, being sure to end with shredded cheese. If mixture seems dry, add some of the reserved broth from the chicken. Bake at 350° for about 1 hour or until bubbling. A dinner knife inserted and held in the center for about 10 seconds comes out very hot to the touch when done.

NOTE: King Ranch Chicken became one of our *go-to* recipes for dinners. It's deceivingly delicious. While chicken breasts are easier and have less fat, nothing beats the flavor of whole chicken. Even if the measurements aren't followed exactly, it still tastes great. Sometimes I use Velveeta cheese instead of the Cheddar. Velveeta adds a creamy texture and really blends the flavors together. But, absolutely nothing could beat the government cheese we used to get from the cafeteria. It was very similar to the American cheese found in a block or by the slice in the deli department of the grocery store.

ANOTHER NOTE: Strain remaining liquid from cooking chicken and freeze for the next time you need chicken broth.

I can't think about "go-to" recipes and not recall Mrs. Nickleberry. She became my coworker in the late 70s when Mrs. Fuller retired and I returned to work after my second maternity leave. Mrs. Nick and I supervised the inflation of at least a million helium balloons for football spirit grams and Veteran's Day programs, traveled to teacher and student conferences together, coordinated and prepared countless dinners, supervised FHA projects and competitions too numerous to name, spent hours and hours filling out those darn home ec reports every year, and shared tons of other responsibilities. I still smile when I remember our belly laughs at student stories and good times. Toward the end, we forwarded some pretty funny emails, too. Her parents and mine even became well-acquainted from sitting side-by-side at our awards banquet every year. Lest I forget, Mrs. Nick and I left a few sprigs of parsley unserved, too!

Orange Peel Chicken

Jennie

4 boneless chicken breasts
Pepper
Flour & milk
Olive oil
5–6 shakes of reduced-sodium soy sauce
Zest of ½ orange
Juice from ½ orange

Pepper chicken breasts; dredge in flour, dip in milk, and dredge again. Sauté in olive oil–just enough to coat the pan. Cook until done. Add remaining ingredients to skillet and heat through. Use just enough soy sauce to turn brown color. Remove and slice crossways.

NOTE: Avid cookbook readers: you'll make the connection—serve this over Jennie's Chinese Cabbage Salad featured on page 75. What's good about this recipe? The same thing: the second day.

"The two biggest sellers in any bookstore are the cookbooks and the diet books. The cookbooks tell you how to prepare the food, and the diet books tell you how not to eat any of it." – Andy Rooney

Mother's Chicken & Dumplings

My Mama
As She Learned It from My Grandma, Daddy's Mama

1 (5½–6 lb.) hen
1 onion, chopped
2 bay leaves
4 eggs
1 tsp. salt
1 c. water
3–4 c. flour
Pinch nutmeg

Cut up chicken and place in large dumpling pot, 8–10 quart size. Add onion and bay leaves; cover with water. Cook until tender. This will take several hours. Remove the cooked chicken from the pot and cool. Remove from bone. Add enough water to fill the dumpling pot at least half full and bring to a boil before dropping dumplings. Make dumplings by beating eggs well. Add water. Mix 2 cups flour with salt and nutmeg; add to water and egg mixture, stirring quickly to blend. Stir enough additional flour into egg mixture to make dough stiff enough to knead and roll out. (Don't stir too much as the dough will absorb as much flour as it is given. Use the least amount of flour possible so dumplings will be light and fluffy. Avoid over-handling or dumplings will be tough and doughy.) Spoon about ⅓ of dough on to floured surface, knead a few times and roll out until about ¼-inch thick. (See instructions below) Cut dumplings into 2-inch squares and drop individually into boiling liquid; stir occasionally as dumplings are added. Repeat with remaining ⅔ of dough. After dumplings are all in liquid, reduce heat, cover, and simmer until done. Add the boned chicken; heat through and serve. Depending on how many are being made, the dumplings take 20–30 minutes after all are dropped to get tender.

ROLLING INSTRUCTIONS: This dough is very soft so handle it gingerly to keep it from sticking to the surface and the rolling pin. Roll from the center to the edges so it's all the same thickness. Don't press too hard or the dough will stick. We often roll on brown paper or freezer wrap to make the job easier to clean up. A granite counter works beautifully–just clean before rolling. Also, many times dumplings are made the day before and allowed to dry.

NOTE: This is our family's favorite and the most requested birthday meal. For Mama's 80th Birthday, we hosted a dinner in her honor at the community center–100 friends and family members attended. Of course, we had chicken and dumplings along with green beans, cole slaw, and hot rolls. In preparation, family and friends gathered at Mama's house the day before. Daddy cut up the old hens, using a hammer, and the ladies made dumplings and made dumplings and made more dumplings. We had dumplings laid out all over the house–on the beds, tables, the sofa, even the ironing board! Early the next morning, using every big pot the stove would hold, plus the turkey-frying and crawfish-boiling pots outside on propane burners, we cooked the dumplings. It was a wonderful time of celebration, with grandchildren serving the food and beverages and the great-grandchildren passing around baskets of hot rolls for all. With both German Chocolate and Italian Crème Cake, dessert was luscious. Presenting Mama with a photo book of her life was the highlight–preserving all those memories...writing down history for generations to follow. In fact, a few of those photos are featured within these covers.

We didn't even let Mama stir the pot and, as a result, we all learned how to mix, roll, cut, and cook Mother's Chicken and Dumplings–passing down those cooking skills from one generation to the next. A pizza wheel works great for cutting the dumplings.

I'll never forget making dumplings one hot summer with David's family in Bakersfield. This was before I had honed my dumpling-making skills, but since David was homesick, I gave it a try. The first batch was a disaster we threw out. After calling Mama and finding out it's one cup water–not five as printed in the ever-faithful, but not always correct, church cookbook, David made a trip to the store for more flour. Another call to Mama and we were ready to roll. We watched the girls hold their arms out and lay dumplings all up and down them so they could carry more to the pot at a time. The next day the ruined dough had risen, burst out of the garbage bag, and taken over half the garage in the summer heat. Moral of the story? Find out how to make your family's special recipes while there is someone to teach you.

Louisiana Chicken & Sausage Jambalaya

½ c. cooking oil
2 c. onions, chopped
1 c. celery, chopped
3 cloves garlic, minced
2 lb. raw chicken, cubed
2 lb. smoked hot *cooked* sausage, sliced ¼–in. thick
2 tsp.salt
½ tsp. black pepper
½ tsp. thyme
¼ tsp. cayenne (red pepper)
½ can (6 oz.) tomato paste
2 c. cold water
1 c. rice
½ c. green onion tops
½ c. parsley, chopped

Put cooking oil in heavy iron pot. Add onions, celery, and garlic. Cook over medium heat in uncovered pot until onions are wilted. Add chicken and sausage. Season with salt, black pepper, thyme, and cayenne. Cook in uncovered pot over medium heat until meat begins to brown. Stir well. Add tomato paste, cold water, and rice; cover and cook over medium-low heat for about 40 minutes, stirring occasionally. Taste and adjust seasonings. Add additional water to maintain a moist combination. When rice is tender, add green onion tops and parsley. Serves a crowd, 12–16 people, or 2 Cajuns if a bunch of Louisiana Hot Sauce is added.

Elaine's Cajun friends prepared jambalaya for her wedding. Wow, it was so good and it's one of the only times we have broken away from barbecue. Later, we came up with this recipe for my brother's crawfish boil. I keep a container of Tony Chacere's or Slap 'Yo Mama beside the pot to adjust seasonings. I've even been known to stir in a little Gumbo Filé into the jambalaya a time or two. We are nearing honorary Cajun status–our jambalaya just keeps on getting better and better and David's crawfish is the real Louisiana thing. Combine this all with his awesome musical ability and the only thing that's left to do is "Laissez Les Bon Temps Roulez."

VARIATION: The last time I made this for the crawfish boil, it was unbelievably good. People just couldn't get enough–not a grain of rice was left! I diced a couple of small pork loins, browned them in oil, and added them to the pot. I also added a generous shaking of Chesapeake Bay style seafood seasoning, leaving out the red pepper and not adding any Cajun seasoning. We multiplied the recipe by 6 and prepared in a big roaster. I don't know if it was the Chesapeake Bay or the pork or what, but this batch of jambalaya was the best ever. Everyone was asking for the recipe–I just told them it would be in the cookbook coming out soon.

Pecan-Crusted Chicken with Raspberry-Chipotle Sauce & Goat Cheese

Jennie

4 boneless, skinless chicken breasts (4 oz. or more ea.)
1 c. Italian bread crumbs
1 egg
½ c. milk
1 c. flour
Olive oil
2–3 cloves fresh garlic, minced
½ c. pecans, chopped
Raspberry-chipotle sauce
Goat cheese

Pepper the chicken breasts. In one bowl whisk egg and milk; add pepper to mixture. In another bowl have your Italian bread crumbs. In yet another bowl have your chopped pecans. Add olive oil and fresh minced garlic to sauté pan and sauté. Dredge chicken breast through milk and egg mixture, then the Italian bread crumbs, then the milk again, then the bread crumbs again. Cover the thoroughly coated chicken breast with chopped pecans and add to the pan with olive oil. Cook covered on medium heat, turning frequently as to not burn the outer layer of pecans. Uncover about 7 minutes through and cook until chicken breast is done throughout. Plate and drizzle with raspberry-chipotle sauce and sprinkles of goat cheese.

NOTE: Jennie says, "It's a mess to make, but boy is it good. Best if served with rice pilaf and spinach salad."

Stuff # 5

Julie

7–9 chicken tenders
1–2 T. oil
¼ tsp. cumin
¼ tsp. oregano
¼ tsp. ground black pepper
1 clove garlic, minced
1 can (10 oz.) Ro-tel tomatoes
1 can (2.25 oz.) black olives, sliced
1 can (4 oz.) mushrooms, sliced
1 T. flour
1 T. water
1 can (8 oz.) tomato sauce
1 c. macaroni, cooked

Heat oil and brown chicken. Add spices, tomatoes, mushrooms, and olives with juice. Mix flour and water and then add to chicken to thicken. Add tomato sauce. Add cooked macaroni and heat through.

Savory Rock Cornish Hens

School Dinner Recipe

4 Rock Cornish hens (1 lb. ea.)
Melted butter or margarine
Savory Rice Blend

Thaw hens if frozen. Heat oven to 350°. Wash hens and pat dry. Rub cavities lightly with salt. Place hens breast side up on rack in open shallow roasting pan; brush with melted butter. Do not cover. Roast 50 minutes, brushing hens 3–4 times with butter. Increase oven temperature to 400°; roast hens 10 minutes longer or until brown. To serve, place hens on bed of Savory Rice Blend and pour remaining butter over hens. For smaller appetites, have butcher saw hens in half while frozen and serve one half to each person. Hen halves will cook in about 35 minutes.

Savory Rice Blend

¼ c. uncooked wild rice
3 T. butter or margarine
1 sm. onion, chopped
½ c. celery, chopped
2½ c. chicken broth
1 T. parsley flakes
½ tsp. salt
½ tsp. bottled brown bouquet sauce
½ tsp. basil
1 can (4 oz.) mushrooms, drained
¾ c. uncooked rice
1 c. dairy sour cream

Heat oven to 350°. Melt butter in small skillet. Add onion, celery, and wild rice; cook and stir until onion is tender. Pour into an ungreased 1½-quart casserole. Heat chicken broth to boiling and pour over wild rice mixture. Stir in parsley flakes, salt, brown bouquet sauce, basil, and mushrooms. Cover tightly and bake 45 minutes. Remove from oven, stir in regular rice. Cover and bake 40–45 minutes longer or until all liquid is absorbed and rice is tender. Stir in sour cream. (One cup wild rice may be used instead of wild and regular rice. Bake 1½ hours.) Yield: 7 servings, about ½ cup each

Eggs

Breakfast Sausage Casserole

Teacher Bake-Off

6 slices bread
Butter, softened
1 lb. bulk pork sausage
1½ c. Cheddar cheese, shredded
1 doz. eggs, well beaten
2 c. milk
1 tsp. salt

Remove crusts from bread; spread butter on bread. Place in bottom of a greased 9 x 13 x 2-inch baking dish; set aside. Cook sausage until browned, stirring to crumble; drain well. Spoon sausage over bread slices. Sprinkle with cheese. Combine eggs, milk, and salt; mix well. Pour over cheese. Cover and chill overnight. Remove 15 minutes before baking. Bake uncovered at 350° for 45 minutes or until set–a knife inserted in the center comes out clean.

Cheese Eggs

My Grandson, Peyton

6 eggs
3 T. milk
Salt & pepper
Pam spray
Cheddar cheese, grated

Beat eggs, milk, salt, and pepper together. Spray skillet with Pam and heat at medium; add beaten eggs and *regularly cook** them for about 10 minutes. Put a layer of cheese on top and let melt. Then stir them to mix together and let cook another 2–3 minutes. Put another layer of cheese on top and let it melt. Serve it.

NOTE: Peyton has loved to cook since he was old enough to stand on a step stool. He used to cook rubber snakes for me on his little play grill. He flips a pancake like a pro! *By *regularly cook*, Peyton means stirring only enough to let uncooked egg get to the bottom of the pan, just like I taught his mom.

Breakfast Tacos on Vacation

With Narration

1 lb. Jimmy Dean Hot Sausage
1 doz. or less eggs
1 sm. pkg. flour tortillas
2–3 c. Cheddar cheese, shredded
Picante sauce

Brown sausage in a non-stick skillet and drain fat. While sausage is browning, beat 2 eggs per person together. Season by salting and peppering as if seasoning each egg individually. That way the seasoning is always right. When I say *beat*, I mean really vigorously so the under-side of the upper arm flaps. This adds air and makes the eggs light and fluffy. Reduce heat under sausage to medium-low and pour in beaten eggs. Allow to cook a little before disturbing. Take a couple of sips of your bloody mary...*what, no one has made a bloody mary?* Fold the egg/sausage mixture over gently allowing all the egg to cook yet maintain its fluffiness. When eggs are almost done, stir in cheese. *The bloody mary maker should have wrapped the tortillas in a clean dish towel and placed them in the microwave for a minute or two so they are steaming hot when the cheese is added to the eggs.* Carry everything out to the balcony or deck and don't forget to bring the picante sauce and paper plates. Each person fills their own tortilla, rolls it, and eats. *Bloody mary maker needs to make everyone another drink.* Enjoy!

Bloody Mary

Hot Spicy V-8 Juice
Vodka
Tabasco sauce
Limes for juice
Lime slices, slit ½ through
Margarita salt
Tall celery sticks

Squeeze a little lime juice in a saucer. Dip the rim of each glass–12 ounce tumblers–in the juice and dip in margarita salt. Remove any salt that may be clinging to the inside of the glass with your fingertip. Fill with ice. Measure a jigger or pour about 1½ inches of vodka in each glass. Splash a little Tabasco sauce in each glass. Fill with V-8 juice, top with a squeeze of fresh lime juice and stir. Add a lime slice to the rim of each glass and finish off with a celery stick. Serve. Warn everyone to be careful not to poke their eye out with the celery, especially if it doesn't contain any leaves, or if the night before was a rough one.

NOTE: I have been blamed for many a thing, but I am absolutely responsible for teaching my friend Rosemary how to relax and have a good time and how to spend money. In turn, she has taught me to always, always start with fresh ice when mixing another drink. My family and friends have spent many a morning on the balcony overlooking the Gulf of Mexico in Destin, sipping a bloody mary, eating these delicious breakfast tacos, and psyching ourselves up to slather on the sunscreen.

Cheese Soufflé

From the Food Lab

¼ c. margarine or butter
¼ c. all purpose flour
½ tsp. salt
Dash of ground red pepper
1 c. milk
1 c. (4 oz.) Swiss or Gruyère cheese, shredded
4 eggs, separated
¼ tsp. cream of tartar

Heat margarine in 2-quart saucepan over low heat until melted. Blend in flour, salt, and red pepper. Cook over low heat, stirring constantly, until mixture is smooth and bubbly; remove from heat. Stir in milk. Heat to boiling, stirring constantly. Boil and stir 1 minute. Stir in cheese until melted; remove from heat. Place oven rack in second to lowest position and remove other rack(s). Heat oven to 325°. Beat egg whites and cream of tartar in large mixing bowl until stiff but not dry. Beat egg yolks in small mixing bowl until very thick and lemon-colored, about 5 minutes; stir into cheese mixture. Stir about ¼ of the egg whites into cheese mixture. Fold cheese mixture into remaining egg whites. Carefully pour into greased 1½-quart soufflé dish or deep casserole. Cook uncovered in oven until knife inserted halfway between the center and edge comes out clean, 50–60 minutes. Serve immediately.

SOUFFLÉ SUCCESS

Line up all ingredients and tools before starting. Have eggs at room temperature and be very careful separating them; remember one speck of yolk in the whites will prevent them from beating up. Use a wire whip to fold the egg whites and cheese mixture together. Watch the milk carefully while cooking to prevent scorching or boiling over. Do not open the oven or shake the stove while baking and serve a soufflé immediately.

"The only thing that will make a soufflé fall is if it knows you are afraid of it."
– James Beard

When a group of my advanced students wanted to try their hand at a soufflé, I said, "Why not?" After much studying, advice seeking, and divvying up of duties, the group completed their lab plans and the soufflé was finally under way. They made arrangements with their next period teachers to come back to take their soufflé out of the oven, most likely promising to bring them a sample. Their very French cheese soufflé was a masterpiece and I almost broke my arm patting myself on the back!

Egg Cookery

Classroom Standard

The first year of home economics was not complete without my egg cookery demonstration. Thanks to federal funding for vocational classes in the seventies and eighties, our classroom had a demonstration table complete with a hot plate and adjustable mirror and, in my new state-of-the-art lab, there was a demonstration mirror over one kitchen counter and range. Here is a synopsis of how to cook all of the different kinds of eggs. Remember, breakfast is the most important meal of the day and it literally *breaks the fast* your body has been on for the past 10 or more hours. So, break some eggs and get your day off to a great start!

Margarine, butter, bacon fat, or cooking oil
Salt & pepper to taste
Fresh eggs

SCRAMBLED
½ T. milk per egg

OMELET
½ T. milk per egg
1 oz. cheese, grated
1–2 T. sautéed onion, peppers, or mushrooms
Hot ham, sausage, or bacon, chopped

Use a heavy non-stick skillet. Over low to medium-low heat, melt/heat the cooking fat. Break egg into a cup or saucer before slipping into the skillet.

Scrambled

Beat together eggs, salt, pepper, and milk. (Salt and pepper each egg individually to get the seasoning right. For example, if scrambling 6 eggs, pretend to salt six eggs, one at a time.) Pour into prepared skillet. Allow to begin to set and rise before stirring. Gently lift and turn over portions of uncooked egg until all egg is cooked. Serve immediately.

NOTE: Remember, make the skin on the underside of the arm wiggle when beating the eggs so lots of air is incorporated. Invariably, I had students who stirred their scrambled eggs too much while cooking, chopping them into small pieces. Allow the eggs to rise, stirring only enough to let uncooked egg get to the bottom of the pan. The result will be light, fluffy scrambled eggs.

Omelets

Prepare two eggs as for scrambled. Pour into prepared skillet. Allow to begin to set; then gently lift edges of egg and tilt skillet to allow uncooked egg to run underneath. When eggs are almost completely set, place cheese and other ingredients on one-half of the omelet. Carefully fold the other half over the ingredients and cook a couple of minutes more. Covering the omelet either before or after folding, lowering the heat, and cooking 3–4 minutes like this will produce a fluffy omelet. Turn onto a heated plate for serving.

NOTE: Some chefs sauté omelet ingredients first and then pour the beaten eggs into the skillet with them, adding the cheese just before folding. Either way, you'll experience success following these general instructions.

Blind-Folded

Use enough cooking fat to splash over the top of the egg yolk, cooking the egg white, and thus *blind-folding* or hiding the yolk with cooked egg white. Continue cooking and splashing with fat until egg reaches desired doneness.

Soft & Hard-Cooked

Place eggs in a saucepan and cover with cold water. Bring to a boil; carefully stir the eggs, trying to turn them over so the yolks will settle in the center of the egg; cover and turn the burner off. Set timer for 3–5 minutes for soft-cooked eggs. Set the timer for 20 minutes for hard-cooked eggs. Immediately drain hot water and serve soft-cooked eggs. Rinse hard-cooked eggs in cold water and place in ice water until completely cooled. Begin peeling the hard-cooked egg at the blunt end. That's where the air cell is, so it's easier to start there. When making egg salad or adding chopped hard-cooked eggs to a recipe, try this technique: place the shelled eggs in a bowl and break them apart with a pastry blender. The more the blender is used, the smaller the egg pieces get–it works perfectly.

NOTE: Boiling eggs will make them tough and rubbery, so be sure to turn off the heat source as soon as eggs come to a boil. If hard-cooked eggs are allowed to remain hot after cooking, the outside of the yolks will turn a grayish-green color, so be sure to do the cold water bath unless serving immediately.

Over Easy

Slip the egg into the skillet and allow to cook until the white is completely white/set. Lightly salt and pepper, if desired. Carefully insert a wide spatula under the egg and turn it over without breaking the yolk. Cook to desired doneness.

Sunny-Side-Up

Slip egg into skillet and cook over low heat until desired doneness is reached. Do not do anything to cover the yolk–it should remain yellow–the *sunny-side* showing.

EGG FACTS

This may be TMI: too much information–it is just about all I know about eggs. Perhaps there is a useful tidbit or conversation starter somewhere within.

- Eggs are sized by the weight per dozen. A dozen PeeWee eggs weigh 15 ounces, Small–18 ounces, Medium–21 ounces, Large–24, Extra-Large–27, and Jumbo–30 ounces per dozen.
- Most recipes use medium or large eggs. If using other sized eggs and the recipe calls for 6 or more eggs, use one more or one less egg to achieve the best results.
- The grade of the egg is determined by its freshness. An egg can go down a grade or two just sitting on the kitchen counter a few hours, so always keep them refrigerated.
- Always keep eggs covered, preferably in the carton in which they came. The egg shell is porous; if it is left uncovered in the fridge, it will absorb odors from other foods, affecting its flavor.
- Keep the egg in its original carton, with the blunt end up. The blunt end contains an air cell and it will remain intact longer if the weight of the entire egg is not placed on it. As the egg loses its freshness, this air cell gets larger.
- The parts of an egg include: the shell, an outer membrane and air cell, the yolk and its inner membrane, the white and its inner membrane, and the chalaza–that's the white-colored things attached to each side of the yolk. No, the chalaza is not a baby chicken. The chalaza serves the purpose of holding the yolk in the center of the egg.

- ✦ The membranes of an egg hold the shape of the egg white and yolk when the egg is cracked. The white of a fresh egg will be *together* much like Jello as it begins jelling. The yolk of a fresh egg will be round like a slightly deflated ball. An older egg will spread out very thinly and the yolk will be flat and break easily.
- ✦ Always check the carton of eggs for cracks in individual eggs before adding to your grocery cart. Bacteria can enter through a crack, so make sure the eggs are not cracked so they are safe to eat.
- ✦ The color of the shell of an egg is determined by the type of hen that laid it. Nutrition is the same. Yard eggs, from chickens raised by individuals, usually have a yolk that is a darker yellow and have a slightly different flavor. This is due to fact that the hens are allowed to roam free, finding bugs and worms and other nutritious additions to their laying chow. My aunt and uncle in Missouri had some weird chickens that laid colored eggs–pale pink, yellow, orange, and blue. They always knew which chicken had laid an egg and, though we were never there at Easter, I guess they didn't bother to dye their eggs.
- ✦ When hard-cooking eggs, older eggs will peel more easily because the membrane that holds the egg together is weaker.
- ✦ Don't know if an egg is fresh or hard-cooked? Just spin the egg. If it wobbles, it's raw. If it spins easily, it's hard-cooked.
- ✦ To determine if an egg is too old to use, place in a bowl of water. A fresh egg will sink; a stale egg will float. If it floats, throw it away. Don't make yourself gag by cracking it open.
- ✦ Always use low to medium-low heat when cooking eggs.
- ✦ Use fresh eggs at room temperature for baking. They are easier to separate and will provide more volume to your finished product.
- ✦ Eggs provide nutrition, texture, thickening, color, and leavening when used in recipes. Try cooking a scrambled egg in a custard cup in the microwave–watch it rise! Eggs do the same thing in baked products.
- ✦ Eggs are used as a binding agent in foods such as meatballs–they help hold ingredients together. Eggs are also used to coat foods such as chicken fried steak.
- ✦ Eggs may contain salmonella, a bacteria that causes food-borne illness. Cooking destroys these bacteria. If a raw egg must be used, make sure it is fresh, clean, and not cracked.
- ✦ Use an egg slicer for hard-cooked eggs to make perfect slices for salads and garnishes.
- ✦ Always crack each egg into a small bowl before adding to recipe to insure its wholesomeness.

"Do vegetarians eat animal crackers?" – Author Unkown

Since I mentioned federal funding earlier, now would be a good time to explain a little about the nuts and bolts of being a vocational home economics teacher. It's simply this: As Mrs. Fuller used to say, "If I go to hell, it will be from lying on these darn reports!" Understand please, that she would not do this intentionally–they were just so complicated. We had to count students every which way, and sometimes it was just impossible to get the numbers to add up. Let's see, there was ethnicity, sex, age, grade level, income level, special education placement, and I can't remember how many other classifications we had to identify. Then we also had to write stories to justify our program. In those years, we were required to make after-school home visits to all students to supervise their home projects. Parent contacts had to be recorded. We offered adult classes to the community and were required to report on those, too. For all this, we were granted an additional conference period. Other teachers were extremely jealous, but we would have given them that hour a day just to get rid of those extra responsibilities and those "darn" reports.

Gourmet Omelet

Jennie

3 eggs
⅛ c. white onion
1 sm. clove fresh garlic
6 slices reduced-fat honey ham
2 fresh mushrooms, sliced
Cracked pepper
2–3 pinches dill
Olive oil
¼ c. Feta cheese
1 green onion, chopped
Parmesan cheese, grated

Dice a quarter of a white onion, and mince some garlic. Place a splash of olive oil and the diced onions and minced garlic in a skillet; sauté on medium. Meanwhile dice 6 slices of the honey ham, slice a couple mushrooms, and whisk the eggs. Add the mushrooms and ham to the skillet when the onions are becoming transparent. Add fresh ground pepper and dill to the skillet. Then, when the ham is browning, pour in the 3 whisked eggs. Make sure the eggs cover the bottom of the skillet and the toppings that have been sautéing. When this gels, add in Feta cheese, more cracked pepper, and dill. Once the cheese starts to melt, fold the omelet over and let cook until golden brown. Plate the omelet and cover with a bit of Parmesan cheese and some chopped green onions; serve with fresh fruit on the side.

NOTE: Jennie explains, "Can be made with pretty much anything in your refrigerator, but this one comes straight out of mine. Delicious served with sliced strawberries sprinkled with powdered sugar and a hot cup of coffee." I think Jennie has inherited my attention to detail.

Ham & Cheese Egg Bake

1½ c. (6 oz.) Cheddar cheese, shredded
1½ c. (6 oz.) Mozzarella cheese, shredded
½ lb. fresh mushrooms, sliced
6 green onions, sliced
1 med. sweet red pepper, chopped
2 T. butter
1¾ c. fully cooked ham, cubed (can use turkey ham)
¼ c. all purpose flour
8 eggs
1¾ c. milk
Salt & pepper to taste

Combine the cheeses; sprinkle into a greased 13 x 9 x 2-inch baking dish. In a large skillet, sauté the mushrooms, onions, and red pepper in butter; stir in ham. Spoon over the cheese. In a bowl, combine the flour, eggs, milk, salt, and pepper. Pour over ham mixture; cover and refrigerate overnight. Remove from the refrigerator 30 minutes before baking. Bake, uncovered, at 350° for 35–45 minutes or until a knife inserted near the center comes out clean. Let stand for 5 minutes before serving. Yield: 8-10 servings

NOTE: I love waking up in the morning and slipping this casserole into the oven. This recipe is great for carb-watchers as there's no bread.

MEASURING CHEESE

Four ounces of cheese yields one cup of shredded cheese—no need to measure. So, a one pound (16 ounce) block of cheese will yield 4 cups shredded cheese. To get the 1½ cups used above, simply cut a 16 ounce block in half (yield: two 8 ounce pieces), then cut ¼ of one piece off; the amount remaining will be 6 ounces or 1½ cups when shredded. Or, it could just be grated and measured, but it is more fun to divide and conquer. I know you are probably thinking, I'll just buy the grated cheese, thank you very much. Remember though, additional ingredients–many of which are chemical in nature–are added to prevent the cheese from sticking together. The more processing a food goes through, the less natural it becomes.

Holiday Strata

Marilyn's Mother

16 slices white or brown bread, crust removed
15 slices cooked lean bacon or ¾ lb. ham, cut in strips
3 c. Cheddar cheese, grated
¼ c. onion, chopped
¼ c. green pepper, chopped
3 c. whole milk
6 eggs
½ tsp. salt
½ tsp. pepper
½ tsp. dry mustard
1½ tsp. Worcestershire sauce
Dash of Tabasco sauce
½ c. margarine, melted
1 c. corn flakes, crushed

Line a 9 x 13 x 2-inch greased pan with 8 slices of the bread. Layer bacon or ham, cheese, onion, and pepper. Cover with remaining 8 slices of bread. Beat together milk, eggs, salt, pepper, mustard, and sauces. Pour over top. Let set in refrigerator overnight. Next morning, pour melted margarine over mixture and sprinkle with corn flakes. Bake in 325° oven for 1 hour. Let stand 10 minutes and serve hot.

NOTE: This recipe is from Marilyn's mother, a wonderful cook–although she was always very skinny. I often wonder about skinny cooks, but in her case, it must have been great metabolism because everything she made was delicious.

WHEN ARE BAKED DISHES DONE?

To tell when a quiche, egg dish, or custard is done, insert a dinner knife into the center and if it comes out clean, it's done. To tell when a casserole or lasagna is done, insert a dinner knife in the center, wait about 10 seconds; then remove the knife and feel the blade. If it's hot, the casserole is hot through and through.

"Ham and Eggs – A day's work for a chicken; a lifetime commitment for a pig" – Anonymous

More Cheese Than Deviled Eggs

6 hard-cooked eggs
¾ c. mayonnaise
2 T. Monterey Jack cheese, finely shredded
2 T. Swiss cheese, finely shredded
2 T. chives, minced & divided
⅛ tsp. ground mustard
⅛ tsp. white pepper
2 oz. Velveeta cheese, cubed
Dash paprika

Peel eggs and slice in half lengthwise. Remove yolks; set whites aside. In a bowl, mash the yolks. Add the mayonnaise, shredded cheeses, 1 tablespoon chives, mustard, and pepper. In a microwave-safe bowl, melt the Velveeta cheese on high for 1–2 minutes; stir until smooth. Stir into yolk mixture. Pipe or spoon into egg whites. Sprinkle with paprika and remaining chives. Refrigerate until serving. Yield: 1 dozen

NOTE: This recipe is a scrumptiously different deviled egg. I double or triple the recipe because it seems the first thing to disappear at our family get-togethers is the deviled eggs. When preparing this recipe, combine the melted Velveeta with the remaining ingredients before it cools too much or there will be lumps. I love making these eggs because there is always more than enough yolk mixture to fill all the egg halves.

WHEN IS EASTER?

Deviled eggs always remind me of Easter. I guess it's the cooking and coloring of all the eggs. My birthday has fallen on Easter Sunday several times during my life, and unless I live to the ripe old age of a hundred and something, it won't happen again. That brings me to the reason for bringing this up. Do you know how Easter Sunday is determined? It's always the first Sunday after the first full moon in spring. Why put this in my cookbook? I thank and praise my Lord for every birthday and for all the blessings He has given me, especially His Son, Jesus Christ, who takes away the sin of the world and mine, too. May God bless you always!

Sharon's Breakfast Squares

Sharon

1 pkg. refrigerated crescent rolls
¾ c. half & half cream
1 lb. Jimmy Dean Sausage
Salt & pepper
8 eggs
1½ c. Mozzarella cheese

Spread crescent rolls evenly on bottom of 9 x 13 x 2-inch casserole dish. Crumble and brown sausage in frying pan. Then spread evenly over crust. Sprinkle cheese on top of sausage. Mix eggs, cream, salt, and pepper; spread on top. Bake in 325° oven until brown, about 25–30 minutes.

NOTE: Prepare and bake the night before so that everyone can just pop a piece in the microwave the next morning.

"You don't have to cook fancy or complicated masterpieces–just good food from fresh ingredients." – Julia Child

PORK

Bacon & Zucchini Pie

1 refrigerated pie crust
6 eggs, well beaten
2 c. zucchini, grated
1 pkg. (2 oz.) Hormel fully cooked bacon, finely chopped

Preheat oven to 400°. Unroll crust and place into an ungreased 8" pie pan. Gently press edges down on the edge of the pie pan. Poke holes into bottom and sides of the crust with a fork. Bake 5 minutes. Add the zucchini and bacon pieces to the beaten eggs and pour into the pie shell. Bake for 20 minutes or until eggs are firm. Cool slightly before cutting.

NOTE: Of course, some will say that real cooks make their own crust. Not! Here's a trick to making pie crust that I used before the days of refrigerated ones. Buy the frozen crust, thaw it completely, and transfer to your favorite pie pan. Then reshape the pre-formed edge into a fluted edge. No one, and I mean no one, will know and everyone will be impressed.

Bacon-Wrapped, Boudin-Stuffed Pork Chops

Jennie

4 butterflied pork chops
1 lb. peppered bacon, thick sliced
2 links (6 in. ea.) boudin

Select really thick-cut pork chops (about 2-inches) and have the butcher butterfly them. Pepper chops inside and out. Cut a 3-inch length of boudin, remove from casing and stuff into a chop. Wrap with bacon slices; secure with toothpicks. Place on a foil-lined baking sheet. Repeat with other chops. Broil or grill. Cook until well done–160°. Serve immediately.

NOTE: Jennie warns, "When grilling, turn often as the bacon will burn easily. Goes great with julienned green beans and French bread–a feast fit for a king…or a redneck!"

HOW TO USE A FOOD THERMOMETER

"Is It Done Yet?"–a question that even experienced cooks ask, brings me to food safety and the use of a food thermometer. We don't want to overcook foods, yet realize that undercooking can compromise quality and place food in danger of causing food-borne illness. Use a temperature guide and follow these simple instructions to determine if foods are indeed done.

- ✦ Use an instant-read food thermometer to check the internal temperature toward the end of the cooking time, but before the food is expected to be done.
- ✦ The food thermometer should be placed in the thickest part of the food and should not be touching bone, fat, or gristle. Check the temperature in several places to make sure the food is evenly heated.
- ✦ Compare your thermometer reading to the USDA Recommended Safe Minimum Internal Temperatures to determine if your food has reached a safe temperature.
- ✦ Make sure to clean your food thermometer with hot, soapy water before and after each use.

USDA RECOMMENDED SAFE MINIMUM INTERNAL TEMPERATURES

Steaks & Roasts - 145 °F
Fish - 145 °F
Pork - 160 °F
Ground Beef - 160 °F
Egg Dishes - 160 °F
Chicken Breasts - 165 °F
Whole Poultry - 165 °F

SOURCE: U.S. Department of Agriculture, Food Safety and Inspection Service

- ✦ Poultry, pork, and ground meat should always be cooked well done.

"Taking your food's temperature is the only way to assure your item is properly cooked." – Mark R. Vogel

Baked Pork Chops and Rice

Janis

6 pork loin center rib chops, ¾-inch thick (about 2 lb. total)
1 tsp. chili powder
1 tsp. salt
Dash pepper
1 c. long grain rice, raw
1 sm. onion, chopped
2 cans (15-oz. ea.) stewed tomatoes
1 c. Cheddar cheese, shredded

Preheat oven to 350°. Trim fat from chops. Heat cooking spray or a small amount of oil in a large skillet over medium heat. Brown both sides of chops. Transfer chops to a shallow 2-quart baking dish. Sprinkle chops with chili powder, salt, and pepper. Evenly layer rice, then onion and stewed tomatoes. Cover lightly with foil. Bake for 1½–2 hours or until chops are tender and rice is done. Sprinkle with cheese, if desired. Bake 5 minutes longer or until cheese melts. Serves 3–6, depending on appetites

NOTE: Janis adds, "Use Mexican-style tomatoes for spicier taste. Also, if cans are only 14½ ounces, add ¼ cup water–important for cooking the rice. One of my husband's favorites! Down-home cooking, slightly spicy, great comfort food."

Friday Nite After a Few Drinks Hungries

1 link beef sausage
½ c. rice
½ c. water
2 tsp. Cajun seasoning (low salt)
1 can (15 oz.) pinto beans
1 can (15 oz.) Trappey's Creole Okra Gumbo*

Slice sausage diagonally. Heat stainless steel saucepan (1½–2 quart). Brown sausage; add rice and brown. Scrape bottom often. Add everything else, including juices. Cover and bring to boil. Lower heat and simmer 20 minutes. Serve with ice water, as you've had enough alcohol already. Serves 3–4 depending on appetites. To serve more, add 1 cup rice and 1½ cups water instead of original amount. *Substitute another brand if not available. Add additional Cajun seasoning if needed.

My BFF Rosemary was over one Friday afternoon and we enjoyed a few gin and tonics and then all of a sudden we were starved. I found a link of sausage in the fridge, so I checked the pantry and this is what resulted. It has become one of my favorite "go-to" quick recipes.

Luscious Pork Loin Chops

3 pork loin chops, center cut, fat removed
Salt, pepper, and flour
1 med. onion, sliced ¼ in. thick
8 oz. fresh mushrooms, sliced
Olive oil
¾ c. dry sherry
Cooked rice

Heat iron skillet and cover bottom with a scant ⅛-inch depth of olive oil. Lightly salt and pepper chops and dredge in flour. Brown chops on both sides. Coating will stick to skillet. Remove chops. Deglaze skillet with the dry sherry and return chops to skillet. Cover with the onions and mushrooms. Cover and cook over low heat until chops are done, about 20 minutes for ½-inch thick chops. Mushrooms will make juice. Serve over rice.

Maple Sugar-Ginger Roast Pork

2½ pounds boneless pork loin roast, tied
2 garlic cloves, thinly sliced
2 T. maple sugar
1½ tsp. fresh ginger, grated
¼ tsp. crushed red pepper
2 T. extra-virgin olive oil
Brown Gravy

Using a small, sharp knife make thin slits all over the pork loin roast and slip a garlic slice into each one. (I kept losing the holes, so finally figured out to cut and insert one slice at a time) In a small bowl, mix the maple sugar with the ginger, salt, red pepper, and olive oil. Rub the paste all over the pork, wrap it well in plastic and refrigerate overnight in a small roasting pan; let stand at room temperature for 1 hour before roasting. Preheat the oven to 450°. Remove plastic wrap and roast the pork for 15 minutes. Lower the oven temperature to 350° and roast the pork for about 50 minutes longer, until an instant-read thermometer inserted in the thickest part registers 160°. Transfer the roast to a cutting board and let rest for 15 minutes before slicing. Discard the string and carve the pork in thin slices. Arrange on a platter and garnish. Serve immediately with brown gravy. 8 servings

NOTE: Maple sugar, made from reduced maple syrup, is available at specialty-food stores. Substitute granulated brown sugar if unavailable. (I used plain old brown sugar. The maple sugar produces a glaze as the meat roasts.) Be sure to use a roasting rack so loin does not sit in juices.

Brown Gravy

Dash of red pepper flakes
2 T. pure maple syrup
1 T. brown sugar
Milk

Add the above to pan drippings and stir in enough milk to make a thin gravy.

Millennium Italian Casserole

Teacher Bake-Off

1 pkg. (12 oz.) lg. pasta shells
½ lb. ground beef
2 cloves garlic, minced
1 tsp. dried oregano leaves
Salt & pepper to taste
8 oz. cottage or ricotta cheese
6 T. butter or margarine, melted
2 cans (8 oz. ea.) tomato sauce
1 c. fresh or canned mushrooms, drained
1 green pepper, diced
1 c. pepperoni, thinly sliced
2 pkg. (6 oz. ea.) pre-sliced Mozzarella cheese

Cook shells as directed on package. Drain. Sauté ground beef. Season with oregano, garlic, and a little salt and pepper. Mix cottage or ricotta cheese, butter, and tomato sauce until well blended. Stir in mushrooms and green pepper, blending well. Place layer of cooked shells in bottom of lightly buttered casserole. Cover with layer of cheese mixture. Top with half the pepperoni. Place two slices Mozzarella cheese on top. Crumble ⅓ ground beef evenly over cheese. Repeat layers until all ingredients are used, ending with Mozzarella cheese on top, ringed with pepperoni slices. Bake at 350° for 45 minutes until hot and bubbly. Serve with a fresh green salad and a red table wine. Yield: 4 servings

"Tomatoes and oregano make it Italian; wine and tarragon make it French. Sour cream makes it Russian; lemon and cinnamon make it Greek. Soy sauce makes it Chinese; garlic makes it good." – Alice May Brock

Our Family Sausage

Original Recipe Sausage

The First Year Recorded, Sometime in the 70s, with Narrative

50 lb. meat
4 T. preservative (purchase at a meat processing plant)
1¼ c. salt
¾ c. pepper
¼ tsp. garlic powder

We used to laugh at the amount of garlic we used–only ¼ teaspoon for 50 pounds of meat. Daddy was a picky eater, and I am still amazed that we added any garlic at all. Over the years our original recipe evolved and the ingredients listed in the Last Recorded Version are the result of much haggling, bickering, and discussion between siblings and sausage factory workers. 1996 is the last year we made sausage. We would tie a red piece of yarn on the string of hot sausages so things didn't get mixed up. Much to Daddy's chagrin, we made more hot sausage than regular in the last few years of production; but we still didn't use as much garlic as I put in a pot of spaghetti sauce.

Last Recorded Version

Circa 1996

50 lb. meat
3 T. preservative
¾ c. salt
¾ c. black pepper
3 tsp. garlic powder
3 tsp. ground cayenne
HOT SAUSAGE
Add these additional ingredients:
½ c. crushed red pepper
2 T. ground cayenne

We were quite the farm family. Daddy raised pigs and we butchered hogs the old fashioned way. I was a cold, shivering observer of the slaughtering and this is what I remember from watching the action that began on Friday evening. A 50-gallon oil drum was buried on a slant in the ground. Water was brought to a boil in the giant cast iron wash pot. A bucket was used to pour the boiling water into the drum. Next, the slaughtered hog was lowered into the drum and sloshed around. More boiling water was poured over the hog. Next, the hog was removed and the scraping began. Our fearless men and boys scraped off all the hair and the hog was left a perky pink color. After throwing a rope over a stout, high limb in one of those big oak trees, the hog was strung up on a single-tree and dressed. I would go get everyone a beer or hot cup of coffee for this part. Mama and Aunt Vera would use Grandma's *schweppas* (old, old, flat wooden sticks worn smooth with use) to clean out the large intestines. I stayed as far away as possible from this event. The clean intestines were then soaked in water until the next day and used for the liverwurst (head sausage).

NEXT MORNING: After arising bright and early, we began to bone the hog meat. Daddy usually bought lean beef from the supermarket where Mama worked to mix with our sausage. A couple of years we used some deer meat, but beef and pork was our standard. We ground the meat, putting one handful of beef to two handfuls of pork. Then it was carefully measured on the same scale we used to weigh our chickens for the fair. (Don't get excited about contamination–we placed the meat in a clean pan. We also smoked the sausage in the chicken house, but there weren't any chickens living there anymore.) All the boning, mixing, and sausage-making was done on a 4 x 8-foot piece of plywood that Daddy had reinforced to make Elaine and I a pingpong table years before. It sat on saw horses. That old piece of wood is so seasoned, it will never rot.

Fifty pounds of meat were laid out in this huge patty and sprinkled with the mixed seasonings. When the grandkids got old enough to help, they did the mixing. Mixing was done with your hands until the preservative changed the meat's color from a bright red to a dull reddish/brown. After smoking, the sausage would turn bright red again. The hands of those mixing would be bright red and almost frozen. The sausage stuffer required two people, one to turn the handle and one to feed the casings onto the spout, twist if making links, and yell *whoa* and *go*. The sausage was stuffed into casings (small intestines, cleaned of course) bought at the store. We used almost every part of the hog, even the tail which was very convenient for getting that last bit of sausage out of the stuffing pipe. Oink, oink. Sausages were hand-tied, placed on a long stick, and hung in the smokehouse. Believe it or not, we never had a sausage fall during smoking.

We never put the pork tenderloins in the sausage. They waited in the freezer and when everything else was finished, Daddy would use his meat saw (a hand one) and a knife to cut pork chops. I remember how cold that loin was because I often got to hold it while Daddy sawed. After everything was cleaned up, Daddy would start the smoke for the smoke house. He used pecan or oak chips in a bucket covered with a piece of tin and would go and check the smoke during the night and the next morning. The following afternoon we would all get back together to divide the sausage among the workers–weighing and sorting who wanted hot, who wanted regular, who wanted both. The head sausage was divvied out very carefully, with Mama and Daddy keeping the majority–that was just fine with all of us. The total cost per pound was figured and everyone paid for the amount they received. We never figured in time and labor on Daddy's part because he wouldn't allow it–he loved every minute of it.

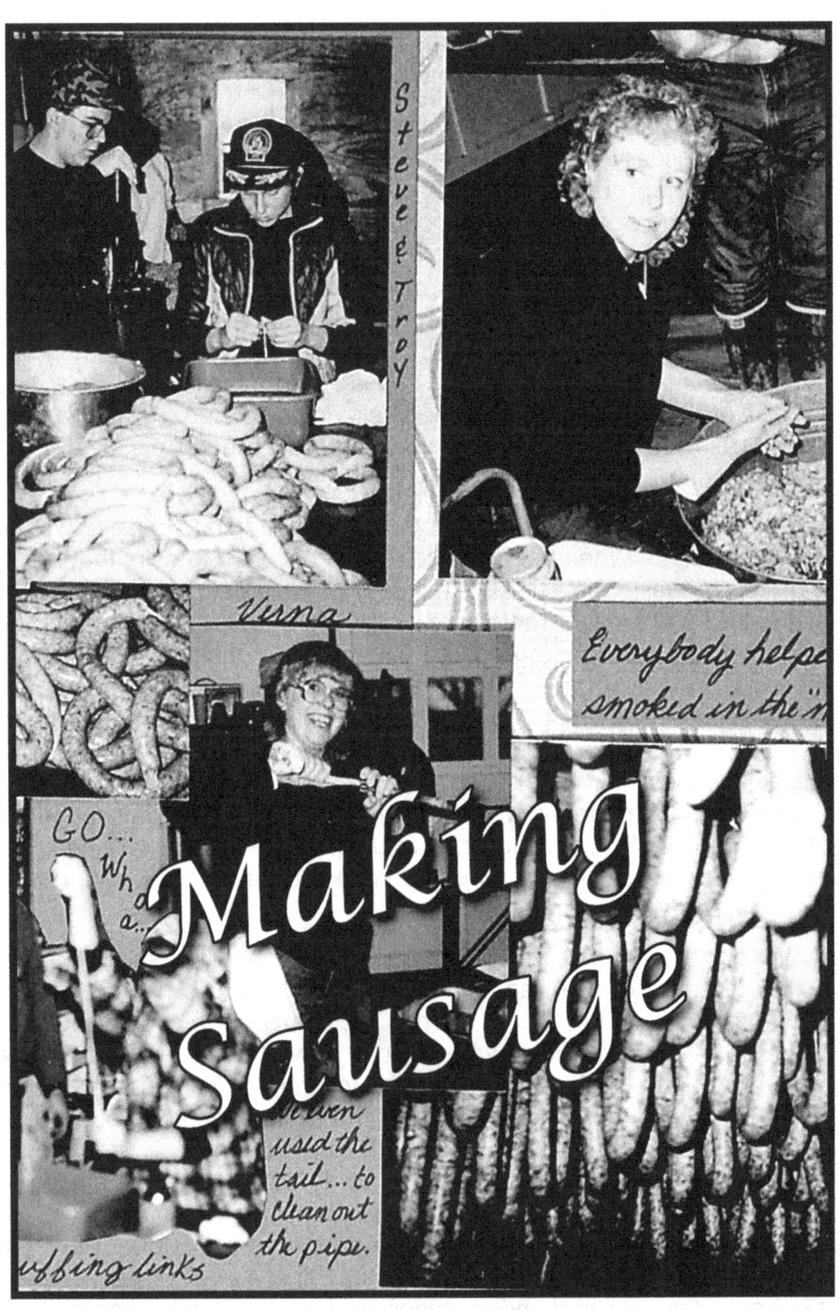

If I didn't see the pictures, I probably wouldn't believe we did this either.

Liverwurst or Head Sausage

I had to ask Mama about making the head sausage as we never wrote it down. Mama said, "Boil the head, bones, jowls, heart, the long brown thing —I think it's called milts or something–and liver in the big black cast iron wash pot I drove all over Houston trying to find. Wait to add the liver until later or it will fall apart. Build a fire around the bottom of the pot." This was quite a task as it had to be cold weather to butcher and it usually was raining or sleeting. Keeping the fire going was quite the chore, involving the use of tin and stakes to protect it. That was the brothers-in-law's job. Daddy had a long-handled three-prong fork he would use to test to see when the hog parts were done. They were dipped out, laid on the table to cool, the meat was boned, and the whole mess was put through an antique hand-grinder. Then it was laid out on our old pingpong table and Mama seasoned it with salt, pepper, and allspice. "Use your judgment and taste it a lot." Stuff into cleaned large intestines, tie and return to the boiling pot. Mama adds, "Careful watching is required and you must poke holes in the sausages or they will bust." It seems I remember that if they begin to float in the boiling pot, Daddy would poke them. Remove from the pot, let cool, and hang in the smokehouse.

I remember one year we had a lot of head sausage and ran out of casings. Daddy said you just couldn't use regular casings, so Mama and Aunt Vera stuffed the head sausage into nylon stockings. It turned out pretty good. Necessity is the mother of invention. Daddy always waited to cook the boudin after the head sausage was done–no cross-contamination allowed. He just didn't venture into hot foods.

Boudin

7 c. cooked rice
1 bottle Trappey's Tabasco Peppers
¼ head sausage, seasoned (about 1¾ c.)

Drain and finely chop the peppers. Combine all ingredients and stuff loosely into regular sausage casings. Boil carefully (not as long as the head sausage). Cool and hang to smoke.

"Asking a critic to name his favorite book is like asking a butcher to name his favorite pig." – John McCarthy

Norman's Layered Sausage Supper

Mom & Grandpa Norman

1 T. oil
2 lg. potatoes, thinly sliced
1 head cabbage, shredded
1 c. onions, chopped
1 link sausage, about 1½ lb.
Salt & pepper

Slice sausage diagonally, ¼-inch thick and set aside. Pour oil in bottom of large iron skillet. Add potatoes in a layer and lightly sprinkle with salt and pepper. Top with onions. Next, add cabbage in layers, lightly sprinkling each layer as it is added. Mash down cabbage–it will shrink dramatically when it gets hot and starts to cook. Place sausage in a single layer on top of the cabbage. Cover and cook over medium heat. Do not stir. After about 5 or 6 minutes, lower heat and cook until done. It takes about 20 more minutes. Dig to the bottom to serve so everyone gets some of those wonderfully brown potatoes.

> This is one of those skillets Mom would leave on our stovetop for us to find when we came home from a long day at school. It is so good and it doesn't take much effort to make it yourself. I usually leave the potato peelings on and sometimes I use new red potatoes just to change it up a little. I don't always add the onions. Yummy!

Prosciutto Provolone Panini

8 slices coarse bread
8 slices Provolone cheese
4 thin slices prosciutto
6 T. basil pesto

Spread one side of each bread slice with basil pesto. Layer a slice of cheese, a slice of prosciutto, and a second slice of cheese on four pieces of bread, pesto side up. Top each with remaining bread slices, pesto side down. Spray outsides of each panini with olive oil. Cook in panini grill and press until bread is toasted and cheese is melted.

NOTE: A griddle or cast iron skillet, in conjunction with a bacon press or a heavy ceramic oven-proof plate and a brick, can be used instead of a panini grill. Another alternative is to simply mash down with a large spatula while cooking.

Quiche Lorraine

Debbie

8-in. pie crust
4 slices bacon
4 thin slices onion
3 eggs
¼ tsp. dry mustard
1 c. light cream, heated
8 paper-thin slices ham, shredded
8 paper-thin slices imported Swiss cheese
Nutmeg

Bake the pie crust at 450° for 10 minutes. Fry bacon until crisp; chop. Sauté onion in bacon fat until soft; drain. Sprinkle the bacon and onion over bottom of baked pie crust. Add half of the shredded ham; lay 4 slices of the cheese over the ham. Add rest of ham, topping with remaining cheese. Beat the eggs and mustard; add the hot cream and continue beating. Pour over the ham and cheese; let stand 10 minutes. Sprinkle a tiny bit of nutmeg on top and bake at 350° until custard is set, around 30 minutes.

NOTE: This is from my younger sister, Debbie. She says it is a no-fail recipe for quiche, always a big hit at luncheons, and it reheats well. Debbie has published two family cookbooks and I only hope that my cookbook comes close to being as great as hers are.

I mentioned before that Debbie was in my class the first year I taught. Well, I might as well tell the story about her floor plan. (I taught all areas of home economics–housing, interior design, consumer economics, child development, family relations, clothing and textiles–not just foods.) The advanced assignment was to draw up a floor plan for your dream home. This was 1971 and, using a 12-inch ruler, students created architectural plans with a scale of ¼ inch equals 1 foot. Debbie's floor plan was a work of art. I could only find one thing not quite perfect: her pencil lead had dulled a little and some of her lines were thicker than others. So, I gave her a 99. She has never forgiven me. To show the significance of this, I need to say that her success in the oil industry lies partly in the fact that she can read seismographic charts and make accurate predictions as to where oil will be found. Use your imagination: the variations in the width of lines on her floor plan and on the seismograph charts are related, aren't they? Debbie drew up the plans to the home that she and her husband built. Years later she drew plans for their home addition. She makes me proud!

Pulled Pork, Barbecue Style

Rosemary

3 lb. pork loin
1 jar (16 oz.) barbecue sauce
1 can (12 oz.) coca cola
Ciabatta bread
1 lg. onion, sliced
2 T. cooking oil

Place pork loin, sauce, and coke in crock pot and cook on low for 6–8 hours. Remove pork and shred using two forks. Place remaining liquid in a saucepan and cook until reduced by half. Strain. Sauté onions in oil. Spoon generous amounts of pulled pork on sliced and toasted Ciabatta bread. Top with sautéed onions and sauce.

NOTE: While there's no pit involved in this dish, it's lick your lips and fingers good. Try Jack Daniels Barbecue Sauce if available. Rosemary and I perfected this recipe while watching the sun go down over Caddo Lake during spring break just recently. We shopped for antiques all day while the pork cooked–crock pots are great!

When Rosemary and I started traveling together many years back, we adopted the "bootle" as a means of sharing expenses. Rosemary's mother had introduced this idea back when Rosemary was young. It's simple and we love it; everyone antes up at the beginning of the trip, usually $50 or $100, depending on the length we'll be gone. Then, when we stop for snacks, have lunch or dinner, or buy groceries for the duration, we pay from the bootle. If the bootle runs out, we all ante up again. If someone decides to have an extravagant meal, usually crab, they just pitch in a little extra. It takes the pain out of dividing checks and constantly thinking about money. We can't let Gary keep the bootle–he always gets it mixed up with our personal funds. We make quite a group traveling–Gary introduces us like this: "This is my wife, Verna, and my girlfriend, Rosemary." People just look at him and wonder....

"Pork fat rules!" – Emeril Lagasse

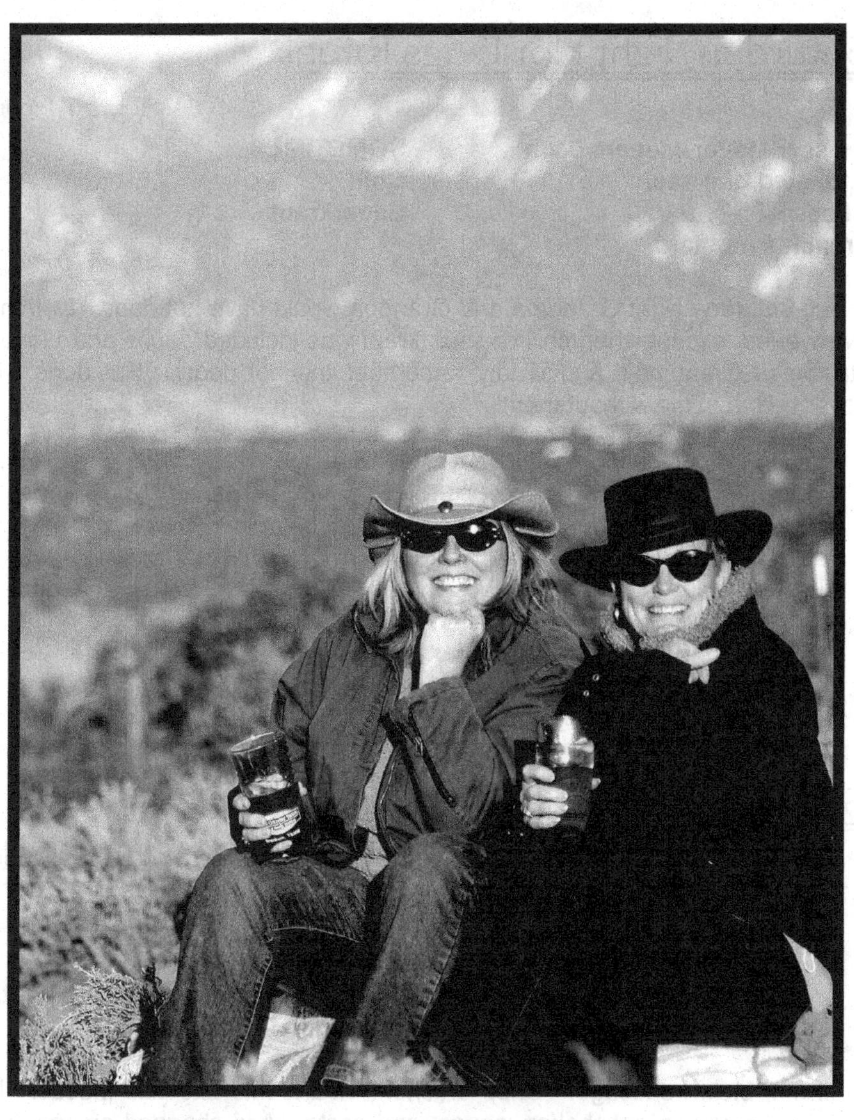

Rosemary and I contemplate the glorious view while sipping gin and tonics. Rosie declares, "Oh man, that was fun!" and decides she wants her ashes spread over the Rio Grande. Everyone is to sing *Shall We Gather at the River*. Then she adds, "Well, everyone but Verna can sing." Taos, New Mexico

Saturday Night Hot Dogs Ritual

As Told by Jennie

2 Oscar Meyer wieners each
1 toasted bun each
Cheese
French's mustard

<u>SOMETIMES</u>
Chili
Sauerkraut

Every Saturday night Grandma and Grandpa would have hot dogs. Nothing ever varied, except when chili or sauerkraut was included. Julie and I loved staying at Grandma's and vividly remember the hot dogs. Hot dogs will never be the same without them.

It must be a German thing, because I remember having hot dogs on Saturday night when growing up, too. Then, later in my life, my girls would sing, "Oh, I wish I were an Oscar Meyer Weiner, that is what I'd really like to be-e-ee." That makes me think about all the miles we clocked while looking for places that served hot dogs during our travels when the girls were small–ordering hot dogs with cheese only. After we iterated all the things not to include, one waiter asked if we wanted a bun with the hot dog. Memories, food, and family intertwine, weaving the fabric of our lives.

Sausage & Artichoke Casserole

Julie

1 can (8½ oz.) artichoke hearts, either plain or marinated
1 lb. Jimmy Dean pan sausage
1 jar (26 oz.) 4 cheeses spaghetti sauce

Onions, chopped
Bell peppers, chopped
2 c. Mozzarella cheese
2–4 c. cooked Penne Rigate pasta
Shredded Parmesan

In skillet, brown sausage. Chop artichoke hearts into bite-size pieces. In bowl mix sausage, artichokes, sauce, and pasta. Add chopped onions and bell peppers. Place half the mixture into Pyrex baking dish. Cover with half the cheese; add rest of mixture and cover with remaining cheese. Add shredded Parmesan to top if desired. Cover; bake at 375° for 20 minutes, until cheese is melted and pasta is warmed though. Can use Italian sausage or other varieties of spaghetti sauce.

"The noblest of all dogs is the hot-dog; it feeds the hand that bites it."
– Lawrence J. Peter.

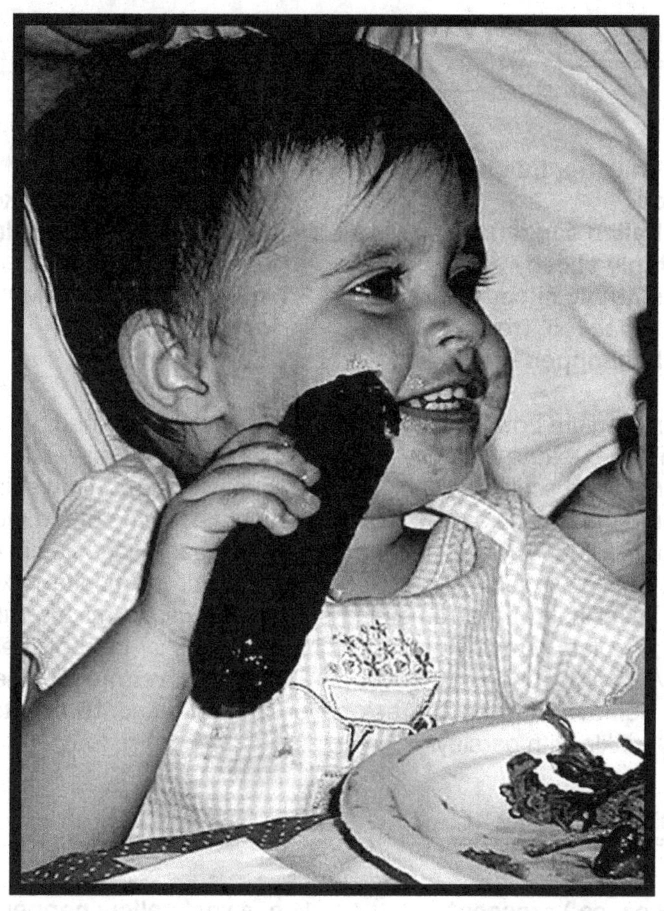

Speaking of German traditions, how about my granddaughter loving sausage? Must be an inherited trait.

"...there are more different sausages in Germany than there are breakfast foods in America, and if there is a bad one among them then I have never heard of it. They run in size from little fellows so small and pale and fragile that it seems a crime to eat them to vast and formidable pieces that look like shells for heavy artillery. And they run in flavor from the most delicate to the most raucous, and in texture from that of feathers caught in a cobweb to that of linoleum, and in shape from straight cylinders to lovely kinks and curlycues." – H.L. Mencken (1880-1956)

Skillet Lasagna

1 egg
1 lb. skim-milk ricotta cheese
2 T. olive oil
1 lb. bulk Italian sausage
1 onion, thinly sliced
2 scallions, thinly sliced
1 c. loosely packed, fresh spinach, chopped
4 c. tomato sauce
6–8 lasagna noodles, broken in half, uncooked
½ lb. skim-milk Mozzarella cheese, thinly sliced
2 T. minced fresh parsley for garnish

Beat egg in medium bowl. Stir in ricotta cheese until combined. In a 12-inch skillet with cover, sauté Italian sausage in olive oil until browned. Drain off fat. Add onion and scallions; cook with meat until tender. Stir in spinach until wilted. Stir in the tomato sauce. Remove about two-thirds of the meat sauce mixture from skillet. Arrange half the uncooked lasagna noodles in one layer over meat sauce remaining in skillet. Spread half the ricotta mixture over noodles. Layer half of the remaining sauce over ricotta mixture, then layer remaining noodles, remaining ricotta mixture, and final third of meat sauce. Top with Mozzarella cheese. Cover pan and cook over medium heat for 45 minutes. Remove from heat, crack cover, and let stand 15 minutes before serving. Sprinkle with parsley.

Veggie Ham Circle

2 tubes (8 oz. ea.) crescent dinner rolls
½ c. spreadable pineapple cream cheese
⅓ c. fully cooked ham, diced
¼ c. green pepper, finely chopped
¼ c. sweet yellow pepper, finely chopped
½ c. fresh broccoli florets, chopped
6 grape tomatoes, quartered
1 T. red onion, diced

Remove crescent dough from tubes; do not unroll. Cut each roll into eight slices. (Or use crescent rounds–16 rounds total) Arrange in an 11-inch circle on an ungreased 14-inch pizza pan. Bake at 375° for 15–20 minutes or until golden brown. Cool for 5 minutes before carefully removing to a serving platter; cool completely. Spread cream cheese over wreath; top with ham, peppers, broccoli, tomatoes, and onion. Store in the refrigerator.
Yield: 16 appetizers

NOTE: I love this dish because it looks like it is really time consuming and difficult to make, but it's easy. Place serving plates in the center of the wreath or fit a bowl filled with veggies or fruit into the center for a special look. Since all those veggies have to be cut, here's a few tips to make the job easier.

FOOD CUTTING TIPS

- ✦ *Always* use a cutting board when cutting foods. It's much more pleasant to have the knife cut the board than to have it cut your hand.
- ✦ A sharp knife is less likely to cause harm than a dull one. More force is needed when using a dull knife, increasing the chance of slipping and cutting yourself.
- ✦ Cutting on surfaces other than wooden, resin, or plastic boards will dull your knife–not to mention scar the surface of the countertop.
- ✦ Cut fruits and veggies before cutting meat, fish, poultry, eggs, pork, or cheese thus preventing *cross-contamination*. Meat products contain bacteria that can be transferred to other foods from the knife or cutting board used. Fruits and veggies are great hosts, allowing these bacteria to grow and multiply quickly. Result: food borne illness and/or food poisoning.
- ✦ Either use a separate knife and board, wash and dry board and knife throughly between foods, or just do like I said above, cut meats last.
- ✦ Follow these directions for cutting foods into specified pieces.
    - **Chopped**–cut into about ½-inch pieces, irregularly shaped.
    - **Cubed**–cut into even-sided pieces about ½-inch in size.
    - **Minced**–cut into irregularly shaped pieces ¼-inch or less in size.
    - **Diced**–cut into ¼-inch even-sided pieces.
- ✦ Remember cube and dice are perfect squares; chop and mince are randomly shaped pieces. Sorry, just can't get all that teacher out of me. There will be a pop test tomorrow!

"Food for thought is no substitute for the real thing." – Walt Kelly

Slow-Cooked Orange Pork Roast Tacos

1 med. onion, chopped
Pork loins, about 5 lb.
2 T. soy sauce
1 T. garlic, chopped
2 tsp. salt
1 tsp. black pepper, fresh ground
1 c. orange marmalade
20 corn tortillas

Place the onions in the bottom of a 5-quart slow cooker. Cut pork loins in half lengthwise and place in slow cooker. In a medium bowl stir together soy sauce, garlic, salt, pepper, and orange marmalade. Pour mixture over the pork. Cover and cook on low for 8 hours. Break meat with a fork and place in serving dish. Wrap the tortillas in damp towels, 10 to a towel and microwave on high for 30 seconds. Set out pork and tortillas with your favorite slaw and have guests assemble their own tacos.

NOTE: I like to use the Latin Slaw, page 81, for pulled pork tacos.

SEAFOOD

Citrus Scallops

1 lemon
1 lime
⅛ tsp. salt
⅛ tsp. black pepper, fresh ground
1¼ lb. sea scallops, rinsed
3 tsp. olive oil
1 T. shallot, finely chopped
1 tsp. Dijon mustard
1 bag baby greens (5 to 6 oz.)
¼ c. fresh parsley leaves, chopped

From lemon, zest ¼ teaspoon lemon peel and squeeze 2 tablespoons juice. From lime, zest ¼ teaspoon peel and squeeze 1 tablespoon juice. Set juices aside. In small bowl, combine zests, salt, and pepper. Place scallops on paper-towel-lined plate; pat dry. Sprinkle with citrus-peel mixture. In 12-inch nonstick skillet, heat 2 teaspoons oil on medium for 1 minute. Add scallops; cook 6–8 minutes or until opaque throughout, turning once. Remove from pan; cover to keep warm. To skillet, add 1 teaspoon oil and shallot; cook 3 minutes or until tender. Stir in Dijon mustard and citrus juices, scraping up browned bits; cook 1 minute. Toss sauce with greens; place on plates. Top with scallops and chopped parsley; serve with whole wheat couscous or brown rice.

After retirement, we finally got to head up the east coast for the Lobsterfest. It was the season for soft-shelled lobsters in Maine and we were able to crack them open with our hands. Our trip included a stay in Digby, Nova Scotia. Digby is known as the scallop capital of the world and their scallops were absolutely the most delicious, tender, and sweet ones I have ever eaten. The fresh mussels in Lunenburg and the Malpeque oysters we ate on Prince Edward Island were unforgettable. We enjoyed more fresh lobsters, clams, mussels, and oysters than the law should allow.

"Fish, to taste right, must swim three times–in water, in butter, and in wine." – Polish Proverb

Crab Cakes a la Rosemary

Rosemary

1 lb. lump crabmeat
1 egg
6 saltines, crushed or ⅓ c. coarse bread crumbs
2 tsp. lime zest
Salt & pepper
½ tsp. pepper
¼ c. mayonnaise
1 tsp. lime juice
½ c. flour
½ c. cornmeal
Red Sauce

Carefully sort through crabmeat, removing shell pieces that may be present. Being careful not to break the crabmeat up too much, combine all ingredients except flour and cornmeal. Shape into patties. Dredge in combined flour and cornmeal. Refrigerate 1 hour before frying. Handle carefully as these will be very soft and tend to fall apart. Fry in shallow oil, turning carefully. Serve with lemon or lime wedges and red sauce. Makes 6 generous patties about 2½ inches in diameter.

Our Red Sauce

1 c. ketchup
2–3 T. horseradish or more

IF DESIRED
Juice of ½ lemon
¼ tsp. garlic powder or 1 garlic clove, pressed
3–4 dashes Worcestershire sauce
Louisiana Hot Sauce

Combine ketchup and horseradish. Do not use horseradish sauce; it just does not turn out the same. *Warning:* Horseradish is very hot, so start with less and taste as more is added.

NOTE: Tired of crab cakes that were more like a hush puppy with a little bit of crab meat in it, Rosemary, Jennie, and I created this crab cake recipe several years ago while staying at the condo in Destin. We have perfected it several times and crab cakes this good are hard to find at a restaurant. Serve with our red sauce–we make it plain, but add some or all of the *if desired* ingredients to find a flavor that appeals to your taste. I like to be able to see the little white specks of horseradish in the mixture–good and hot.

Creole Sauce

Mom

2 c. celery, chopped
2 c. onions, chopped
1 c. bell pepper, chopped
2 T. flour
1 c. butter
2 No. 2 cans strained tomatoes (40 oz. in all)
3 tsp. salt
1 T. Tabasco
2 lg. cans tomato juice (46 oz. in all)
2 cans (4 oz. ea.) mushrooms, chopped
3 T. Worcestershire sauce

Sauté celery, onion, and bell pepper in butter; stir in flour and cook a few minutes. Add tomatoes and remaining ingredients. Cook about 3 hours, covered over low heat. Serve over hot rice. Serves 10.

NOTE: It's not really Creole until some protein is added. Add 2–3 pounds small, peeled, and deveined shrimp to the creole sauce and cook until shrimp turn pink. Serve immediately. Remember a No. 2 can holds 2½ cups. Try this sauce with crawfish tails–or maybe even alligator.

Spicy Shrimp Creole

1 Recipe Creole Sauce
1 T. Tabasco sauce
1 T. Worcestershire sauce
Juice of 1 lemon
1½ tsp. crushed red pepper
2–3 lb. shrimp, peeled & deveined

Add these additional ingredients to creole sauce. I've found that the older and wiser I become, the more toward hot and spicy my taste leans. The lemon juice cuts the tomato flavor a little.

"Anyway, like I was sayin', shrimp is the fruit of the sea. You can barbecue it, boil it, broil it, bake it, sauté it. Dey's uh, shrimp-kabobs, shrimp creole, shrimp gumbo. Pan fried, deep fried, stir-fried. There's pineapple shrimp, lemon shrimp, coconut shrimp, pepper shrimp, shrimp soup, shrimp stew, shrimp salad, shrimp and potatoes, shrimp burger, shrimp sandwich. That–that's about it." – Bubba in the movie Forrest Gump

Fish Tacos

Jennie

1 lb. tilapia fillets
Pepper
Garlic powder
Tony Chacere's
Olive oil
Juice and zest of 1 lime

Flour or corn tortillas
Red and green cabbage, slivered
Fresh cilantro, chopped
1–2 fresh avocados, chopped
Thirds Creamy Jalapeño Dip
Fresh jalapeño slices

Season fillets with pepper, garlic powder, and Tony's; place on foil-lined baking sheet. Drizzle with olive oil; squeeze on lime juice. Broil 15–20 minutes, checking often. Remove and break apart with fork; toss in lime zest and top with additional zest and juice. Warm tortillas and place accompaniments on serving platter. Everyone makes their tacos, topping with Thirds Creamy Jalapeño Dip from appetizer section, page 38.

Fried Shrimp

12–18 fresh extra-large/jumbo shrimp per person
Crushed red pepper
1 recipe Beer Batter for Frying
Vegetable oil

Cocktail sauce
Tartar sauce
Ketchup
Lemon wedges

Peel and devein shrimp, leaving tails intact. Place in a colander and layer with ice cubes and sprinkles of red pepper; top with ice to keep cool until deep fryer is ready. Prepare Beer Batter for Frying, page 317. Fill fryer or deep skillet to fill line or a minimum of 3 inches of oil; heat to 375° and maintain this temperature throughout. Holding shrimp by tails, dip into batter; drop into hot grease one at a time until the surface of oil is full of shrimp, 8–12 depending on the size of your fryer. Shrimp are done when they float. Dip out with slotted spoon and place on layers of paper towel in a 9 x 13 x 2-inch cake pan; drop next batch of shrimp. While it is frying, transfer cooked shrimp to a warmed dish, using additional paper towels to separate shrimp. Keep in warmed oven because there are lots more to fry and no one wants cold shrimp–this also hides them so there are some left for dinner. Serve with French fries, cocktail sauce, tartar sauce, ketchup, and lemon wedges.

When the girls were growing up, we had fried shrimp often. We even owned our own shrimp trawl, and upon occasion hauled in enough to make it worth the trip to the coast–it was really more fun than profitable. I would freeze batches of 12 shrimp per person. We actually counted tails to make sure we each got our fair share. It was such fun–I swear, I still think sometimes the girls would eat the tails to try to wrangle a few more shrimp from their Dad and me!

Rockin' Salmon with Dill Cream Sauce

Debbie

1 fresh salmon fillet, about 2 lb.
¼ c. sour cream
2 T. heavy cream
¼ c. Dijon mustard
2 T. honey
3 T. fresh dill, minced
2 T. fresh lemon juice (about 1 lemon)
1 tsp. capers, drained

Preheat oven to 400° or heat grill to high. In a saucepan, combine sour cream, honey, cream, mustard, lemon juice, and fresh dill. Heat on low. Sprinkle salmon with salt and pepper and cook in oven or grill for 15–20 minutes. Remove salmon and top with dill sauce and capers.

Salmon Patties

Debbie

16 oz. can pink salmon
½ c. flour
1 egg
1½ tsp. baking powder
⅓ c. onion, chopped
1½ c. cooking oil

Drain salmon, keeping 2 T. of the liquid. Mix salmon, egg, and onion in mixing bowl until mixture is sticky. Stir in flour. Add baking powder to the reserved liquid. Stir into salmon mixture. Form into small patties, using hands. Place oil in large skillet. Fry patties over medium heat for 5 minutes. Turn patties once while frying. Place patties on several layers of paper towel to drain.

NOTE: Debbie says when you forget to thaw out meat, try this. Her boys loved them and I remember Mama used to made salmon croquettes shaped like patties when we were growing up. Today it's an inexpensive meal and delicious, too. The onions may tend to burn before the salmon patty is done, so cook over medium to low heat.

VARIATION: Omit flour and baking powder. Add crumbled crackers, fresh-cracked pepper, Tony's, and garlic powder to taste. Coat shaped patties with bread crumbs before frying. While cooking squeeze lime juice over patties. Serve topped with lime zest. This is Jennie's adaptation.

NOTE: Take either of these salmon patties uptown by serving with the Dill Cream Sauce, page 205. It's like wearing stilettos with old, worn jeans!

Sassy & I Do Mean SASSY Shrimp

2 lb. shrimp, peeled and deveined
1 c. fresh pineapple, chopped
½ c. Canyon Foods Sweet Chili Lime Sauce
3 T. garlic, minced
1 T. southwest rub
2 T. extra virgin olive oil
¼ c. cilantro, chopped
1 c. rice, cooked

Heat large skillet over medium-high heat for 3 minutes. In large bowl combine shrimp, garlic, seasoning, and 1 tablespoon oil. Toss well. Pour remaining oil into skillet. Tilt to cover evenly. Add shrimp mixture to skillet and cook for 2–3 minutes. Add pineapple and cook 1–2 minutes more. Add chili lime sauce; mix well and heat through. Garnish with cilantro and serve with cooked rice.

NOTE: Substitute any brand of chili lime sauce or make your own.

Shrimp Scampi

Debbie

1 lb. uncooked shrimp, peeled and deveined
½ c. margarine or butter
¼ c. fresh parsley, finely chopped
¼ c. onion, finely chopped
1 T. lemon juice
1 T. garlic, minced
Salt to taste
Louisiana Hot Sauce or ground cayenne pepper to taste
Onion Rice

Over medium-high heat in a medium-sized frying pan, melt the margarine. Add the parsley and onions and sauté until the onions are tender. Add the lemon juice and garlic; stir and continue to sauté about another 5 minutes. Add the shrimp, salt, and hot sauce and stir to mix well. Sauté until the shrimp are opaque and turn pink, about 5 minutes; do not overcook. Serve over onion rice. Yield: 2–4 servings

Onion Rice

2 c. rice
1 can Campbell's onion soup
1 can water
½ c. margarine
1 tsp. salt

Place rice in 2-quart Corning dish. Add soup, water, and salt; set margarine on top of rice. Cover dish and bake in oven 1 hour at 375°. Stir when done.

Shrimp & Pasta Stir Fry

Debbie

1¼ lb. lg. shrimp, peeled & deveined
2 tsp. Creole seasoning
1 lb. linguini or other favorite pasta, cooked
1 T. garlic, minced
¼ c. green onion, tops only, chopped
2 T. fresh parsley leaves, chopped
½ c. dry white wine
¼ c. fresh lemon juice
1 tsp. lemon zest
2 tsp. olive oil
4 T. unsalted butter, divided
½ tsp. salt
⅛ tsp. black pepper, freshly ground
1 tsp. red pepper flakes, crushed

Toss the shrimp in a medium bowl with the Creole seasoning; set aside. Cook the pasta per package directions. Prepare garlic, green onions, and parsley; do not combine. In a mixing cup, combine the wine, lemon juice, and lemon zest; set aside. When pasta is done, place the olive oil and 2 tablespoons butter in large 14-inch skillet over high heat. Add the shrimp to the pan, spreading them evenly in 1 layer. Cook for 2 minutes then turn them over. Add the garlic to the pan and cook for 30 seconds. Add the wine mixture and remaining 2 tablespoons butter; cook for 1½ minutes. Season shrimp mixture with the salt and pepper. Add the pasta, crushed red pepper flakes, and green onions, tossing to coat well. Remove the skillet from the heat; add the parsley and toss to combine. Serve hot.

NOTE: Debbie adds, "This recipe will feed 4–6. The secret to making this easy is reading the entire recipe before starting. It is especially easy if you buy ready to cook shrimp and use rice noodles. This is my favorite "spicy" stir fry recipe. Try experimenting by adding broccoli crowns and red pepper strips or substituting cooked chicken for the shrimp."

Shrimp Boil

4–5 lb. med. size fresh gulf shrimp, heads off
1 pkg. Zatarain's shrimp boil
Sm. red potatoes
Corn on the cob, 3 in. pieces
2 onions, quartered
Red Sauce
Lemon wedges
Butter

Bring at least 1 gallon of water to boil in a big pot. (Use pasta pot with draining insert if large enough.) While it is heating, figure out how many potatoes and pieces of corn are needed for your crowd. Add shrimp boil package, potatoes, corn, and onions. Cook until potatoes are just about done, then add shrimp. Bring to a boil and cook until shrimp turn pink, about 3–4 minutes. Drain and serve with butter, red sauce, page 202, and lemon wedges.

NOTE: The shrimp boil package can be used intact or cut open allowing spices to get mixed up with food–it's a personal preference. This is a vacationing on the coast standard meal for us. We always boil enough shrimp to have leftovers for shrimp salad the next day. When on the coast, eat food from the local waters. It's a requirement!

Spicy Garlic Shrimp Scampi

Jennie

1 lb. shrimp (peeled & tails removed)
2–3 cloves fresh garlic
1 white onion
Olive oil
Basil pesto (found in grocery stores–I prefer Bertolli from the cold section)
Lime juice and zest
Pepper
Tony Chacere's
French bread, Texas toast, or linguine
Parmesan cheese, fresh grated

Chop white onion and mince garlic. Heat sauté pan and add olive oil to barely coat the bottom. Add onion and garlic; sauté until translucent. Add fresh cracked pepper and Tony Chacere's liberally to the onion and garlic mixture as it begins to sauté. Zest the lime and cut in half; squeeze in lime juice from one half and add a bit of lime zest. Add two tablespoons of basil pesto. Let this meld together for about a minute. Add the shrimp, placing evenly in the pan so one side of the shrimp can cook. Squeeze the other half of the lime over the shrimp and add more lime zest to it. Sprinkle with pepper and more Tony's. At this point the mixture should smell delicious.

Make sure not to overcook the shrimp–as soon as they begin to turn color, flip them. Turn the shrimp and add two more tablespoons of pesto with another squeeze of lime. (Depending on how the scampi is served, more pesto can be added.) When the other side of the shrimp is done remove from the heat. Serve over cooked linguine, combined with additional olive oil and basil pesto, or my personal favorite–pour over garlic-buttered French bread or Texas toast. Top with fresh-grated Parmesan cheese.

NOTE: From Jennie, "This is one of the quickest meals you can make–less than ten minutes for a variety of serving options. Here are my favorite choices. Choose one or try them all."

- Nice served with crisp, steamed broccoli and topped with fresh Parmesan cheese to add in a veggie and some color.
- For lunch, make a French bread sub instead of an open face bread, and serve with a broccoli slaw or fruit salad.
- To make a cream sauce, prepare exactly as described above, but remove just the shrimp when they are cooked and add some heavy whipping cream, fresh grated Parmesan cheese, and a handful of Ricotta cheese to the basil pesto, lime, onion, garlic mixture. Heat cream, scrapping all the dredges from the bottom of the pan and simmer until heated throughout and bubbles appear. Pour this over cooked noodles or toasted French bread, and top with the shrimp–adding a bit of Parmesan on top for show and flavor.

This recipe gives a glimpse into the complexity of my youngest child. She, like most members of our family, is an overachiever. Her attention to detail, no doubt, is responsible for her success in the corporate world.

Do you get the picture that we all love shrimp? Thank goodness we live near the coast. We could give Forrest a run for his money!

"Bubba's momma cooked shrimp. And her momma before her cooked shrimp, and her momma before her momma cooked shrimp, too. Bubba's family knew everything there was to know about the shrimpin' business."
– Forrest from the movie Forrest Gump

Stuffed Crabs

1 lb. white crabmeat
4 stale hamburger buns or 6 slices stale bread
3 eggs
1 c. evaporated milk
½ c. margarine
1 c. onions, chopped
½ c. celery, chopped
½ c. bell pepper, chopped
2 cloves garlic, minced
½ c. green onion tops, chopped
½ c. parsley, chopped
Salt, black pepper, & cayenne to taste
½ tsp. Worcestershire sauce
Bread crumbs

Pick through crabmeat for shells. Crumble bread and soak in beaten eggs and milk. Sauté onions, celery, garlic, and chopped bell pepper in a heavy pot in the margarine until wilted. Add Worcestershire sauce and crabmeat; season to taste with salt, red pepper, and black pepper. Cook over medium heat about 15 minutes, stirring constantly. Add onion tops and parsley. Then add soaked buns. Mix well. Stuff crab shells with mixture or bake in shallow ramekins (greased). Sprinkle tops of stuffed crabs with bread crumbs and bake in 375° oven for 10 minutes or until well browned. Stuffs 12 crab shells.

Stuffed Red Snapper

1½ c. onions, chopped
½ c. celery, chopped
½ c. margarine
½ tsp. sugar
1 tsp. salt
½ tsp. cayenne (red pepper)
½ c. bread crumbs
¼ tsp. black pepper
4 lb. red snapper fillets
1 lb. shrimp, peeled & deveined
3 stale hamburger buns
4 eggs, beaten
1 heaping T. all purpose flour

Boil shrimp until barely pink, drain water, cool, and chop them–not too fine. Dice one pound of fillet of red snapper and set aside. Wilt onions and celery in margarine. Add sugar, black pepper, and salt. Add diced red snapper to wilted onions. Cook for 5 minutes. Put buns and eggs in bowl; mix well and add flour and bread crumbs. When well mixed, add shrimp and diced red snapper and onion mixture. Stir well. Butterfly large fillets and stuff; season and butter each side of them; broil in oven, 4–6 inches from heat source, 10 minutes to each side. For small fillets, place a layer in 9 x 13 x 2-inch buttered baking dish, cover with stuffing and top with another layer of fillets. Butter top of fillets. Bake in 450° oven for 35–40 minutes or till done. Serve piping hot with drawn butter or garlic butter. Yield: 6 large servings

NOTE: I have prepared this with whole red snapper, and it is delicious. Allow longer cooking time and bake at 350° instead of broiling. Only thing was, I had to place a slice of lemon over the poor guy's eye. I just couldn't look him in the eye and eat him, too.

Shrimp Stuffed Mushrooms

My daughter, Jennie, uses the stuffing part of this recipe for stuffed mushrooms. She just adds the shrimp and no fish to make it simpler. Clean mushrooms; remove stems. Chop and combine stems with stuffing; fill mushrooms and bake at 350° until stuffing is firm and brown, about 15 minutes. Serve immediately.

Tilapia with Broccoli-Quinoa Pilaf

3 tsp. olive oil
½ sm. onion, chopped
¾ tsp. salt
¼ tsp. pepper
1 c. quinoa, rinsed well
1½ c. water
2 c. broccoli, chopped
¼ c. raisins
½ c. toasted almonds, coarsely chopped or sliced
2 scallions, sliced
4 pieces (6 oz. ea.) tilapia, skinless cod or striped bass fillet
½ tsp. paprika
Kosher salt & pepper

Heat 1 teaspoon of the oil in a medium saucepan over medium-high heat. Add the onion, salt, and pepper. Cook, stirring occasionally, until softened and starting to brown, 3–4 minutes. Add the quinoa and water and bring to a boil; reduce heat to low, cover, and simmer gently until almost all the water has evaporated, 10–12 minutes. Fold in the broccoli and raisins, cover and cook until the quinoa and broccoli are tender, 8–10 minutes more. Remove from heat and fold in the almonds and scallions. While the broccoli is cooking, heat the remaining 2 teaspoons of oil in a large nonstick skillet over medium-high heat. Season the fish with the paprika, salt, and pepper. Cook until opaque throughout, 3–4 minutes per side. Serve with the pilaf.

NOTE: I never knew quinoa existed until I developed an allergy to wheat, corn, oats, barley, rye, and much more. I had to go in search of something else to eat. Quinoa is really quite tasty. I especially like the Red Inca variety. Tilapia is a very popular fish–very economical and tasty without a fishy odor or flavor.

Tuna Casserole

8 oz. macaroni or noodles
1 can (5 oz.) Starkist tuna, water-packed, drained
1 can cream of mushroom soup
1½ c. Velveeta cheese, cubed
¼ tsp. garlic powder
Salt & pepper to taste
1 can baby green peas, drained

Cook pasta according to package instructions until almost done. Drain. Stir in remaining ingredients and heat until bubbly. Sit on the couch and veg out. If it's a badly needed veg-time, leave the peas out.

"I refuse to believe that trading recipes is silly. Tuna fish casserole is at least as real as corporate stock." – Barbara Grizzuti Harrison

QUICK BREADS

QUICK BREAD GUIDELINES

- ✦ Quick breads are fast to prepare, using baking powder or baking soda for the leavening agent. Stir together quickly as over-stirring will cause tunnels, a wet texture, a peaked top, and toughness.
- ✦ When the recipe calls for *sifted flour*, that means to sift and then measure. When it calls for *flour, sifted*, measure the flour and then sift it, using the entire amount. The difference between "1 cup flour" and "1 cup flour, sifted" is about 2 tablespoons. So, it really does make a difference when baking. If a recipe calls for just *flour*, that means to measure without sifting.
- ✦ Sifting adds air and helps produce a lighter texture in baked products.
- ✦ All purpose flour is used unless specified otherwise.
- ✦ Shortening is a solid fat and will perform differently than oil in a recipe. When shortening is melted, it becomes a liquid. Then, when it cools, it turns back into a solid. Because of this property, shortening affects the texture of the finished product. Shortening and oil are usually not interchangeable in a recipe.
- ✦ This brings up the subject of margarines: do not use reduced-fat margarines or vegetable oil spreads when baking. They have more liquid and less solid fat, so your recipe will not turn out right. Once Julie was baking chocolate chip cookies and mistakenly used reduced-fat margarine; they ran all over the pan. With all the hoopla about fats, I just use butter—an all-natural ingredient with great flavor. I make sure I grab the unsalted package.

Quick Bread Guidelines, continued

- ✦ Flour contains gluten which forms the structure of the baked product. Mixing, stirring, kneading–any handling of the dough–develops the gluten. Quick breads are handled just enough to begin the development of gluten so they remain soft and tender.
- ✦ The gluten must harden to hold the shape of the risen product. Thus, bake according to instructions, being careful not to knock out air while baking and allow to cool according to instructions for best results.
- ✦ When using the oven for baking quick breads, yeast breads, cakes, etc., be sure to *preheat* to the desired temperature. Quick breads rise two times: once when the baking powder comes in contact with liquid and again when it gets hot. That's why it's called double-acting baking powder. (Maybe you have noticed that pancake batter starts rising in the bowl–that is the first action of the baking powder triggered by moisture.) Have ingredients and baking pans ready; combine quickly, stirring only enough to moisten dry ingredients, and get in the oven immediately.
- ✦ Baking soda requires the addition of acid such as buttermilk, chocolate, or lemon juice to make a product rise.
- ✦ The *muffin method* of mixing involves mixing the dry ingredients in one bowl and making a well in the center. Then mix the liquid ingredients in another bowl and pour all at once into the well in the dry ingredients bowl. Stir around the bowl just until moistened. Batter should be lumpy.
- ✦ When baking muffins, if there is not enough batter to fill all the muffin cups, place about ½ inch of water in the empty ones to prevent burning the pan and insure even baking.
- ✦ The *biscuit method* involves cutting the solid fat into the dry ingredients and then adding the combined liquid ingredients. This creates delicate layers in the finished product much the same as in pastry-making, which uses the same technique. Again, do not over-handle.

Banana Bread

⅓ c. cooking oil
1 c. sugar
1½ c. ripe bananas, crushed
3 eggs, well beaten
½ tsp. vanilla
2⅓ c. baking mix
1 c. nuts, chopped

Preheat oven to 350°. Grease the bottom of a 9 x 5 x 3-inch loaf pan. Place all ingredients in pan and stir with fork until moistened; still using fork, beat vigorously for 1 minute. Bake 55 minutes to 1 hour until a toothpick inserted in the center comes out clean. Cool in pan for 5 minutes. Loosen sides of pan, remove, and cool on wire rack.

HOW TO PEEL A BANANA

My former teacher, dear friend, and neighbor Evelyn, told me a little while back that she just learned how to peel a banana properly. She was struggling to peel a particularly tough banana when one her coworkers in the lunchroom of her elementary school said, "Eat a banana like a monkey does–that is peel it from the bottom. It opens easily and all those stringy things hang on to the banana peeling." I tried this and discovered an added benefit: the stem end of the banana serves as a handle. Evelyn quietly retired this year after 54 years of teaching. Just think of the countless number of lives she has touched. I can attest to the positive influence she had on mine. Evelyn recently told me, "I just realized I have spent all but 8 years of my life in a classroom of one kind or another." That's dedication! By the way, Evelyn says people ask her, "After that many years of teaching, how have you kept your sanity?" She just looks at them with her beautiful smile and replies, "Who says I have?"

Banana-Nut Pumpkin Bread

Julie

¾ c. butter, softened
1 pkg. cream cheese, softened
2 c. sugar
2 eggs
2 mashed bananas
¾ c. canned pumpkin (bananas & pumpkin should total 1½ c.)
½ tsp. vanilla
3 c. all purpose flour
½ tsp. baking powder
½ tsp. baking soda
½ tsp. salt
2 c. chopped pecans, divided & toasted

ORANGE GLAZE

1 c. powdered sugar
3 T. minus 1½ tsp. orange juice
1 tsp. orange extract
½ tsp. vanilla

In large mixing bowl, cream the butter, cream cheese, and sugar until light and fluffy. Add eggs, one at a time, beating well after each addition. Add bananas, pumpkin, and vanilla; mix well. Combine the flour, baking powder, baking soda, and salt; add to creamed mixture. Fold in 1 cup pecans. Transfer to two greased 8 x 4 x 2-inch loaf pans. Sprinkle with remaining pecans. Bake at 350° for 1–1¼ hours. In a small bowl, whisk the glaze ingredients and pour over the loaves. Cool for 10 minutes before removing from the pans.

Belgium Waffles

2 c. baking mix
1 c. milk
2 T. oil
2 eggs, separated

Beat egg whites to soft peaks. Blend baking mix, milk, oil, and egg yolks together. Fold in egg whites. Use ½ cup mix per waffle, or enough to fill the center two-thirds of waffle iron.

Blintz Bubble Ring or Fancy Monkey Bread

2 pkg. (3 oz.) cream cheese
2 pkg. refrigerated biscuits
½ c. sugar
1 tsp. ground cinnamon
3 T. butter or margarine, melted
⅓ c. pecans, chopped

Cut cream cheese into 20 pieces; roll into balls. Roll each biscuit into a 3-inch diameter circle. Combine sugar and cinnamon. Place one cheese ball and 1 teaspoon cinnamon mixture in each biscuit; pinch to seal. Pour melted butter or margarine into bottom of a 5-cup ring mold. Sprinkle half the nuts and half the remaining sugar mixture into the mold. Place half the rolls on top of mixture, seam side up. Repeat layers. Bake in 375° oven for 20 minutes, until browned. Cool 5 minutes in pan; invert onto serving plate.

NOTE: Don't have a 5-cup ring mold? Use a tube cake pan or a bundt pan. However, don't use an angel food cake pan. The melted butter and sugar will run out of the bottom making a terrible mess in the oven.

"As for butter versus margarine, I trust cows more than chemists."
– Joan Gussow

Biscuits

Classroom Standard

2 c. sifted all purpose flour
3 tsp. baking powder
⅓ c. shortening
1 tsp. salt
¾–⅞ c. milk

Sift four, measure, and sift again with baking powder and salt. Cut or rub in shortening until the mixture resembles coarse meal. Add enough milk to make a soft dough that can be handled. Turn dough onto a lightly floured surface, sprinkle with a little flour and knead lightly about 30 seconds. Roll or pat out to ½-inch thickness, fold in half and roll out again to ½-inch thickness. (For thin crisp biscuits, roll ¼-inch thick.) Cut with floured cutter and place on an ungreased shallow baking pan. If crisp sides are desired, place biscuits 1-inch apart; if soft sides are preferred let the biscuits touch. Bake in a very hot oven (450–475°) for 10–12 minutes or until golden brown. Yield: 14 two-inch biscuits

Cheddar Biscuits

2½ c. baking mix
¾ c. cold milk
4 T. cold butter
¼ tsp. garlic powder
1 c. Cheddar cheese, grated

BRUSH ON TOP
2 T. butter, melted
¼ tsp. parsley flakes
½ tsp. garlic powder
Pinch salt

Preheat oven to 400°. Combine baking mix with cold butter in a medium bowl using a pastry blender. There should be small chunks of butter about the size of peas in the mixture. Add cheese, milk, and ¼ teaspoon garlic powder. Mix until combined using a wooden spoon or use your hands. Do not over mix. Drop one-fourth cup portions of dough onto an ungreased cookie sheet using an ice cream scoop. Bake 15–17 minutes or until the tops of the biscuits begin to turn light brown. Combine melted butter, parsley flakes, garlic powder, and salt; brush over tops of biscuits using a pastry brush when biscuits are done. Yield: 1 dozen biscuits

Peyton loves spending the night and we always make pancakes on Saturday morning. He and Grampa Gary have developed their own *best practices* for making them. Peyton says, "Even tough guys with scars can cook."

MAKING PANCAKES

Pancakes are cakes made in a pan and they are supposed to be light and fluffy. Many of my students would flip their pancakes and then mash them down. Mashing pancakes down makes them tough and rubbery. Pancakes are ready to flip when the bubbles that have formed on the surface start to break. After flipping, cook a couple of minutes longer, turning only once.

Buttermilk Pancakes

Donna's Granny

2 c. sifted all purpose flour
1 tsp. soda
2 tsp. baking powder
1 tsp. salt
2 eggs
2 c. buttermilk
2 T. butter, melted

Sift dry ingredients together. Stir into milk and eggs; add butter. Beat until smooth. Drop from spoon onto hot griddle, 375°. Cook on one side 2 minutes, turn over, and bake about 2 minutes longer.

NOTE: Donna reminisces: "Granny has this recipe marked 'Best.' She always made these for us at the beach house in Galveston. Grandaddy fried bacon and Granny made pancakes, usually in an iron skillet."

Cheese-Nut Bread

3¾ c. baking mix
1½ c. Cheddar cheese, shredded
½ c. pecans, chopped & toasted
1 egg
1 can (12 oz.) evaporated milk

Combine the baking mix, cheese, and pecans in a mixing bowl; make a well in the center. Beat egg and combine with milk; pour into cheese mixture and stir just until all is moistened. Spoon into 12 well-greased muffin cups filling each two-thirds full. Bake in a 375° oven for 12–15 minutes.

Cornbread or Muffins

1 c. cornmeal
1 c. sifted flour
¼ c. sugar
4 tsp. baking powder
½ tsp. salt
1 egg
1 c. milk
¼ c. shortening, melted

Place iron skillet with 1 tablespoon oil or shortening into preheating oven. Combine dry ingredients in a large mixing bowl. Beat egg and combine with milk and shortening. Make a well in the flour mixture and pour in the egg mixture. Stir just until the flour disappears. Pour into hot, greased iron skillet or muffin tins. Bake at 425° for 20–25 minutes.

NOTE: If preparing cornbread for dressing, omit the sugar.

Crunchy Bread Twists

School Dinner Recipe

1 egg, beaten
¼ c. Green Goddess Salad Dressing
½ c. Parmesan cheese, grated
2 c. herb-seasoned stuffing mix, coarsely crushed
1 pkg. refrigerator crescent rolls

Combine egg and salad dressing in a small bowl. Combine stuffing mix and cheese in a shallow dish or on waxed paper. Unroll crescent rolls; separate into 4 rectangles, sealing diagonal perforations. Flatten slightly with rolling pin. Cut each rectangle lengthwise into four 1-inch wide strips. Dip each strip into egg mixture; roll in cheese mixture, coating well. Twist each strip several times and place on ungreased cookie sheet about 1-inch apart. Bake in preheated 375° oven for 15 minutes or until golden brown. Serve warm. Yield: 16 twists

Grandmother Craig's Buttermilk Biscuits

From A Tattered Newspaper Clipping Grandmother Gave Me

2 c. all purpose flour
1 T. baking powder
¼ tsp. soda
½ tsp. salt
⅓ c. butter (or use ½ butter plus ½ shortening to equal ⅓ c.)
¾ to 1 c. buttermilk

Mix flour, baking powder, soda, and salt in a bowl. Cut in butter with a fork or 2 knives until mixture is crumbly. Stir in ¾ cup buttermilk all at once. Add more buttermilk if needed to make a soft dough. Knead dough gently about 10 times on a lightly floured surface. Pat or roll ½-inch thick. Cut dough with 2-inch cutter. Place biscuits in iron skillet; brush tops with a little buttermilk. Place over hot coals. Cover and put coals on lid. Cook about 15 minutes. Yield: 12 biscuits

Grandmother Craig could make the most delicious biscuits. We drove to Missouri to visit family at least twice a year and the girls and I watched and learned to make biscuits just like hers. Grandmother fried bacon and eggs for everyone while we rolled and cut biscuits. Her original recipe was cut from a newspaper and yellowed with age. I have it framed and displayed with my antique cooking collection. For today's modern oven, place in a baking pan that has been brushed with bacon fat and bake at 450° for 10–12 minutes. I think I remember brushing the tops with bacon fat, too, instead of the buttermilk. Place the biscuits close together.

OVEN TEMPERATURES

Grandmother Craig's Buttermilk Biscuit recipe certainly explains why this chart of oven temperatures might be useful. Those recipes of long ago simply used words for baking temperatures, but I'm pretty sure the pioneer woman knew just how bright the coals were burning or how close they could put their hand to the surface for each of these descriptions.

Very slow oven	250°–275°
Slow oven	300°–325°
Moderate oven	350°–375°
Hot oven	400°–425°
Very hot oven	450°–475°
Extremely hot oven	500°–525°

As the chart shows, oven temperature is a range of degrees. Today's modern oven cycles on when it is 10–15° below the set temperature and it cycles off when it is 10–15° above the set temperature. Remember that opening the oven door while baking dramatically lowers the baking temperature and will affect the outcome of baked goods as well as the cooking time required.

Monkey Bread

½ c. sugar
2 tsp. cinnamon
3 tubes biscuits
1 c. sugar
1½ tsp. cinnamon
½ c. butter, melted

Cut each biscuit into 4 pieces. Mix ½ cup sugar and 2 teaspoons cinnamon in a bag. Add some of the biscuit pieces and shake until coated. Arrange the pieces in a well greased bundt pan. Continue coating and arranging biscuit pieces until all are done. Mix the remaining 1 cup sugar and 1½ teaspoons cinnamon with the melted butter and pour over the biscuits. Bake in a 350° oven for 40 minutes.

Muffins

From My High School Homemaking Class

2 c. sifted all purpose flour
3 tsp. baking powder
¾ tsp. salt
2 T. sugar
1 egg
1 c. milk
¼ c. shortening, melted
Table fat

Light oven and set at 425°. Place dot of table fat in each muffin cup; melt fat in oven and remove. Sift flour, baking power, salt, and sugar together twice in a large bowl. Beat egg until thick; add milk and shortening; blend with rotary beater. Make a well in flour mixture; add egg mixture all at once, stirring quickly until flour mixture is just moistened. Push batter into muffin pans or cups quickly. Bake muffins for 20 minutes or until light brown. Yield: 12 muffins

The age of this recipe is revealed by the instruction, light oven, and by the term table fat. In times past, everyone kept a grease can by the stove and recycled the fat from frying bacon–actually all the fat left after frying foods except fish. This fat was then reused. Our can was state of the art as it had a straining tray to catch bits of fried food. Look at the differences between the Muffins from my homemaking class and Mrs. Craig's Muffins to see how food preparation has changed over the years. One of my goals as a home economics teacher was for the students to gain as much knowledge and practical experience as possible. I emphasized planning, following instructions, and evaluation. We searched out recipes that fit within our time frame, pouring over cookbooks and adapting procedures to save time.

Mrs. Craig's Muffins

Classroom Standard

1 egg
¾ c. milk
⅓ c. cooking oil
1¾ c. all purpose flour
¼ c. sugar
2½ tsp. baking powder
¾ tsp. salt

Beat egg; add milk and oil. Beat until combined. Mix dry ingredients in large bowl. Make a well in the center. Add egg mixture and stir around the bowl just until moist. Mixture should be lumpy. Fill greased muffin tins two-thirds full. Bake at 400° for 20–25 minutes until golden brown.

Norman's Cornbread

Grandpa Norman

2 T. shortening or bacon fat
1 c. cornmeal
½ c. flour
3 tsp. baking powder
2 eggs
1 c. milk

Place the shortening or bacon fat in an iron skillet and heat in oven. Meanwhile mix remaining ingredients well and pour into the heated skillet with the fat. Bake at 350° for 30 minutes.

NOTE: Men have a way of just getting things done, don't they? Grandpa Norman also baked fresh bread in a bread machine. He made it from scratch, but we have not been able to locate his recipes. Jennie says it was "sooo good!"

Popovers

2 eggs
1 c. milk
1 c. sifted all purpose flour
½ tsp. salt
1 T. salad oil

Place eggs in mixing bowl; add milk, flour, and salt. Beat 1½ minutes with rotary or electric beater. Add salad oil; beat ½ minute longer. (Do not over-beat.) Fill 6–8 well-greased custard cups one-half full. Bake at 475° for 15 minutes. Reduce heat to 350°; continue baking about 25–30 minutes, until popovers are browned and firm. A few minutes before removing from oven, prick each popover with a fork to allow steam to escape. For popovers that are dry inside, turn off oven and leave popovers there for 30 minutes with door ajar. Split and fill with creamed ham, chicken, or seafood. Yield: 6–8 popovers

"Never eat more than you can lift." – Miss Piggy

Yummy Breakfast Rolls

Marilyn

2 cans crescent rolls
16 oz. cream cheese, softened
1 tsp. vanilla
1¼ c. sugar, divided
1 tsp. cinnamon
½ c. margarine, melted

Unroll one can of the rolls into the bottom of a 9 x 13 x 2-inch pan. Do not press the seams together. Mix cheese with 1 cup sugar and vanilla. Spread over rolls. Place second can of rolls over top (separated same as the bottom layer). Pour melted margarine on top. Sprinkle with mixture of remaining ¼ cup sugar and cinnamon. Bake for 30 minutes at 350° degrees.

I can just smell this baking; it reminds me of a cream cheese kolache, only it's a lot simpler to make. Marilyn gave me this recipe when I started my home party business and needed brunch ideas.

YEAST BREADS

TIPS FOR MAKING YEAST BREADS

- Yeast is a living microorganism and must have the proper temperature, moisture, food, and growth regulation to grow and produce the carbon dioxide that causes bread to rise.
- Measure the liquid's temperature with a thermometer to insure accuracy: Too hot and the yeast will die; too cool and it will grow slowly–neither producing the desired outcome.
- Sugar provides the food for yeast to grow. Do not use sugar substitutes.
- Salt regulates the rate at which yeast grows. Decreasing the salt a bit in a recipe might work, but salt must be included in the yeast bread recipe for it to rise properly.
- Yeast dough will absorb all the flour that is added. Measure all the flour first; then follow instructions, trying hard not to use more flour than originally measured out. Do not over-handle the dough or the baked product will be dry and tough. It is true that a little more flour is needed on a humid or rainy day.
- Mixing and kneading develop the gluten or framework of the yeast bread. Follow instructions for time required for each. Try not to use more than the amount of flour measured out before beginning.
- Granite and marble countertops work wonderfully for kneading–just be sure to sanitize first.
- Knead on a floured surface using the heels and fingertips of the hands. Press the dough with the heels of the hands; fold in half using fingertips as a single unit (don't stick fingertips into the dough); rotate the dough one-quarter turn; press, fold, turn–repeat for number of minutes required.

Tips for Making Yeast Breads, continued

- ✦ Dough must rest after kneading in order for the developed gluten to relax. Dough that is rolled or shaped without resting will simply draw back and not hold the desired shape. You'll need the rest after kneading anyway, so cover the dough with a cloth and take a 20-minute break.
- ✦ To test when yeast dough is doubled in bulk, spread two fingers apart and stick into risen dough. Dough is proofed, or doubled in bulk, if indentions remain.
- ✦ Tapping a fingernail on top of a roll or loaf and listening for a hollow sound indicates the doneness of a yeast bread.
- ✦ Use a string of thread to cut cinnamon rolls; place the thread under the roll at each marking, cross the ends over the top and pull. This cuts a perfect cinnamon roll without mashing it out of shape.
- ✦ Nothing creates a path to a man's heart like the smell of fresh yeast bread baking.
- ✦ When baking in a glass pan, lower the temperature 25°. Glass gets hotter than metal pans.

Batter Rolls

School Dinner Recipe

¾ c. milk
¼ c. sugar
1 tsp. salt
¼ c. margarine
½ c. warm water (105°–115°)
2 pkg. yeast
1 egg
2½ c. unsifted flour

Scald milk; stir in sugar, salt, and margarine. Cool to lukewarm. Measure warm water into large warm bowl. Sprinkle in yeast. Stir until dissolved. Add lukewarm milk mixture, egg, and 2 cups flour. Beat until smooth. Stir in enough remaining flour to make soft dough. Cover, let rise in warm place, free from draft, until doubled in bulk, about 30 minutes. Punch down and shape into 2 dozen rolls. Place on greased baking sheets, cake, or muffin pans. Cover, let rise until doubled in bulk, about 30 minutes. Bake in hot oven at 400° about 15 minutes.

Bow-Knots

Flour hands and take about ¼ cup dough; shape into an 8–10 inch rope with hands. Tie in single knot. Place on baking sheet. Repeat with remaining dough. Brush with melted butter.

Crescent

Divide dough in half. Roll each half into 12–14-inch circle. Spread with melted butter. Cut into 12 wedges (as if cutting a pie). Roll up, beginning with wide end. Place on baking pan with tip tucked under, pulling ends around to form shape of crescent.

Parker-House

Roll out on floured surface to ½" thickness. Cut with 3" round cookie cutter. Brush each roll with melted butter and fold in half to make half-circles. Pinch edge lightly to hold, so the rolls don't unfold as they rise.

Cloverleaf

Pinch off small amount and shape into balls. Place 3 balls in bottom of each greased muffin cup. Brush with melted butter.

I first used this recipe as a student in homemaking class. We always prepared yeast rolls for school board dinners. Things were different back then–we would get out of our other classes all day long to help prepare the dinners. Later on, as a teacher, my students would come in right after school was out and prepare the dough for these rolls. Even though I helped train at least eight different principals during my career, I never could convince any of them that I needed my students to miss their other classes. When I think back to those times, I simply have to ask myself, "What happened to the world?" By the time I retired 30 something years later, it was a chore to get anyone to even open a can of biscuits. The truth be known, I don't make yeast breads very often anymore, either.

"Good bread is the most fundamentally satisfying of all foods; good bread with fresh butter, the greatest of feasts!" – James Beard

RAISING YEAST BREADS QUICKLY

MICROWAVE METHOD

Place yeast dough in a warm, greased bowl. Cover with light towel and put in the microwave. Cook at 10% power for 6 minutes, giving a quarter turn after first 3 minutes. Let set for 15 minutes.

OVEN METHOD

Preheat the oven to 200° and turn off. Place a 9 x 13 x 2-inch pan of hot water on the lower rack of the oven. Put the yeast dough in a warm, greased bowl and cover with a light towel. Place on the rack above the pan of water. Make sure the oven is off. If oven seems too hot, leave open as for broiling. Check after about 30 minutes.

Coolrise White Bread (2 loaves)

From the Food Lab

5½–6½ c. flour
2 pkg. active dry yeast
½ c. warm water (105°–115°)
1¾ c. warm milk or water (105°–115°)
2 T. sugar
1 T. salt
3 T. margarine or shortening
Cooking oil

Spoon flour into dry measuring cup. Level off and pour measured flour onto wax paper. Sprinkle yeast into warm water in a large, warm bowl. Stir until dissolved. Add warm milk or water, sugar, salt, margarine, and 2 cups flour. Beat with electric mixer at low speed until smooth (about 1 minute). Add 1 cup more flour. Beat vigorously with wooden spoon (150 strokes) or electric mixer at medium speed (2–3 minutes) until thick and elastic. Scrape sides of bowl occasionally. Stir in 2½–3 cups of remaining flour gradually with wooden spoon. Use enough flour to make a soft dough which leaves sides of bowl, adding more if necessary. Turn out onto floured board. Round up into a ball. Divide dough into two equal portions (one for each student). Knead 5–10 minutes or until dough is smooth, elastic, and no longer sticky. Cover with plastic wrap, then a towel. Let rest for 20 minutes on board. Punch down. Shape each portion into a loaf. Cover pans loosely with oiled, wax paper then plastic wrap. Refrigerate 2–48 hours at moderately cold setting.

BAKING: When ready to bake, remove from refrigerator. Uncover and let stand for 10 minutes (while preheating the oven). Puncture any surface bubbles with an oiled toothpick just before baking. Bake at 400° for 30–40 minutes or until done. Bake on a lower oven rack position for best results. Remove from pans immediately. Brush top crust with margarine if desired. Cool on racks.

NOTE: Volume decreases slightly as refrigeration time increases beyond 24 hours, but texture and eating quality remain acceptable up to 48 hours.

SHAPING A LOAF OF BREAD

- Place dough smooth-side down on lightly floured board. Roll into 8 x 12-inch rectangle of uniform thickness. Roll out all bubbles in outer edges of dough.
- Roll dough tightly toward you, beginning with the 8-inch edge. Seal dough with thumbs after each complete turn. The final seam should be well sealed by pinching together.
- Seal ends of loaf by pressing firmly with side of hand to make a thin, sealed strip. Be careful not to tear the dough. Fold sealed ends under.
- Place shaped loaf seam-side down in center of greased 8½ x 4½ x 2⅝-inch bread pan. Correct pan size is important for best results. Brush lightly with oil.

English Muffin Bread

Julie

Cornmeal
2 c. milk
6 c. all purpose flour
½ c. water

2 pkg. active dry yeast
1 T. sugar
½ tsp. baking soda
1 tsp. salt

Grease two 8 x 4 x 2-inch loaf pans. Lightly sprinkle with cornmeal to coat bottom and sides. In large bowl, combine 3 cups flour, yeast, and baking soda. In medium saucepan, heat and stir milk, water, sugar, and salt until just warm (120–130°). Using wooden spoon, stir milk mixture into flour mixture. Stir in remaining flour. Divide dough in half, place in pans. Sprinkle tops with cornmeal. Cover and let rise in a warm place until double in size–about 45 minutes. Bake at 400° for 25 minutes until golden brown. Immediately remove from pans and cool on wire racks.

Coolrise Sweet Dough

From the Food Lab

5–6 c. flour
2 pkg. active dry yeast
⅔ c. warm water (105°–115°)
1 c. warm milk (105°–115°)
½ c. sugar
1½ tsp. salt
¼ c. softened margarine or butter
2 eggs
Cooking oil

Spoon flour into dry measuring cup. Level off and pour measured flour onto wax paper. Sprinkle or crumble yeast into ⅔ cup warm water in large, warm bowl. Stir until dissolved. Add warm milk, sugar, salt, margarine, and 3 cups flour. Beat with wooden spoon or electric mixer at low speed until smooth (about 1 minute). Then beat vigorously with wooden spoon (150 strokes) or electric mixer at medium speed (2–3 minutes) until thick and elastic. Scrape sides of bowl occasionally. Stir in 2–3 cups of remaining flour gradually with wooden spoon. Use enough flour to make a soft dough which leaves sides of bowl, adding more if necessary. Turn out onto floured board. Round up into a ball. Divide dough into two equal portions (one for each student). Knead 5–10 minutes or until dough is smooth, elastic, and no longer sticky. Cover with plastic wrap, then a towel. Let rest for 20 minutes on board. Punch down. Shape each portion into coffee cake or cinnamon rolls as desired. Cover pans loosely with oiled, wax paper then plastic wrap. Refrigerate 2 to 48 hours at moderately cold setting.

BAKING: When ready to bake, remove from refrigerator. Uncover. Let stand for 10 minutes (while preheating the oven). Puncture any surface bubbles with an oiled toothpick just before baking. Bake at 375° for 25–30 minutes or until done. Bake on a lower oven rack position for best results. Remove from pans immediately. Brush top crust with margarine if desired. Cool on racks.

Daisy Braid

Roll one half of the CoolRise Sweet dough into a 6 x 18-inch rectangle on lightly greased board. Cut lengthwise into 3 equal strips. Pinch lengthwise edges of each strip together to form an 18-inch rope. Braid the three ropes together. Begin at center and braid to each end. Place in greased 9-inch round pan. Braid loose ends together to form circle. Complete as basic recipe directs. Frost with Powdered Sugar Icing, page 235, and decorate with cherries and nuts.

NOTE: See the Cinnamon Roll instructions included with the Rich Sweet Dough recipe, page 235, for making cinnamon rolls.

I wish I had a dollar for every student I taught how to make yeast bread and cinnamon rolls. When I think about it, I wonder how in the world we had time to complete detailed recipes like these. Of course, it was Homemaking II and Homemaking III classes, or later, the Advanced Food Science classes, that got to the difficult recipes–they did have some experience under their belt. The cool-rise method was great for a two-day project.

Ice Box Rolls

2 yeast cakes
2 c. lukewarm water
2 eggs, well beaten
2 tsp. salt
6 T. sugar
3 T. shortening
6½ c. flour

Soak yeast in lukewarm water (110°). Mix all ingredients well and let rise for two hours. Knead and fix the amount to be cooked in pan. Bake at 375° for 10–12 minutes. Put the balance in the refrigerator for future use.

SOURCE: I used to make these rolls all the time–the short-cut method was great for after work. Boy, would it be great to come home and have fresh-baked yeast rolls with dinner.

For some reason this recipe reminds me of Melody, a former student. If memory serves me correctly, she was the president of Future Homemakers of America her senior year. Melody gave me a yellow plaque that begins, "May the Lord be beside you." It hangs in my home to this day. Bet she doesn't know I still remember her. We had almost the same color hair.

"I don't even butter my bread; I consider that cooking."
– Katherine Cebrian

Grandma Wernecke's Cottage Cheese Coffeecake

Known to Great-Grandchildren as "Grams"

Dough

2 pkg. dry yeast—dissolved in ¼ c. sugar & ¾ c. lukewarm water
1½ c. sugar
1½ c. scalded milk
1 c. shortening
⅛ tsp. salt
1 egg, beaten
6 c. flour or more to form soft dough

Put shortening, sugar, and salt in a large bowl. Add scalded milk. Let cool; add yeast mixture and beaten egg. Add flour and have the dough soft, (like biscuit dough). Let rise to double bulk. Grease jelly roll pans and put enough dough to spread thin on pan. Let rise again.

Topping

1 pkg. (8 oz.) cream cheese
1 pt. cottage cheese
2 beaten eggs
1½ c. sugar
⅛ tsp. salt
1½ c. raisins

Mix all ingredients together and spread on dough. Bake in oven at 325–350° until dough is done, about 35 minutes.

What a wonderful person this German lady was and oh, how she could cook. When there were big family gatherings, she would have 4 or 5 jelly roll pans of coffeecake, each covered with a flour-sack dish towel. Before the day was done, they would all have disappeared. She did not use recipes, so one day I took my measuring spoons and cups over to her house and we got it all written down. She would scoop out the amount of flour she was going to use, but before she used it, I would measure and record the amount. We did this for every ingredient, and the result is that I can now make Cottage Cheese Coffeecake almost as good as she did. Grandma Wernecke would also make homemade noodles. They were rolled so thin and cut so precisely, I never even thought about learning how to make them. Now I wish I had.

My Grandma Simon would make coffeecake, but hers would be topped with streusel. As best I remember, it was made with butter, sugar, and maybe a little flour. Wish I had some now! Somewhere way back in my memory, I see streusel on top of cobbler, too. Here's instructions I adapted to be as similar to her's as I could come.

Streusel Topping

¼ c. all purpose flour
¼ c. sugar
1 tsp. ground cinnamon
¼ c. margarine or butter

Stir together flour, sugar, and cinnamon. Cut in butter or margarine. Sprinkle over dough before baking. Makes enough topping for one jelly roll pan.

Heavenly Hot Cakes

⅔ c. warm water
1 pkg. dry yeast
2 c. biscuit mix
1 c. milk
1 egg

Measure ⅔ cup warm water into bowl. Sprinkle in yeast and stir until dissolved. Add remaining ingredients and beat until smooth. Cook hot cakes on a hot, lightly greased griddle. To determine if the griddle is ready, drop a few drops of water on it–they will dance around if it is hot enough. Turn hot cakes only once.

"One can say everything best over a meal." – George Eliot

Grandma Wernecke's Raisin Bread

2 pkg. dry yeast
1 c. lukewarm water
2 T. sugar
10 c. flour
1 tsp. salt
1 c. margarine
1 c. shortening
3 c. sugar
2 tsp. orange rind
3 T. vanilla
½ tsp. nutmeg
4 c. milk
1 box raisins

Mix together the yeast, lukewarm water, and 2 tablespoons sugar. Let stand a few minutes. Meanwhile mix together the flour, salt, margarine, shortening, 3 cups sugar, orange rind, vanilla, and nutmeg. Add the milk, yeast mixture, and raisins to flour mixture to make a soft dough. Leave in bowl and let rise to double in bulk. Work up in loaves; let rise. Sprinkle sugar on top of loaves. Bake at 350° until brown, probably about an hour. Yield: 6 large loaves

NOTE: Beware, the box of raisins is shrinking–it's now 2 ounces less than before. Use about 2 cups.

German women didn't mess around when making bread! If it was baking day, you made enough to last and to share. I don't know about you, but I find it very hard to imagine life where you baked your own bread, carried your dirty dishwater out the back door and dumped in it the flower beds, potty-trained your children on a chamber pot, worked at home from sunup to way past sundown, prepared all your food on the kitchen table, worked alongside the men in the fields, cooked over an open fire or in an oven where you maintained the hot coals, hand-washed, wrung out, and hung the wash on clotheslines, and then ironed the sheets and just about everything else. When my first microwave oven bit the dust, I went out the very same day and bought another one. I do remember washing and drying dishes; but now, if it doesn't go in the dishwasher, it doesn't get used very often. We are so spoiled and we have the audacity to complain about being too busy and are developing arthritis from texting.

Rich Sweet Dough

From My High School Homemaking Class

¾ c. milk
½ c. sugar
2 tsp. salt
½ c. margarine
½ c. warm water (105°–115°)
2 cakes/pkg. yeast
1 egg
4 c. unsifted flour
Filling for Cinnamon Rolls
Powdered Sugar Icing

Scald milk; stir in sugar, salt, and margarine; cool to lukewarm. Measure warm water into large warm bowl. Sprinkle in yeast; stir until dissolved. Stir in lukewarm milk mixture, egg, and half the flour; beat until smooth. Stir in remaining flour to make a stiff batter. Cover tightly with waxed paper or aluminum foil. Refrigerate dough at least 2 hours. Dough may be kept in refrigerator up to 3 days. To use, cut off amount needed and shape as desired.

Filling for Cinnamon Rolls

1½ T. sugar
2 T. butter, melted
2 tsp. cinnamon
½ c. pecans, chopped

Roll half the dough into a rectangle approximately 9 x 12-inches. Brush with melted butter. Combine sugar, cinnamon, and pecans. Sprinkle evenly over the buttered dough. Roll up along the 12-inch side. Stretch the dough slightly as you roll to make it nice and tight. Pinch edge shut. Take care to make sure the roll is an even diameter. The ends of the roll tend to be thinner, so squash them up. Make 1-inch interval markings along the roll with the back of a knife. Using a piece of thread, cut into 1-inch pieces and place cut-side-down into a greased baking pan. (Slip the thread under the roll, cross the ends over the top and snap.) Cover and allow to rise until doubled in bulk. Bake in 375° preheated oven for 15–20 minutes or until golden brown on top.

Powdered Sugar Icing

1 c. powdered sugar
2–3 tsp. milk, coffee, or orange juice

Combine and drizzle over cooled rolls. When using milk add a few drops of vanilla extract.

Sourdough Bread

1 pkg. active dry yeast
1½ c. warm water (110°)
1 c. Sourdough Starter (at room temp.)
5½–6 c. all purpose flour
2 tsp. salt
2 tsp. sugar
½ tsp. baking soda

In large mixing bowl soften yeast in warm water. Blend in 2½ cups of the flour, Sourdough Starter, salt, and sugar. Combine 2½ cups of the flour and the baking soda; stir into flour-yeast mixture. Add enough remaining flour to make a stiff dough. Turn out onto a lightly floured surface and knead until smooth and elastic (5–7 minutes). Shape in ball. Place in greased bowl; turn once. Cover and let rise in warm place until double (about 1½ hours). Punch down; divide in half. Cover and let rest 10 minutes. Shape into 2 round loaves. Place on lightly greased baking sheets. With sharp knife, make diagonal slashes across tops of loaves. Let rise in warm place until double (1–1½ hours). Bake at 400° for 35–40 minutes. Remove from baking sheets; cool. If desired, brush with butter. Yield: 2 loaves

NOTE: Sourdough bread, having no butter, shortening, or margarine, will be more dense and tough. Serve with a hunk of cheese and a great bottle of wine.

Sourdough Starter

1 pkg. active dry yeast
½ c. warm water (110°)
2 c. warm water (110°)
2 c. all purpose flour,
1 T. sugar

Soften yeast in ½ cup warm water. Stir in remaining water, flour, and sugar. Beat until smooth. Cover with cheesecloth; let stand at room temperature 5–10 days, stirring 2–3 times a day. (Time required to ferment depends on room temperature; if room is warm, let stand a shorter time than if room is cool.) Cover and refrigerate until ready to use.

TO KEEP STARTER GOING: After using some starter, add ¾ cup water, ¾ cup all purpose flour, and 1 teaspoon sugar to remainder. Let stand at room temperature until bubbly, at least 1 day. Cover and refrigerate for later use. If not used within 10 days, add 1 teaspoon sugar. Repeat adding sugar every 10 days.

Sourdough French Bread

1 pkg. active dry yeast
5–5½ c. all purpose flour
1 c. Sourdough Starter (at room temp.)
3 T. sugar
2 T. butter, melted
2 tsp. salt
½ tsp. baking soda
Yellow cornmeal

In large mixing bowl, soften yeast in 1½ cups warm water (110°). Blend in 2 cups of the flour, Sourdough Starter, sugar, butter, and salt. Combine 1 cup of the flour and the soda; stir into flour-yeast mixture. Add enough remaining flour to make a moderately stiff dough. Knead on floured surface until smooth (5–8 minutes). Place in greased bowl; turn once. Cover; let rise until double (1–1½ hours). Punch down; divide in half. Cover; let rest 10 minutes. Shape in 2 oblong or round loaves. Place on greased baking sheet sprinkled with cornmeal. Cover; let rise until almost double (about 1 hour). Brush with water and make diagonal slashes across tops. Bake at 375° for 30–35 minutes. Remove from sheet; cool. Yield: 2 loaves

Notes

DESSERTS

Brennan's Banana Foster

From the Food Lab

2 T. butter
4 sm. bananas
2 T. brown sugar
Dash cinnamon
1 T. banana liqueur
½ c. rum
Ice cream

Melt butter in small skillet. Cut bananas in half lengthwise and brown them in butter. Sprinkle with brown sugar and dash of ground cinnamon. Add banana liqueur and rum; set aflame. (See Flaming Cherries Jubilee, page 241, for instructions.) Serve blazing over ice cream. Yield: 4 servings

NOTE: If bananas are large, use fewer and cut in half crosswise also.

Brownie Cupcakes

¼ c. butter
¼ c. semisweet chocolate chips
1 egg
¼ c. sugar
¼ tsp. vanilla extract
¼ c. all purpose flour
¼ c. pecans, chopped

In a microwave-safe bowl, melt butter and chocolate chips; stir until smooth. Cool slightly. In a small mixing bowl, beat egg and sugar. Stir in vanilla and chocolate mixture. Gradually add flour to chocolate mixture; fold in pecans. Fill paper-lined muffin cups two-thirds full. Bake at 325° for 20–25 minutes or until tops begin to crack. Cool for 10 minutes before removing from the pan to a wire rack to cool completely. Yield: 4 cupcakes

NOTE: This is a great snack and the small amount is perfect for satisfying the sweet tooth yet preventing overindulgence. The muffin cups will be a little more than two-thirds full, but they bake up with perfectly rounded tops.

Cheesecake Cups

<u>CRUST</u>
1 pkg. moist deluxe yellow cake mix
¼ c. butter or margarine, melted
<u>CHEESE FILLING</u>
2 pkg. (8 oz. ea.) cream cheese, softened
3 eggs
¾ c. sugar
1 tsp. vanilla extract
<u>TOPPING</u>
1½ c. dairy sour cream
¼ c. sugar
1 can (21 oz.) cherry pie filling

Preheat oven to 350°. Place paper or foil liners in 24 muffin cups. Combine dry cake mix and melted butter. Beat at low speed with electric mixer. (It will be crumbly.) Spoon into muffin cups. Level but do not press. Combine cream cheese, eggs, ¾ cup sugar, and vanilla. Beat at medium speed until smooth. Spoon into muffin cups. Bake at 350° for 20 minutes or until mixture is set. Remove from oven. Combine sour cream and ¼ cup sugar. Spoon over cheesecakes. Return to oven and bake 5 minutes. Cool. Garnish with cherry pie filling. Refrigerate.

NOTE: I only use about half the crust mix and freeze the rest for another time. After reading the desserts section of <u>Making Memories</u>, it will be obvious that I have a love affair with cheesecake.

Cheesecake Phyllo Cups

4 oz. reduced-fat cream cheese
½ c. reduced-fat sour cream
Sugar substitute equivalent to 2 T. sugar
1 tsp. vanilla extract
2 pkg. (2.1 oz. ea.) frozen miniature phyllo shells
<u>GARNISH</u>
1 can (11 oz.) mandarin orange slices, drained
1 kiwi, peeled, sliced and cut into quarters

Remove phyllo shells from freezer in advance. In a bowl, whisk together the cream cheese, sour cream, sugar substitute, and vanilla until smooth. Pipe or spoon the mixture into phyllo shells. Top each with a mandarin orange segment and kiwi piece. Refrigerate until served. Yield: 2½ dozen

Cherries Jubilee

¾ c. currant jelly
1 can (1 lb.) Bing cherries, pitted
1 tsp. orange rind, grated
1 tsp. brandy flavoring

Melt jelly in chafing dish over direct heat. Add cherries and orange rind. Heat slowly till simmering, stirring occasionally. Serve hot over scoops of vanilla ice cream. 8–10 servings

Flaming Cherries Jubilee

Swirl in ½ cup brandy just before serving. Heat 1 tablespoon additional brandy in spoon, holding match underneath it. When it flames, pour over cherries jubilee and all will flame.

NOTE: It might be a good idea to practice this near a fire extinguisher before serving this at the dinner table. Watch your eyebrows.

Speaking of fire, we had a full-fledged grease fire in the foods lab one time. It was back in the day of fondue pots. I told the students to heat their oil in a saucepan on the stove to get it hot before putting it in the fondue pot. The fondue pot would just take too long to get it hot enough to fry. Well, they heated it alright–right to the point of ignition. Luckily, no one was hurt and I managed to keep calm. I grabbed a lid (use metal, not glass) and slid it over the pot, depriving the fire of oxygen. After a few minutes, the students removed the lid and the grease re-ignited. After that, we let it sit until the next day before trying to clean up.

PUTTING OUT A GREASE FIRE

- The best way to put out a grease fire in the kitchen is to cover it with a lid, covering it from one side to prevent flames from burning your arm.
- Another way to put out a grease fire is to wet a towel, wring it out, and lay it over the pan.
- Baking soda is also effective, but it takes a large amount of baking soda to do the job.
- NEVER put water on a grease fire.
- By all means, do not try to carry the fire out of the house.

BURNING MEMORIES: Not only is "Burning Memories" one of my favorite Ray Price songs, but all this talk about fire reminds me of another hot time when my friend Donna and I lived together in an apartment at Sam Houston. We were so excited to be back together again. We were best friends all through jr. high and high school, but college had separated our paths. It was our senior year in college and our apartment was just a step above a dump. The kitchen had an efficiency unit with the stove on one end, the sink in the middle and the refrigerator under the counter–about five feet of space in all. Well, the first time we used the stove was to boil water, so we turned the burner on high. It's a lucky thing that we stayed in the kitchen, because all of a sudden huge flames jumped to the ceiling. We covered the burner with a lid and flames jumped out of another burner. Somehow we survived and so did the little kitchen, but we ate salads the rest of the semester.

Cherries Over Snow

Teacher Bake-Off

1 pkg. (8 oz.) cream cheese
1 c. powdered sugar
¼ c. sweet milk (whole)
16 oz. Cool Whip
1 Angel Food Cake
1 can (21 oz.) cherry pie filling

Blend cream cheese, powdered sugar, and milk. Add Cool Whip; stir until blended. Tear angel food cake into bit-sized pieces. (Some recipes say to cut off all brown edges first so it really looks like snow.) Fold into cream cheese mixture. Pour into serving dish. Top with cherry pie filling. Refrigerate for one hour before serving.

"Just think of all those women on the Titanic who said, 'No, thank you,' to dessert that night. And for what!" – Erma Bombeck

Chocolate Panini

2 crescent rolls, split
2 T. cream cheese, softened
1 milk chocolate candy bar (1.55 oz.), divided
½ c. fresh strawberries, sliced
¼ c. heavy whipping cream, whipped

Spread cream cheese over the inside bottom of each crescent roll. Place candy bar on the cream cheese and cover with top half of crescent roll. Cook on the Panini Grill and press for 2–3 minutes or until bread is browned and candy bar is melted. Cut in half; top with strawberries and whipped cream.

Creamy Cream Puffs

School Dinner Recipe

1 c. water
½ c. butter or margarine
1 c. flour, sifted
4 lg. eggs
Cream Filling
Chocolate Glaze

Heat oven to 400°. Heat water and butter or margarine to a rolling boil in a saucepan. Stir in flour. Stir vigorously over low heat until mixture forms a ball that leaves sides of the pan–about 1 minute. Remove from heat and beat in eggs, one at a time, until mixture is smooth and breaks off when spoon is raised. Drop by rounded tablespoonfuls, 2 inches apart, onto an ungreased cookie sheet. Bake at 400° for 45—50 minutes or until puffed and golden brown. Cool on wire rack away from any draft. Cut in half horizontally, remove tops and scoop out centers. Fill with cream filling and drizzle chocolate glaze over the tops. Yield: 12 large puffs

Cream Filling

⅓ c. sugar
2 T. cornstarch
⅛ tsp. salt
1½ c. milk
2 egg yolks, slightly beaten
2 tsp. vanilla

Blend sugar, cornstarch, and salt in medium saucepan. Combine milk and egg yolks; gradually stir into sugar mixture. Cook over medium heat, stirring constantly, until mixture thickens and boils. Boil and stir 1 minute. Remove from heat; stir in vanilla. Cool to room temperature.

Chocolate Glaze

2 oz. unsweetened chocolate
3 T. butter or margarine
1 c. powdered sugar
1 tsp. vanilla
2 T. hot water

Melt chocolate and butter over low heat in a heavy saucepan. Remove from heat; stir in sugar and vanilla. Mix in hot water, 1 teaspoon at a time, until glaze is of proper consistency. Drizzle over filled cream puff. Dust tops with powered sugar just before serving.

VARIATION: You can make a faster version of the filling by using a box pudding mix. Use a little less liquid than it calls for so the pudding will set up good and thick. No croissants available? Just use cream puffs for that chicken salad sandwich.

Miniature Cream Puffs or Finger Sandwiches

Drop cream puff mixture by teaspoonfuls, shorten the baking time to 25–30 minutes and fill with pimiento cheese, chicken salad, or your favorite sandwich spread. These smaller versions also make great cream-filled dessert puffs for the buffet table.

Date-Filled Baked Apple

4½ tsp. brown sugar, divided
1 T. dates, chopped
1½ tsp. walnuts, chopped
⅛ tsp. ground cinnamon
1 lg. tart apple
¼ c. water
Whipped cream

In a small bowl, combine 1½ teaspoons brown sugar, dates, walnuts, and cinnamon. Peel top half of apple and remove core; place in a small baking dish. Fill with date mixture. Combine water and remaining brown sugar; pour over apple. Cover and bake at 400° for 35–40 minutes or until apple is tender, basting occasionally. Serve warm with whipped cream.
Yield: 1 serving

"A spoonful of honey will catch more flies than a gallon of vinegar."
– Benjamin Franklin

Death By Chocolate

Marilyn

1 chocolate cake mix, baked as directed
3 T. Amaretto
4–5 Heath bars
16 oz. Cool Whip, thawed
Chocolate Bavarian Mousse

Bake cake according to package instructions. When done, poke holes in cake and drizzle with Amaretto. Crumble. Crush Heath bars in food processor or chopper; reserve about ⅛ cup for garnish. Prepare Chocolate Bavarian Mousse when everything is ready to go. In a large crystal or trifle bowl, layer the ingredients in this order: cake crumbs, mousse, Heath bar crumbs, Cool Whip. Continue layers until all ingredients are used, usually 3 rounds of layers, depending on the diameter of your bowl. Garnish with reserved Heath bar crumbs, chocolate curls, or grated chocolate.

Chocolate Bavarian Mousse

2 envelopes unflavored gelatin
¾ c. boiling water
1 pkg. (6 oz.) semisweet chocolate chips
1 T. sugar
2 egg yolks
1 c. heavy cream
½ tsp. vanilla
1 heaping c. crushed ice

Combine gelatin and hot water in blender. Cover and blend for 30 seconds. Add chocolate chips and sugar. Blend until smooth. Add egg yolks, heavy cream, vanilla, and crushed ice. Cover and blend until ice dissolves.

NOTE: The mousse sets up quickly, so be ready to use immediately. This has become the girls' and my traditional Christmas dessert. It makes a full trifle bowl; you could use two smaller bowls and have one for home and one to share. It is so good and rich, thus its name.

Double-Easy Fruit Dessert

Home Management Special

1 No. 2½ can (3½ c.) fruits for salad, well drained
1 c. tiny marshmallows
1 c. dairy sour cream
1 T. lemon juice
1 T. sugar
¼ tsp. salt
Maraschino cherries

Mix all ingredients except cherries and chill several hours. Garnish with maraschino cherries. Yield: 5–6 servings

Mama's Bread Pudding

My Mama

8–10 slices bread, toasted
¾ c. sugar
2 eggs
Milk to make right consistency
2 hands full of raisins
1½ tsp. vanilla (pure)
½ c. pecans, sometimes used
¼ c. butter
Cinnamon

Break bread into small pieces in large mixing bowl. Add sugar, eggs, about 1½–2 cups milk, raisins, vanilla, and pecans. The consistency should be soupy, but not too thin. (I'm thinking this is why mine never turns out like Mama's. It's a judgement call–thicker than dressing, but not too thin or it will bubble over in oven.) Place in greased 9 x 13 x 2-inch pan; dot with butter slices and sprinkle with cinnamon. Bake 50 minutes to 1 hour or until a knife inserted in the center comes out clean.

NOTE: Mama's bread pudding is dense. It reminds me of home and I hope one day that I can capture its essence in my home. Bread pudding was not made because someone wanted it for dessert. It was made because the bread was getting old and stale and so women came up with a way to use the bread before it spoiled.

For some reason, I am reminded of my students' community service activities. One of their most inspiring projects was an Adopt the Elderly program at local elderly care facilities. Students adopted grandparents and once a month we climbed on a school bus and went to visit them, conducting special activities for them. Students assumed individual responsibilities as well. I will always remember the year students invited their adoptees to our awards banquet–such a heartwarming experience; I can still see the grandparents, sporting their walkers, canes, and wheelchairs, entering the cafeteria on the arms of their grandchildren. The closer I get to being a member of that population, the more thankful I am that we devoted our time to the elderly.

PLUMPING RAISINS

Soaking raisins in boiling hot water for 5–10 minutes before using in baked recipes will plump them up nicely. Be sure to drain off all the liquid before adding to recipe.

Mama's Cobbler

My Mama

1 qt. peaches + sugar*
1 c. milk
1 c. sugar
1 c. Pioneer Biscuit Mix
1 tsp. vanilla
¼ c. butter, sliced very thin
Cinnamon

*Taste peaches to make sure they are sweet. If not sweet enough, add some sugar, maybe about ½ cup. Spread peaches on the bottom of a greased 9 x 13 x 2-inch pan. Blend milk, sugar, biscuit mix, and vanilla. Pour over peaches. Sprinkle with cinnamon and arrange butter slices on top. Bake at 350° for 40–50 minutes until golden brown.

VARIATION: Mama also makes a blueberry cobbler with this recipe, but does not add any sugar to the blueberries. If using fresh-picked dewberries, be sure to add enough sugar to make them sweet. Leave the cinnamon out for berry cobblers.

Daddy loved fresh peaches–he and Mama would always go to Fredericksburg or Fairfield to buy a bushel or so every year. They preferred freestone peaches. Daddy would help Mama peel them (blanch in boiling water a couple of minutes, plunge in cold water, and the peeling just slips off. This works for tomatoes, too). After slicing and putting a little Fruit Fresh on the peaches, they would package them in quart Ziplocs and put in the freezer. One of the best presents we ever bought Daddy was a fruit of the month club membership from Harry and David–it was a gift that kept on giving! If you have someone who is difficult to buy for, try this idea.

Original Recipe Dessert

Rosemary

BOTTOM LAYER
1 box yellow cake mix
1 c. pecans, chopped
1 egg
½ c. butter, melted

TOP LAYER
1 box powdered sugar
2 pkg. (8 oz. ea.) cream cheese
2 eggs

Mix bottom layer ingredients well and press into a 13 x 9-inch pan; it will be thick. Beat together top layer ingredients and pour over crust. Bake at 350° until golden brown, about 35 minutes.

NOTE: This is a great bar or a yummy dessert. Rosemary says, "For the version you tasted, I used a lemon cake mix and I have also used a chocolate mix. I also use walnuts instead of pecans and I always have to cook it longer than the recipe states." Where would we be without special instructions like this? The lemon dessert that she made for a party at my house tasted just like old-fashioned lemon bars.

Our Favorite Cheesecake

From the Food Lab

FILLING
2 pkg. (8 oz. ea.) cream cheese, softened
3 eggs
1 can (15 oz.) sweetened condensed milk
1 graham cracker crust (10")

TOPPING
1 c. sour cream
3 T. sugar
½ c. crushed pineapple, well-drained

Cream the cheese and blend in eggs. Add milk and blend until smooth. Pour into crust and bake at 300° for 25 minutes. Remove; very carefully spread on topping. Return to oven for 10 minutes. Cool and chill for several hours before serving. Use the simple topping below if pineapple is not desired.

Simple Topping

1 c. sour cream
3 T. sugar
1 tsp. vanilla

Combine and spread over baked cheesecake. Return to oven for 10 minutes. Cool, cover, and chill at least 1 hour.

Quick Pineapple Dessert

1 c. flour
1 c. brown sugar
1 tsp. baking soda
½ tsp. salt
1 egg
1 sm. can (8½ oz.) crushed pineapple
<u>TOPPING</u>
¼ c. brown sugar
¼ c. chopped nuts

Place all ingredients (except topping) in bowl and mix; pour into greased 8 x 10-inch pan. Combine topping ingredients and sprinkle over surface. Bake at 350° for 30–40 minutes. Serve with whipped or ice cream.

Quick Rice Pudding

Leftover rice, still in pot
Milk
2–3 T. sugar, more if needed
Cinnamon
Raisins
2–3 tsp. butter

Add enough milk to the leftover rice to barely cover it. Add sugar, a sprinkling of cinnamon, and a handful of raisins. Cook slowly until mixture thickens. Taste; adjust sugar and cinnamon. Stir in butter. Serve warm or hot.

NOTE: I often cook too much rice just so I can make pudding out of the leftovers. It reminds me of home. To make sure there is rice left over, remember this formula: 1 cup uncooked rice equals 3½ cups cooked rice. A serving of rice is about ½ cup, but allow more for gumbo.

"My kitchen is a mystical place, a kind of temple for me. It is a place where the surfaces seem to have significance, where the sounds and odors carry meaning that transfers from the past and bridges to the future."
– Pearl Bailey

MILK FACTS

- Evaporated milk has had one half of the water removed. To reconstitute and use as fresh milk combine equal parts of evaporated milk and water. For example: 1 cup evaporated milk + 1 cup water = 2 cups milk
- Whole milk contains 3½–4% milk fat.
- Low-fat milk contains 2% milk fat. That's why it's often called 2% milk.
- Skim milk contains less than ½% milk fat.
- Whipping cream contains 30% or more butterfat and can be mixed with air to form whipped cream. The result is roughly double the volume of the original cream. If, however, the whipping is continued, it will turn to butter.
- Heavy cream contains 36% butterfat.
- Half and half, which is commonly used as cream for coffee, contains 10% fat. Light cream is about 18% fat and is also used for coffee.
- Sour cream, made from cream, contains from 18–20 percent butterfat and gets its characteristic tang from the lactic acid created by the helpful bacteria that is added.
- Homogenized milk has been processed so the milk fat (cream) does not rise to the top–it's homogeneous.
- Pasteurized milk has been heated to destroy harmful bacteria. All milk should be pasteurized. I remember when Mama used to milk Rosie, our cow. She would always heat the milk in a big pot on the stove, allow it to cool, and then refrigerate it. For those who milk a cow or goat: be sure to pasteurize the milk before using.
- Nonfat dry milk has had all the milk fat and water removed. To reconstitute, use ⅓ cup nonfat dry milk powder plus about ¾ cup water. Just put the dry milk in a liquid measuring cup and add warm water; stir and fill to the 1 cup line. I keep a box of nonfat dry milk in the refrigerator to use when I am out of fresh milk or when I want to reduce the fat and calories in a recipe. There is not a discernible difference in baked products when nonfat dry milk is substituted for whole milk. If used for something like pudding, whose main ingredient is milk, a difference in flavor and texture can be noticed.
- To scald milk, heat in saucepan until bubbles form around the edges. Milk will form a skin on top if it is not stirred when heating; that skin will hold in air causing the milk to boil over–nine-tenths of the milk will wind up on the stove. To avoid boil-overs, stir milk while heating and since milk scorches easily, cook over low heat.

- ✦ Nearly all milk in the United States has been fortified with Vitamin D. Our body needs the right proportion of calcium, phosphorus, and Vitamin D to build and maintain bones and teeth. Vitamin D, known as the sunshine vitamin, is produced by fair skin when exposed to sunlight. To insure that everyone, regardless of skin color and sun exposure, gets the nutrients needed, the government began adding Vitamin D to milk which already contains the proper proportion of calcium and phosphorus. Rickets is the deficiency disease caused from lack of Vitamin D.
- ✦ The date stamped on milk and milk products sold in retail stores is the *pull* or *sell by* date. This is the date that these products are removed from the grocery shelf. However, milk products can remain fresh and useable for quite a while after that date, so don't get rid of them just because they have passed the stamped date. I have kept fresh milk in the refrigerator for several weeks and it remains the same as the day I bought it. The more often milk products are removed from the refrigerator and allowed to set on the kitchen counter, the sooner they will sour. Do as Mama used to say, "Put the milk back in the icebox and don't just stand there looking–get what you want and close it." Of course, don't drink from the milk container.

Buttermilk

The term buttermilk originally applied to the watery byproduct of churning butter. Today's buttermilk is cow's milk that has had bacterial cultures added to it. Sour milk can be substituted for buttermilk in recipes.

Sour Milk

Place 1 tablespoon lemon juice or white vinegar in a glass measuring cup. Add in milk (2% or richer) to equal 1 cup. Stir. Let stand for 15 minutes until it looks like it is beginning to curdle. Buttermilk and sour milk can be used interchangeably in recipes. Milk that has spoiled is not *sour* milk and should not be used as it can cause illness.

Whipped Cream

When whipping cream, be sure to use chilled beaters and bowl. Do not add sugar until soft peaks have formed. Keep chilled and serve soon.

Whipped Nonfat Dry Milk

Sprinkle an equal amount of nonfat dry milk powder over ice-cold water or fruit juice. Beat with electric mixer until thick. Place the bowl and beaters in the freezer a few minutes before whipping.

Whipped Evaporated Milk

Chill bowl and beaters. Place evaporated milk in a shallow pan and put in the freezer until ice crystals begin to form around the edges. Pour milk into the chilled bowl and beat until it begins to thicken. Gradually add 2 tablespoons lemon juice and 2 tablespoons sugar for each cup of milk being whipped. Beat until very stiff and serve immediately.

Tiger Pudding

Julie & Jennie

1 sm. pkg. vanilla instant pudding
1 sm. pkg. chocolate instant pudding
Milk
Cool Whip

In separate bowls, prepare pudding mixes according to package instructions. Spoon into 4 parfait glasses–first vanilla, then chocolate–making it look like tiger stripes. Repeat until glasses are full and/or the pudding is all used. Refrigerate. Top with dollops of Cool Whip before serving.

NOTE: This is our extra-special dessert reigning from the days when the girls could barely reach the countertop–seems like I remember them standing on a step stool at first.

Vanilla Pudding

Classroom Standard

¾ c. sugar
3 T. cornstarch or ⅓ c. flour
3 c. milk
4 egg yolks, beaten
1 T. butter or margarine
1½ tsp. vanilla

In a heavy 2-quart saucepan combine sugar and cornstarch or flour. Stir in milk. Cook and stir constantly over medium heat until mixture is thickened and bubbly. Cook and stir for 2 minutes more. Remove from heat. Gradually stir about 1 cup of the hot mixture into beaten egg yolks. Return all the egg mixture to the saucepan. Bring to a gentle boil; reduce heat. Cook and stir for 2 minutes more. Remove from heat. Stir in margarine and vanilla. Pour pudding into a bowl or individual dishes. Cover the surface with clear plastic wrap, pressing it down into the bowl or serving dishes so it actually touches the pudding, thus preventing the formation of a skin on top. Chill. Do not stir. Yield: 6 servings

Chocolate Pudding

Prepare as above, except add ⅓ cup unsweetened cocoa powder to sugar. Use 2 tablespoons cornstarch or ¼ cup flour, 2⅔ cups milk and egg yolks (not whole eggs).

NOTE: Combining flour, cornstarch, and cocoa with sugar before adding liquid separates the starch particles and prevents lumping.

Warm Chocolate Soufflé

5 T. unsalted butter, plus more for greasing
All purpose flour, for dusting
12 oz. bittersweet chocolate, chopped
9 lg. egg yolks
½ c. plus 2 T. sugar
3 lg. egg whites

Preheat the oven to 350°. Butter a 5-cup soufflé dish and dust with flour, tapping out the excess. In a large saucepan, melt the chocolate with the 5 tablespoons of butter over very low heat, stirring constantly. In a large bowl, using an electric mixer, beat the egg yolks with ½ cup of the sugar until thick and pale, about 4 minutes. Fold in the melted chocolate mixture. In a clean bowl, using clean beaters, whip the egg whites at high speed until soft peaks form. Gradually add the remaining 2 tablespoons of sugar and beat until the egg whites are glossy, about 1 minute. Fold the egg whites into the chocolate mixture and pour into the soufflé dish. Bake in the center of the oven for about 25 minutes, until the soufflé is risen, cracked and slightly jiggly. Carefully transfer the soufflé to a trivet and serve right away. Serve with ice cream, Blue Bell Homemade Vanilla is my choice.

NOTE: Try under baking this a little bit to make the center gooey. It's also remarkably good when left a little longer in the oven, too, particularly topped with a scoop of coffee ice cream. Serve the soufflé warm or even at room temperature. So, even a cook who has never made a soufflé can succeed. Simply say, "I like to under-bake my soufflés so they are gooey in the middle." or "I like to bake my soufflés a little longer. It makes them so good with ice cream." Be careful not to let the potholders touch the soufflé when removing from the oven or it will fall before its time.

"I doubt the world holds for anyone a more soul-stirring surprise than the first adventure with ice cream." – Heywood Broun

West Yellowstone Stagecoach Cheese Cake

Inspired by Stage Coach Inn

CRUST
¾ c. Zweiback, ground
½ c. blanched almonds, slivered & chopped
¼ c. butter, melted
FILLING
11 oz. cream cheese, room temperature
1 c. sour cream
1 c. sugar
1 tsp. vanilla
3 med. eggs or 2 lg. eggs
TOPPING
1 c. sour cream
½ c. sugar
1 tsp. vanilla

Combine crust ingredients and press into bottom of 9-inch spring-form pan. Blend filling ingredients, leaving lumpy. Pour over crust. Bake at 350° for 20–25 minutes. Reduce temperature to 300° and continue baking until barely brown on top. Remove from oven and place on cooling rack. Stir topping ingredients together until sugar dissolves and spread on warm cheese cake.

FAMILY VACATIONS: I could write a book about our experiences. We beheld the most beautiful scenery imaginable on a trek from our house to the Grand Tetons, Yellowstone where it snowed on us, San Francisco, and looping back home through Scottsdale, Arizona, where it was 121°. The best cheesecake I ever remember eating was at this inn in West Yellowstone. I have reconstructed it as close as possible–the zweiback cookies made all the difference. Although the original cheesecake was prepared in a very high altitude, when I made this back home, 90 feet above sea level, it came out almost as good–the only thing missing was the view.

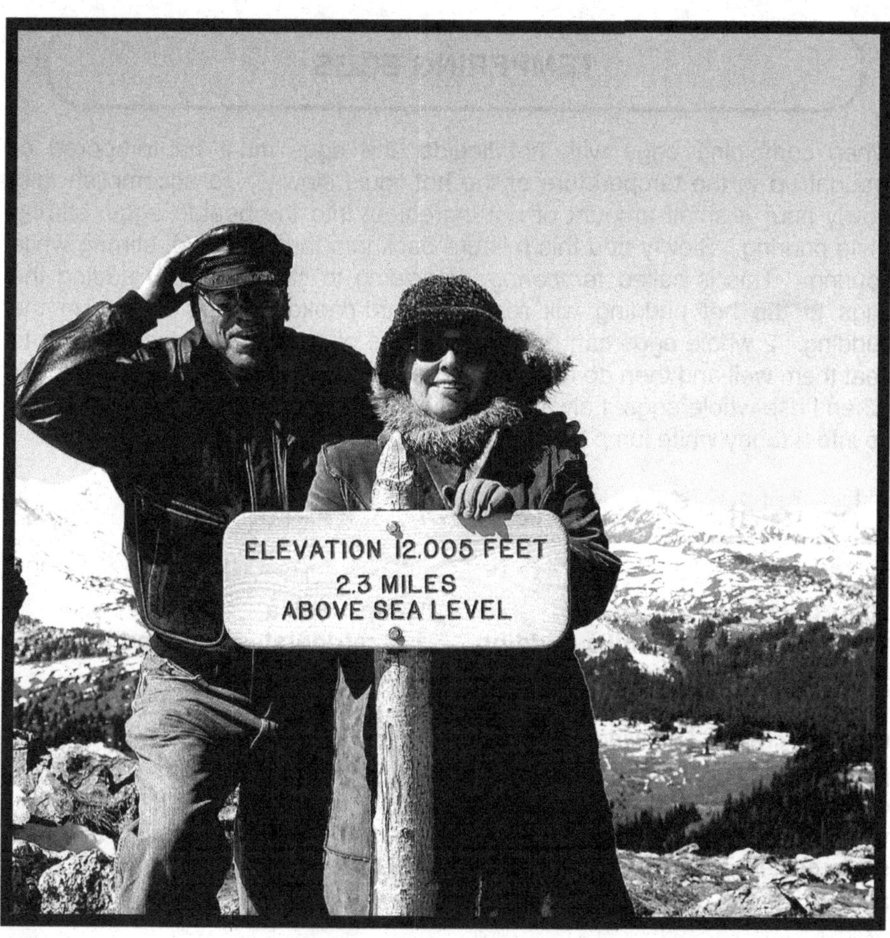

Gary and I walked to the this highpoint on Trail Ridge Road in Rocky Mountain National Park. High altitudes require adjustments when baking and walking takes on a whole new meaning.

TEMPERING EGGS

When combining eggs with hot liquids, the eggs must be tempered or brought up to the temperature of the hot liquid slowly. To accomplish this, slowly pour a small amount of hot ingredient into the beaten eggs, stirring while pouring. Slowly add this mixture back into the hot liquid, stirring while pouring. This is called *tempering*. Deciding to short-cut it by adding the eggs to the hot pudding will result in hard-cooked lumps of egg in the pudding. 2 whole eggs can be used in place of 4 egg yolks, just be sure to beat them well and then do not boil after adding–just cook until nearly bubbly. When I use whole eggs, I always remove the chalaza from the eggs–it cooks up into a funny white lump.

Chocolate Éclair Crepes

Janis

10 to 12 cooked crepes
1 sm. pkg. instant vanilla pudding
1½ c. milk
½ tsp. vanilla
1 c. refrigerated whipped topping
Chocolate Glaze

Prepare crepes following All Purpose Crepe Batter, page 328. Prepare pudding mix according to directions on box, except use 1½ cups milk instead of 2 cups as box directs; add vanilla while preparing pudding. Fold in whipped topping. Fill cooked crepes down center with pudding and fold sides over filling. Drizzle with Chocolate Glaze. Arrange on serving plate and refrigerate.

Chocolate Glaze

2 T. butter or margarine
2 oz. unsweetened baking chocolate bar or squares
5 T. sugar
¼ c. water
1 tsp. vanilla

In small saucepan, combine first four ingredients. Stir over low heat until chocolate melts and mixture is smooth. Stir in vanilla. Let stand about 5 minutes. Drizzle over filled crepes. Refrigerate until ready to serve.

CAKES

MAKING BEAUTIFUL CAKES

- ✦ Gently dusting ingredients like pecans and coconut with all purpose flour before adding to the cake batter will keep them suspended in the batter instead of sinking to the bottom or rising to the top.
- ✦ Eggs and butter or margarine should be room temperature for best results when baking. Eggs can be placed in a bowl or warm water for 10–15 minutes to bring to room temperature quickly.
- ✦ When a recipe calls for cake flour, which has less gluten and is lighter, either use cake flour or make the following adjustment: 1 cup cake flour equals 1 cup minus 2 tablespoons all purpose flour
- ✦ When preparing layer cake pans: grease only the bottom of the pan. This allows the cake to rise evenly and not slip back down on the sides of the pan as it attempts to rise.
- ✦ Cut wax paper to fit the bottom of layer cake pans. Grease bottom of pan, press in wax paper; grease wax paper and dust lightly with flour. This technique will insure that the cake always releases from the pan.
- ✦ Fill the layer pans evenly, making the center of the batter a little lower than the sides. This will help insure that the layers are flat on top for easy stacking and frosting.
- ✦ Place pans as close to the center of the oven as possible. For 3 layers, place two layers on one rack–one near the front and one near the back of the oven. Place the third layer on another rack, staggered so it is not directly under another pan.
- ✦ Do not allow the sides of the pan to touch each other or the oven walls or door. This stops the flow of heat and the part that touches the side will dry out or even burn.
- ✦ Be sure to set a timer, as opening the oven door can cause the cake to fall. Always time for the lesser amount of time specified. For example, if the cake is to bake 27–30 minutes, set the timer for 27 minutes. Remember, the window is placed in the oven door so you can see what is happening in there–use it instead of opening the oven.

- ✦ There are three ways to determine if a cake is done.
  - It turns loose from the sides of the pan.
  - A toothpick inserted in the center of the pan comes out clean.
  - When touched in the center, an indention will not be left.
- ✦ When layer or sheet cakes test done, allow to cool on a rack for 10 minutes. Then remove from pan and complete cooling on a rack. For tube or bundt cakes, follow recipe directions for cooling. Generally they are cooled completely in the pan.
- ✦ If cake layers did not come out perfectly flat, turn them so they offset each other when frosting, creating a level cake. If a layer is high in the center, simply slice the high part off.
- ✦ Tear 3-inch strips of wax paper and slip under the bottom layer of cake before frosting. When cake is frosted, slip the wax paper out for a perfectly clean cake plate.
- ✦ Frosting a 2-layer cake: Place the bottom layer upside down; frost. Top with the second layer right side up. Frost the sides and then the top.
- ✦ Frosting a 3-layer cake: Place the bottom layer upside down and frost top. Place the second layer right side up; frost the top. Place the third layer right side up. Frost the sides and then the top. Italian crème and German chocolate cakes are usually not frosted on the sides. Push the frosting on each layer all the way to the edges if not frosting the sides.

Angel Food Cake

1½ c. egg whites (10–12 lg. eggs)
1½ c. sifted powdered sugar
1 c. sifted cake flour or sifted all purpose flour
1½ tsp. cream of tartar
1 tsp. vanilla
1 c. sugar

Bring egg whites to room temperature. Sift powdered sugar and flour together 3 times. In a large bowl beat egg whites, cream of tartar, and vanilla with an electric mixer on medium speed until soft peaks form (tips curl). Gradually add sugar, about 2 tablespoons at a time, beating until stiff peaks form (tips stand straight). Sift about one-fourth of the flour mixture over beaten egg whites; fold in gently. (If bowl is too full, transfer to a larger bowl.) Repeat, folding in remaining flour mixture by fourths. Pour into an ungreased 10-inch angel food cake pan. Bake on the lowest rack in a 350° oven for 40–45 minutes or until top springs back when lightly touched. Immediately invert cake. Cool thoroughly. Loosen outside edges of cake. Remove from outside part of pan. Loosen center and bottom of cake. Remove cake from center part of pan.

NOTE: Follow the instructions carefully; I know they are time consuming, but that's what works. Make sure to use a glass or metal bowl (no plastic) and beaters that are spiffy clean so the egg whites will beat up. Having eggs at room temperature produces greater volume. Use a wire whisk to fold in the flour; the flat-antique ones work the best, but any wire whisk will do. (A whisk knocks less air out of the beaten egg whites.) An angel food cake pan has two parts: the outside and the bottom-center piece. This allows easy removal of the cake. Using this pan for most other cake recipes doesn't work; the batter will drip out into the oven. Invert the angel food cake immediately when it comes out of the oven or it will fall. Most angel food cake pans have three little projections around the top edge of the pan that hold the cake up in the air while it cools. If pan doesn't have those, position the center hole of the cake over a soda or liqueur bottle.

CRACKING EGGS

When cracking eggs for this cake, or for any other purpose, it is a good idea to crack each egg into a custard cup before adding to mixture. That way if an egg is bad, it won't contaminate the whole recipe. Believe it or not, I was making an angel food cake and the twelfth egg was yucky. I had to throw it all out and start again. If a piece of the egg shell happens to get in the eggs, use the edge of the shell to remove it easily.

My favorite birthday cake is angel food. I didn't get to go home for my birthday that first year in college, so Mama, Daddy, and Grandma Simon came to Beaumont bringing an angel food cake, strawberries, and whipped cream. I felt so special and blessed. I lived on the second floor and my grandma walked up with her crutches and her left knee that wouldn't bend. She made it up all those stairs for my birthday!

"When baking, follow directions. When cooking, go by your own taste."
– Laiko Bahrs

Angel Food Waldorf

School Dinner Recipe

1 pkg. (15–16 oz.) white angel food cake mix
FILLING
3 c. whipping cream, chilled
1½ c. powdered sugar
¾ c. cocoa
¼ tsp. salt
⅔ c. slivered almonds, toasted & divided

Bake cake mix as directed or make an angel food cake from scratch. Cool completely. Place cake upside down; about 1-inch down, slice off entire top of cake and set aside. Make cuts down into cake 1-inch from outer and center edges all the way around, leaving substantial walls on each side. With a curved knife or spoon, remove cake within cuts, being careful to leave a base of cake 1-inch thick. Place cake on serving plate.

In chilled bowl using chilled beaters, beat the chilled whipping cream, sugar, cocoa, and salt until stiff. Divide into two portions. Fold ⅓ cup toasted almonds into half the whipped cream mixture. Spoon into cake cavity. Press mixture firmly into cavity to avoid holes in cut slices. Replace top of cake and press gently. Frost cake with remaining whipped cream mixture. Sprinkle with ⅓ cup toasted almonds. Chill at least 4 hours or until set. Cut cake with serrated bread knife, using it like a saw to prevent mashing the cake slices. Yield: 12–16 servings

NOTE: This cake has the center removed and my students loved getting to eat that part right away. The center of the cake contains a square of chocolate pudding when sliced, making a very impressive dessert.

My advanced classes would make angel food cakes from scratch. They are just so much better than the boxed mixes or ready-made ones. Once I took my samples to the cafeteria at lunch and shared with my coworkers. Rosemary was so impressed with the difference in flavor that I decided to surprise her and make an angel food cake for her birthday. Well, I forgot to put in the sugar but remembered it just as I was putting the cake in the oven. Even after removing the cake and carefully adding the sugar 2 tablespoons at a time, the cake turned out flat as a flitter. I told her it was a white devil cake. We enjoyed the flavor and a good laugh–too much love invested to throw it away. Let me stress again that recipes are created and tested; following the instructions given usually produces the best results.

Baker's Basic Cake

1 pkg. yellow or white cake mix
4 eggs (for white cake use 6 egg whites)
¼ c. oil
1 c. buttermilk

Combine ingredients and beat on medium speed for 4 minutes. Bake according to package instructions. Sweet milk can be substituted for the buttermilk.

Baker's White Icing

1 heaping c. nonfat dry milk
½ c. water
1 tsp. clear vanilla or ¼ tsp. almond extract
2 egg whites (med. to lg. eggs)
2 c. Crisco shortening
2–3 lb. powdered sugar

In a large bowl beat milk, water, and extract until foamy. Add shortening and egg whites; beat until smooth. Add sugar gradually. Leave one half of the icing as is. Divide remainder in half.

SOFT ICING: ½ of the icing used as is for frosting

MEDIUM ICING: ¼ of the icing used for decorating
Add 1 teaspoon corn syrup and 1 cup powdered sugar.

THICK ICING: ¼ of the icing used for decorating
Add up to 2 additional cups powdered sugar.

CHOCOLATE ICING: Add 1 package Hershey's hot chocolate mix, individual serving size.

NOTE: This recipe comes from a cake decorating class. It's delicious and easy to use. Cake decorators freeze the cake layers, keeping them fresh until ready to assemble. Thaw before frosting. Giving the layers a very thin coating of icing first helps to seal in the crumbs.

I never had the patience to make all the fancy flowers and trims, but I did decorate the girls' birthday cakes when they were little: Winnie the Pooh, Cinderella, Strawberry Shortcake, Mickey Mouse. If you are interested in trying your hand at cake decorating, this is definitely the recipe to use.

Basic Cake

From My High School Homemaking Class, as Copied by Donna

2 c. cake flour, sifted
2 tsp. baking powder
¼ tsp. salt
⅔ c. shortening
1⅓ c. sugar
3 eggs
⅔ c. milk
1 tsp. vanilla

Preheat oven to 375°. Grease and flour two 8-inch cake pans. Sift the flour with the baking powder and salt; set aside. Cream the shortening until soft and smooth by rubbing it; add sugar and continue creaming. Add the unbeaten eggs, one at a time, beating well. Add ¼ of dry ingredients; beat until well-blended. Add ⅓ of milk. Add another ¼ of dry ingredients. (I think Donna started talking here because she never adds the rest of the dry ingredients and milk.) So, continue adding dry ingredients and milk alternately, beating after each addition, ending with an addition of dry ingredients. Add vanilla and mix well. Pour the batter into (prepared) pans and bake 25–30 minutes, or until it tests done. Remove from oven. Leave in cake pan for 7 minutes. Loosen from sides and turn onto a cake rack. Cool; brush crumbs and frost.

I have so many memories of my high school homemaking teacher; let's just say she must have been my inspiration for choosing home economics as my teaching field. I remember her tests were pages and pages consisting of questions and huge expanses of blank space between for answers. We would write and write and write!

Brown Stone Cake

Aunt Geraldine

2¼ c. sugar
1 tsp. vanilla
1 c. shortening
5 eggs, separated
2 tsp. soda
3 c. all purpose flour
½ tsp. salt
4 tsp. cocoa
2⅓ c. buttermilk
Brown Stone Frosting

Cream sugar, vanilla, and shortening together. Add egg yolks and beat until smooth. Sift all dry ingredients together 3 times. Add dry ingredients alternating with buttermilk to creamy mixture. Beat egg whites to form stiff peaks. Last, fold in beaten egg whites. Place in 3 (8 or 9-inch) prepared cake pans. Bake at 350° for 25–30 minutes.

NOTE: Referring to sifting the dry ingredients three times, Aunt Geraldine says, "You don't have to do that with the flour different now." In earlier years flour was compact and required sifting before using. However, your cake will be lighter in texture if you sift.

Brown Stone Frosting

2 c. sugar
1 c. heavy cream
½ c. butter

Combine and cook until thick. Frost as desired.

Our Aunt Geraldine made Brown Stone Cake for just about every occasion. It's absolutely delicious and holds many happy memories. We played many a hand of 42 in her garage, sitting on old wooden chairs from Tin Hall–one of the oldest dance halls around. Tin Hall was a place where men had to check their hats, the windows were always open, and everyone tried their best to dance in front of one of the fans on hot summer nights. Babies slept on the tables while kids slid on the floor during band breaks. I can still hear Randy and Rockets playing Jolie Blonde....

Cajun Cake

Janis' Mother

2 c. flour
1½ c. sugar
2 tsp. soda
1 can (2½ c.) crushed pineapple
2 eggs
Boiled Icing

Mix together dry ingredients. Add pineapple with juice and eggs. Mix well. Bake in a greased 9 x 13 x 2-inch cake pan for 30–40 minutes in 350° oven. Ice while warm.

Boiled Icing

¾ c. sugar
½ c. evaporated milk
½ c. margarine
½ c. pecans, chopped
1 c. coconut
1 tsp. vanilla

Bring sugar, milk, and margarine to a boil and add the pecans, coconut, and vanilla. Pour over warm cake.

Canned Apple Cake

1¾ c. sugar
1 c. oil
2 eggs, beaten
3 c. sifted flour (sift flour and then measure)
1 tsp. baking soda
1 tsp. cinnamon
¾ tsp. salt
Dash of nutmeg
1 can apple pie filling
2 tsp. vanilla
2 c. pecans, chopped (or less)
Caramel Frosting

Combine sugar and oil. Add remaining ingredients. Mix well and pour into a well-greased and floured tube pan. Bake for 1 hour at 350°.

Caramel Frosting

1 c. sugar
1 c. brown sugar
1 c. evaporated milk
2 T. margarine
1 tsp. vanilla

Cook to soft-ball stage, add vanilla, and remove from heat. Beat well and frost cake. If frosting gets too hard to spread, add a tiny amount of cream.

NOTE: "Delicious and moist. This recipe is tested. A family favorite. Great for the busy homemaker!" These are the comments made in our church cookbook. It always seemed like too much trouble to make an apple cake until I found this recipe. It really is delicious–tastes just like fresh apple cake.

Coconut Pound Cake

Mom

1 c. margarine
½ c. Crisco shortening
3 c. sugar
5 eggs
3 c. flour
½ tsp. baking powder
1 can (1⅓ c.) flaked coconut
1 c. milk
1 tsp. vanilla

Cream butter, shortening, and sugar; add eggs, one at a time, beating after each addition. Sift flour and baking powder together; add coconut to flour mixture and stir; add the flour mixture to the creamed mixture alternating with the milk. Add vanilla and blend. Bake in loaf or tube pan at 325°. To test for doneness, use a broom straw or knife and stick into cake. If no dough sticks to it, the cake is done. Bake 45 minutes or more.

Carrot Cake

4-H Food Show Winner

1½ c. cooking oil
2 c. sugar
4 eggs
3 tsp. cinnamon
2 tsp. baking powder
1 tsp. salt
2 tsp. vanilla
2 c. flour
3 c. grated carrots
Butter Icing

Mix and blend all ingredients well, adding carrots last. Bake in 3 greased or lined 8-inch cake pans at 350° for 35–40 minutes until done. Frost with Butter Icing.

Butter Icing

½ c. margarine
1 pkg. (8 oz.) cream cheese
1 lb. powdered sugar

Allow margarine and cream cheese to come to room temperature. Cream and gradually beat in powdered sugar until fluffy.

> I've talked about other 4-H adventures; this was my most successful food endeavor. I still have the tiny gold medal I won at the district food show. I guess at heart, I love competition. I'll see how my cookbook does in the sales market...will I appear on Good Morning America?

Fluffy White Frosting

(a.k.a. Seven-Minute Frosting)

1 c. sugar
⅓ c. water
¼ tsp. cream of tartar
Dash salt
2 egg whites
1 tsp. vanilla

In 2-quart saucepan combine sugar, water, cream of tartar, and salt. Bring to boil, stirring until sugar dissolves. *Very slowly* pour sugar syrup into unbeaten egg whites in mixing bowl, beating constantly with electric mixer, about 7 minutes or until stiff peaks form. Add vanilla and beat until combined. Frost.

NOTE: This recipe doesn't require using a double boiler and it makes enough frosting to really pile it on your cake layers.

Dump Cake

School Dinner Recipe

1 #2 can* (20 oz.) crushed pineapple, drained
1 can (1 lb. 5 oz.) cherry pie filling
1 box white or yellow cake mix
½–1 c. pecans, chopped
½ c. butter, sliced thinly

Pour pineapple in greased 9 x 13 x 2-inch cake pan. Pour cherry pie filling over pineapple. Pour cake mix directly from the box over cherry filling. Spread pecans over the cake mix. Cover with thin layer of butter—spread it all around or you will have dry mix when cake is done. Bake at 350° for 1 hour.

*See the can sizes chart that follows.

NOTE: May be topped with whipped cream or ice cream. As a home ec teacher, this was my standard *go-to* recipe for large luncheons and dinners. For one, it was easy for students to prepare and it nearly always turned out great–although the cakes never all looked quite the same. For another, it can be changed up and no one will realize it's the same recipe. Leave out the pineapple. Use apple or blueberry pie filling. Use a chocolate cake mix with the cherry pie filling. Bake in a ceramic pan for a beautiful presentation.

CAN SIZES

What is a #2 can? Old recipes often rely on knowledge we don't use anymore. Back in the dark ages, cans were numbered, the larger the number, the more it held, sometimes. A Number 2 can held 2½ cups. When scraping around, finding old recipes, chances are some will include references to can sizes that are not familiar, like the No. 2 can I found in many of my recipes. Here's a chart to help determine the correct amounts to use.

No. 1 flat = 1 c. or 9 oz.
No. 1 tall = 2 c. or 16 oz.
No. 303 = 2 c. or 16 oz.
No. 2 vacuum = 1¾ c. or 12 oz.
No. 2 = 2½ c. or 20 oz.
No. 2½ = 3½ c. or 28 oz.
No. 3 cylinder = 5¾ c. or 46 oz.
No. 10 = 13 c. or 6 lb.-10 oz.

Earthquake Cake

My Mama

1 c. coconut
1 c. pecans, chopped
1 box German chocolate cake mix
8 oz. cream cheese, softened
1 lb. powdered sugar
½ c. oleo, softened (margarine)

Grease 9 x 13 x 2-inch pan. Spread coconut and pecans on bottom. Mix cake mix according to package directions. Pour over pecans and coconut. In a medium bowl, combine oleo and cream cheese with powdered sugar. Drop by spoonfuls on top of the cake. Do not stir. Bake at 350° for 45–50 minutes or until done. Allow to cool.

I must talk about oleo. Many older recipes call for oleo, which was the precursor to modern-day margarine. I can hardly believe that we used to say oleo–that's kinda like calling the refrigerator an icebox. Mama told me that when oleo was first introduced, it was almost white and came with a packet of yellow coloring that could be added to make it look like butter. Oh, that manufacturers would give us a choice about food additives today.

Fruit Cocktail Cake

2 c. flour
1½ c. sugar
½ tsp. salt
2 tsp. soda
2 c. fruit cocktail with juice
2 eggs
½ c. brown sugar
1 c. nuts
Evaporated Milk Icing

Sift together flour, sugar, salt, and soda. Add fruit cocktail and eggs. Mix well and pour into a greased 13 x 9 x 2-inch pan. Sprinkle top with brown sugar and nuts. Bake in 350° oven for 30 minutes.

Evaporated Milk Icing

1½ c. sugar
¾ c. margarine
1 c. evaporated milk

Bring to boil in saucepan and boil 1 minute. Pour over above cake while hot.

Flourless Chocolate Cake

1 c. unsalted butter, cut into pieces, plus more for the pan
¼ c. unsweetened cocoa powder plus more for pan
1¼ c. heavy cream, divided
8 oz. bittersweet chocolate
5 lg. eggs
1 c. sugar
½ c. Crème Fraîche or sour cream
¼ c. powdered sugar, plus more for dusting

Heat oven to 350°. Butter a 9-inch spring-form pan and dust with cocoa powder. In a medium saucepan, heat the butter with ¼ cup of the heavy cream over medium-low heat until the butter is melted. Chop the chocolate, add to pan, and stir until melted and smooth; remove from heat. In a medium bowl, whisk together the eggs, sugar, and cocoa powder; whisk in the chocolate mixture. Transfer the batter to the prepared pan and bake until puffed and set, 35–40 minutes. Let cool in the pan for 1 hour. Run a knife around the edge of the cake before removing from pan. Using an electric mixer, beat the remaining 1 cup of heavy cream with the crème fraîche and powdered sugar until soft peaks form. Dust the cake with powdered sugar and serve with the whipped cream.

NOTE: This cake is like a cross between a brownie and a gooey candy bar. The flavor is delicious. The whipped cream mixture keeps in the refrigerator for a couple of days, too. Also, since there is no flour, this would be perfect for someone who can't have any gluten. To top this cake, try homemade crème fraîche. It's easy to make and widely used by chefs. For about a dollar, sour cream's fancy French cousin can be made in your kitchen. It's typically about $7.50 for 8 ounces. Just two ingredients transform into this thick, rich, tangy cream after a quick stir and a day on your countertop. Dollop it on desserts or stir into savory dishes for a touch of *tastes-like-a-million-bucks* decadence. Just call yourself a gourmet chef!

Crème Fraîche

1 c. heavy cream
2 T. low-fat buttermilk

Stir together cream and buttermilk in a large, clean glass jar or bowl. Cover tightly with lid or plastic wrap. Let mixture stand at warm room temperature overnight or until the consistency of sour cream. Refrigerate 5 hours or until very cold. Crème fraîche can be kept, refrigerated, up to 1 week. Yield: 1 cup plus 2 tablespoons

German Chocolate Cake

1 pkg. (4 oz.) Baker's German Sweet Chocolate
½ c. water
2 c. flour
1 tsp. baking soda
¼ tsp. salt
1 c. margarine or butter, softened
2 c. sugar
4 egg yolks
1 tsp. vanilla
1 c. buttermilk
4 egg whites
Coconut Pecan Frosting

Heat oven to 350°. Line bottoms of 3 (9-inch) round cake pans with wax paper. Microwave chocolate and water in large microwavable bowl on high 1½–2 minutes or until chocolate is almost melted, stirring halfway through heating time. Stir until chocolate is completely melted. Mix flour, baking soda, and salt; set aside. Beat margarine and sugar in large bowl with electric mixer on medium speed until light and fluffy. Add egg yolks, 1 at a time, beating well after each addition. Stir in chocolate mixture and vanilla. Add flour mixture alternately with buttermilk, beating after each addition until smooth. Beat egg whites in another large bowl with electric mixer on high speed until stiff peaks form. Gently stir into batter using a wire whisk. Pour into prepared pans. Bake 30 minutes or until cake springs back when lightly touched in center. Immediately run spatula between cakes and sides of pans. Cool 10 minutes; remove from pans. Remove wax paper. Cool completely on wire racks. Spread Coconut-Pecan Frosting between layers and over top of cake, allowing a little to hang down the sides.

TOP OF STOVE PREPARATION:
Heat chocolate and water in heavy 1-quart saucepan on very low heat, stirring constantly until chocolate is melted and mixture is smooth. Remove from heat. Continue as above.

Coconut Pecan Frosting

1 can (12 oz.) evaporated milk
1½ c. sugar
¾ c. margarine or butter
4 egg yolks, slightly beaten
1½ tsp. vanilla
1 pkg. (7 oz.) Baker's Angel Flake Coconut (2⅔ c.)
1½ c. pecans, chopped

Mix milk, sugar, margarine, egg yolks, and vanilla in large saucepan. Cook and stir on medium heat about 12 minutes or until thickened and golden brown. Remove from heat. Stir in coconut and pecans. Cool to room temperature and of spreading consistency. Yield: about 4½ cups

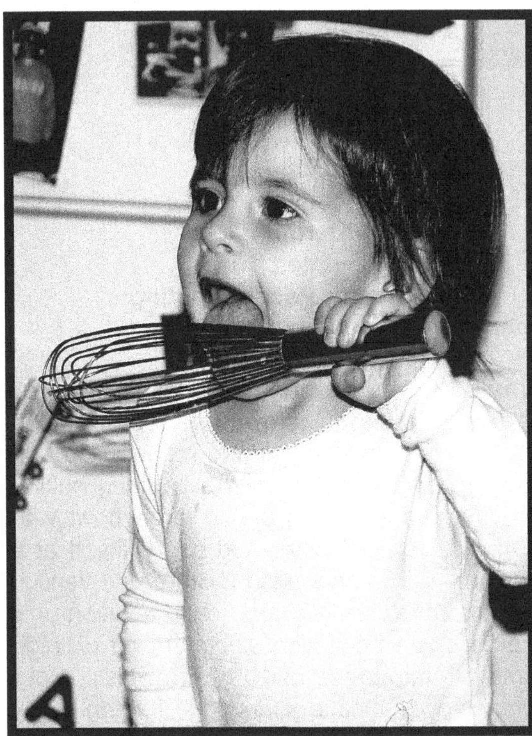

A given when baking: the spoon or, in this case the wire whisk, just has to be licked dry as a bone. Lydia's doing such a good job it might not need to be washed.

Italian Crème Cake

Project Show: Grand Champion Cake

1 c. buttermilk
1 tsp. baking soda
5 eggs, separated
2 c. sugar
½ c. butter
½ c. shortening
2 c. sifted all purpose flour
1 tsp. vanilla extract
1 c. pecans, chopped
1 sm. can coconut (1⅓ c.)
Cream Cheese Icing

Preheat oven to 325°. Combine soda and buttermilk and let stand for a few minutes. Beat egg whites until stiff. In a separate bowl cream sugar, butter, and shortening. Add egg yolks, one at a time, beating well after each addition. Add buttermilk alternately with flour to creamed mixture. Stir in vanilla. Fold in beaten egg whites; gently stir in pecans and coconut. Bake in three 9-inch greased, floured layer pans at 325° for 25 minutes or until cake tests done. Frost cooled cake with cream cheese icing.

Cream Cheese Icing

1 pkg. (8 oz.) cream cheese, softened
½ c. butter, room temperature
1 tsp. vanilla
1 lb. powdered sugar

Mix cream cheese and butter well and add vanilla. Beat in sugar, a little at a time, until of a spreading consistency. Frost layers, letting a little frosting hang over the edges, but leaving the sides unfrosted. Garnish by sprinkling top with chopped pecans or by arranging pecan halves on top. Use your imagination. It's easier to cut the cake if chopped pecans are used; or arrange whole pecans so each will end up on a slice of cake.

This cake may have originally been an entry in the teacher bake-off or brought to one of our teacher dinners. I guess I had lead a sheltered life, because it was new to me. It was love at first bite and I began baking it all the time. When Julie was in my class, she baked it for the project show. It was awesome–with three layers and the frosting oozing out from between them–quite a masterpiece. Well, it won grand champion and Julie let us sell it as our chapter cake since she wasn't a member of Future Homemakers of America and couldn't participate in the auction. Later on when Jennie was in my class, being no fool, she also made the Italian Crème Cake for the project show. Naturally, it won grand champion. Remember, I said Jennie was no fool–her cake sold for the astronomical amount of four hundred sixty dollars! She was a dedicated member of FHA, even qualified to go to national conference in Anaheim, California, as a member of our parliamentary procedure team. I used to haul students all over the United States and even to Canada once. I never lost a one.

"Part of the secret of success in life is to eat what you like and let the food fight it out inside." – Mark Twain

Lemon Jello Cake

My Mama

1 pkg. yellow cake mix
1 pkg. lemon Jello
1 can (5½ oz.) apricot nectar
4 whole eggs
¾ c. Wesson oil
Grated rind and juice of 1 lemon
Powdered Sugar Glaze

Put all ingredients in mixing bowl; beat at low speed for 2 minutes; then beat 1 minute at medium speed. Pour into large tube pan or loaf pans, greased and floured. Bake at 350° for 50 minutes to 1 hour, or until done. When removed from oven, let stand 2 minutes; then pour over cake this icing.

Powdered Sugar Glaze

1 c. powdered sugar
Juice of 1 lemon

Let stand until cool before removing from pan.

NOTE: This recipe is in Mama's recipe box. It's typed on the old Remington typewriter and is brown and stained. I remember how good it is and can't wait to try it again. I recently discovered the microplane zester–much more flavor is extracted using one and that bitter taste from getting too much of the lemon or lime peeling is avoided. This zester was created by a carpenter who designed it after one of his woodworking tools.

Mama's Fruit Cake

My Mama

4 slices candied pineapple
½ lb. candied cherries
1 lb. pecans
1 lb. dates
1 c. sugar
1 c. flour
1 tsp. vanilla
1 tsp. baking powder
¼ tsp. salt
3 eggs

Beat eggs first in one bowl. In second bowl, put all dry ingredients and sift flour over all the fruit and nuts that have been cut up. Then mix all together and pour in well-greased brown paper-lined loaf pans and bake in slow oven (275°) about 1 hour until brown.

"Avoid fruit and nuts. You are what you eat." – Jim Davis

Mama used to make fruit cake every year. She never poured bourbon over it until we were grown though. When I asked her to make sure this was the recipe she used, Mama said, "Yes, but I quit making it when I got smart. That Collin's Street fruit cake is very, very good. It costs might near that much to make it. It's just a lot of work, but it sure is good when you get finished. I used to do so many things. I just cannot believe I did all that. All that canning and putting that paste wax on those hardwood floors. That was work."

AVERAGE DRIED FRUIT YIELD

From My High School Homemaking Class

1 lb. dried apples = 10 cups, cooked; 4⅓ cups
1 lb. dried apricots = 5 cups, cooked; 2¾ cups
1 lb. candied cherries = 2¼ cups, sliced
1 lb. dried citron = 2½ cups, sliced
1 lb. currants = 3 cups
1 lb. dates = 2½ cups, pitted (60 dates); 3 cups, chopped
1 lb. figs = 3 cups cut fine = 44 figs
1 lb. crystallized ginger = 2⅔ cups, diced
1 lb. dried peaches = 6 cups cooked
1 lb. dried prunes = 4 cups cooked; 2¼ cups
1 lb. raisins = 3 cups

Mrs. Winn's Crazy Cake

1½ c. flour
1 c. sugar
1 tsp. soda
½ tsp. salt
2 T. cocoa
6 T. salad oil
1 T. vinegar
1 c. water
1 tsp. vanilla

Sift dry ingredients together and mix with remaining ingredients in 7 x 9-inch rectangular or 8-inch square cake pan. Bake at 350° for 30 minutes.

NOTE: My friend's mother used to bake this for us when we got home from school; it is a little crazy–you will see why when you bake it.

Oatmeal Cake

Elaine

½ c. margarine
1 c. quick oats
1¼ c. flour
½ tsp. salt
1 tsp. soda
1 c. sugar
1 c. brown sugar
½ tsp. nutmeg
1 tsp. cinnamon
2 eggs
Brown Sugar Topping

Preheat oven to 350°. In saucepan boil 1½ cups water. Remove from heat and add the margarine and oats; stir and cover. Grease the bottom only of a 9 x 13 x 2-inch pan. Mix remaining ingredients. Add oatmeal mixture and beat 3–4 minutes. Pour in pan and bake 30–35 minutes.

Brown Sugar Topping

6 T. margarine
½ tsp. vanilla
1 c. coconut
1 c. nuts, chopped
½ c. brown sugar
¼–½ c. milk

Cook all ingredients in a saucepan. Spread on baked, hot cake and broil 5–6 inches from heat source until light brown, 3–4 minutes. Watch closely.

NOTE: Don't walk away from the broiler. It gets brown really fast! My sister Elaine used to make this cake all the time and she says, "I couldn't tell you the number of times I burned the coconut." Just watch it close and set the timer. The result is worth the extra watch time.

Pineapple Upside-Down Cake

½ c. brown sugar
¼ c. butter, melted
1 can (20 oz.) sliced pineapple, drained
6 Maraschino cherries
1 yellow cake mix, prepared according to pkg. directions

Heat oven to 350°. Sprinkle brown sugar in bottom of an iron skillet. Drizzle ¼ cup melted butter over brown sugar. Place pineapple slices over this. Place one maraschino cherry in center of each pineapple slice. Pour prepared cake batter over pineapple. Bake at 350° for 50–55 minutes until toothpick inserted in center comes out clean. Immediately turn pan upside down onto serving plate. Serve warm. 8 servings

Pound Cake

Donna

2 c. oleo (margarine)
7 eggs
2¼ c. sugar
2½ c. flour
⅛ tsp. salt
½ tsp. mace
1 tsp. vanilla
1 tsp. lemon extract
Yellow cake coloring to suit

Cream oleo and sugar. Add eggs one at a time; beat well each time. Then add flour, salt, and mace. Beat well again. Add vanilla, lemon extract, and coloring; beat well. Grease and flour 2 loaf pans. Bake at 250° for 20 minutes; then turn oven to 350° and bake 35 minutes or until done.

SOURCE: Another of Granny's golden oldie recipes, she writes a note to Donna about the mace, "This is what you liked." As I copied this recipe from Donna's handwritten one given to her by Granny, Donna told me, "You weren't my only teacher, Granny taught me, too."

Pineapple Orange Cake

Debbie

1 pkg. (18¼ oz.) yellow cake mix
1 can (11 oz.) mandarin oranges, undrained
4 egg whites
½ c. unsweetened applesauce

TOPPING
1 can (20 oz.) crushed pineapple, undrained
1 pkg. (1 oz.) sugar-free instant vanilla pudding mix
8 oz. low-fat whipped topping

In a large bowl, beat cake mix, oranges, egg whites, and applesauce on low speed for 2 minutes. Pour into a 13 x 9 x 2-inch baking dish coated with nonstick cooking spray. Bake at 350° for 25–30 minutes or until a toothpick inserted near the center comes out clean. Cool on a wire rack. In a bowl, combine pineapple and pudding mix. Fold in whipped topping just until blended. Spread over cake. Refrigerate for at least 1 hour before serving.

NOTE: Debbie says, "This recipe is almost guilt-free, deliciously moist and light." I bake this in a pretty casserole pan when I take it somewhere. Be sure to use fruits that are packed in their own juices for less sugar.

Rum Cake

My Mama

1 pkg. yellow cake mix
1 pkg. instant vanilla pudding
½ c. salad oil
½ c. water
½ c. rum
½ c. pecans, chopped
4 eggs (1 at a time)
Rum Glaze

Blend all ingredients except eggs. Add eggs to mixture one at a time, beating after each addition. Pour into well-greased bundt or tube pan. Bake at 325° until done, about 1 hour. About 5 minutes before cake is done prepare glaze.

Rum Glaze

½ c. butter
¼ c. water
1 c. sugar
2 T. rum

Boil first 3 ingredients 1 minute. Add rum. Remove cake from oven when done. Pierce top thoroughly with tines of fork. Pour glaze into holes and over top slowly. Let cool in pan.

NOTE: Mama says, "That recipe doesn't fail." I'm thinking that it could stick in the pan, in which case, I will simply drink rum and eat cake crumbs. I asked Mama if it sticks to the pan and she replied, "Yes, it does. That's the only thing I hate about those bundt pans. You have to really grease them good." Notice the rum is added to the glaze after cooking–that way it still has it's alcohol content.

Tres Leche Cake

Julie

1 yellow cake mix
1 pkg. vanilla pudding
Egg, water, oil as required for cake mix
<u>LECHE:</u>
1½ c. heavy cream
1 can Eagle Brand sweetened condensed milk
1 c. evaporated milk
4 T. brandy, divided
1 pkg. (8 oz.) Cool Whip
1 T. vanilla

Mix cake as directed except add vanilla pudding. Bake as directed. Cool. Mix milks and 2 tablespoons brandy. Poke holes in the cake. Spoon the milk mix over the cake. Refrigerate for a day. Mix Cool Whip, remaining 2 tablespoons brandy, and vanilla. Spread over cake and serve.

Sock It To Me Cake

My Mama

1 pkg. Duncan Hines Butter Recipe Golden Cake Mix
1 c. (8 oz.) dairy sour cream
½ c. Crisco oil
¼ c. sugar
¼ c. water
4 eggs

FILLING
1 c. pecans, chopped
2 T. brown sugar
2 tsp. cinnamon

GLAZE
1 c. powdered sugar
2 T. milk

Preheat oven to 375°. In a large mixing bowl blend the cake mix, sour cream, oil, the ¼ c. sugar, water, and eggs. Beat at high speed for 2 minutes. Pour two-thirds of the batter in greased and floured 10-inch tube pan. Combine filling ingredients and sprinkle over batter in pan. Spread remaining batter evenly over filling mixture. Bake at 375° for 45–55 minutes, until cake springs back when touched lightly. Cool right-side-up for about 25 minutes, then remove from pan. Blend powdered sugar and milk. Pour over cake when cool.

Anyone who lived through the 70s has probably had Sock It To Me Cake. I hope this recipe brings a long-lost memory back and puts a smile on your face. On the other hand, for those too young to have old memories, head to the kitchen and bake this cake right now. You won't believe what you missed!

"There is no love sincerer than the love of food." – George Bernard Shaw

White Fruit Cake

Mom

PART I

1¼ lb. butter (5 sticks)
9 eggs, separated
2¼ c. sugar
1½ oz. or more lemon extract

Cream butter until it is like ice cream; add sugar. Add egg yolks, one at a time. Cream well after each one; add lemon extract; blend.

PART II

1½ qt. pecans, chopped
1 lb. glazed cherries, cut in half
1 lb. candied pineapple, chopped
1 box (about 2 c.) white raisins
5 c. all purpose flour

Place in a large mixing bowl and mix well.

PART III

Combine Part I and Part II mixtures. Beat egg whites to form stiff peaks. Add egg whites to combined Part I and Part II mixture. Mix well. Place in well-greased and floured pans. Start baking at 300° for 20 minutes; reduce heat to 250° or less and bake until done, about 1½ hours. Bake with pan of water under cakes.

NOTE: I am not sure how many fruit cakes this makes, but every one of them will be absolutely delicious. I'm also not sure about the size of the pans, but I remember loaves and a tube cake shape. Be sure to fill all pans to the same level so they bake evenly. It is a toss-up between Mama's Fruit Cake, which is dark, and Mom's White Fruit Cake for me.

PIES

Amazing Coconut Pie

2 c. milk
¾ c. sugar
½ c. biscuit mix
4 eggs
¼ c. butter or margarine
1 c. Baker's angel flake coconut

Combine milk, sugar, biscuit mix, eggs, butter, and vanilla in electric blender container. Cover and blend on low speed for 3 minutes. Pour into greased 9-inch pie pan. Let stand about 5 minutes; then sprinkle with coconut. Bake at 350° for 40 minutes. Serve warm or cool.

NOTE: This pie is a perfect option for people who do not enjoy making pie crusts. I taught students how to make great pie crusts, but in practice, it just wasn't for me. Amazing and impossible pies are perfect choices for anyone who feels the same way–the crust appears like magic.

Banana Split Pie

My Mama

2 c. graham cracker crumbs
½ c. butter or margarine
2 eggs
¾ c. butter or margarine, melted
2 c. powdered sugar
3–4 bananas
1 can (No. 2) crushed pineapple, drained
12 oz. Cool Whip , thawed
½ c. pecans
¼ c. maraschino cherries
½ c. coconut

Make pie crust by melting first stick of butter or margarine and mixing with graham cracker crumbs. Press into the bottom of a 9 x 13 x 2-inch pan. Bake at 375° until golden brown, about 10 minutes. Cool. Blend eggs, melted butter, and powdered sugar at least 15 minutes. Pour over crumb crust; top with bananas, then pineapple. Cover with Cool Whip. Sprinkle with chopped pecans, coconut, and cherries. Chill and serve. Very delicious!

Buttermilk Pie

Julie

3 T. flour
2 c. sugar
3 eggs
1 c. buttermilk
½ c. butter, melted
1 tsp. vanilla
2 unbaked 9-inch pie crusts

Mix flour and sugar. Beat eggs well and add to sugar mixture. Add milk, melted butter, and vanilla. Pour into unbaked pie crusts. It just won't fit into one crust. Bake at 350° for 50–60 minutes or until done. A knife inserted in the center of pie will come out clean when done.

NOTE: "Oh my, this pie is delicious!" is all Julie has to say about it.

Black-Bottom Pie

From the Food Lab

1 envelope unflavored gelatin
¼ c. cold water
1 c. sugar, divided
1 T. cornstarch
2 c. milk
4 egg yolks, slightly beaten
1 tsp. vanilla
1 pkg. (6 oz. or 1 c.) semisweet chocolate pieces
Baked pastry shell
3 T. rum or ½ tsp. rum extract
4 egg whites

Soften gelatin in ¼ cup *cold water*; set aside. In a saucepan combine ½ cup of the sugar and the cornstarch. Stir in milk and egg yolks. Cook and stir until bubbly. Cook and stir 2 minutes more. Remove from heat; stir in vanilla. Divide mixture in half. Add chocolate pieces to one portion, stirring until melted. Pour into pastry shell and cover directly with plastic wrap. Chill. Stir softened gelatin into remaining hot mixture until gelatin dissolves. Stir in rum. Chill to the consistency of corn syrup, stirring occasionally. Remove from refrigerator (gelatin mixture will continue to set). Immediately beat egg whites until soft peaks form. Gradually add remaining ½ cup sugar, beating until stiff peaks form. When gelatin is partially set (consistency of unbeaten egg whites), fold in stiff-beaten whites. Chill until mixture mounds when spooned. Spoon into shell. Chill 8 hours or until set. Serves 8

Here's the memory about Black-Bottom Pie. It was the last food lab of my first year as a teacher; I decided to let the students choose what they wanted to cook. My sister's group selected this pie to make. It's a pretty intense recipe, but they figured out how to get it done. The group right next to them happened to be black girls and they decided to test my racial outlook by choosing to cook chitterlings. I don't think they really liked chitterlings—but they had to try me. (Remember, this was 1971, just two years after desegregation was mandated by the federal government—things could still get a little touch-and-go at times.)

If you are reading this cookbook from cover to cover, you know I have much experience in the hog-killing field, but stayed away from the internal operations. Nevertheless, I was determined to prove my lack of prejudice so I agreed to their choice. We adapted their grandma's recipe to use a pressure cooker. Let me mention that our classroom and lab was wall-bound with no windows for ventilation and you had to walk through our living-dining room to get from the hallway to the lab.

On with the story...the pie was progressing nicely. The pressure regulator on the pressure cooker started bobbling. Things were going great. The pie-makers were putting the final touches on their masterpiece, counting the hours until the next day when they could eat it. Meanwhile, the air was getting pungent—so pungent even the chitterling cookers vacated the lab. The next day, there was still a remnant of chitterling aroma in the air, but the pie-makers were willing to forgive and forget; they shared their pie with the pressure-cookers. (I don't recall what happened to the chitterlings.) The look on the faces of all those girls as they tasted the pie was priceless! Their eyes popped and their mouths twisted—forcing them to confess: they had added the whole bottle of rum extract to their pie, thinking it would give them a nice little buzz.

Afterward everyone laughed about how many times they washed their hair trying to rid themselves of the pungency of pressure-cooked chitterlings. What a bonding experience. I earned a reputation for not being prejudiced; but that was the last time I tried to prove anything. Later, my mentor and fellow homemaking teacher, Mrs. Fuller, called me into her private office and told me that if I ever let anyone cook chitterlings again she would see to it that I lost my job. I'm not sure if it was the smell or the connotation, but her statement didn't even phase me, because there is no way I would ever allow myself to be near a chitterling again—not even in the grocery store's frozen food aisle.

Cherry Cream Cheese Pie

1 pkg. (8 oz.) cream cheese, softened
1 can Eagle Brand sweetened condensed milk
½ c. lemon juice
1 tsp. vanilla flavoring
1 graham cracker crust
1 can (1 lb. 5 oz.) cherry filling, chilled

Beat cream cheese until smooth. Gradually mix in sweetened condensed milk. Stir in lemon juice and vanilla. Spread in crust. Refrigerate 3–4 hours or until firm. Top with chilled cherry pie filling. To remove pie pieces easily, place hot, wet towel around sides and bottom of pan before cutting.

This pie is so good, there's no wonder that it stirs up so many memories. Mama would make this for Sunday dinner quite often and it also brings to mind dinners in Mrs. Riemer's commercial foods kitchen. Her students would prepare and serve sit-down meals for teachers during our lunch period. It was a welcome break to be treated as a special guest and they had their routine down–we only had 25-30 minutes for lunch. This recipe was often prepared in mini-size cupcake pans and it was so cute; plus we could carry them with us while running back to our classes. Mrs. Riemer, who was a senior and one of the FHA officers the first year I taught, wore many hats and, upon my retirement, started wearing mine.

Deep-Dish Pie

1 c. sugar
1 c. flour
1 T. baking powder
1 c. milk
1 egg, beaten
Dash of salt
½ c. butter or margarine
1 c. fruit or berries
1 c. juice from fruit or berries

In a 1½-quart deep dish, mix dry ingredients together. Combine milk and egg; add to dry mixture and blend thoroughly. Melt butter in deep pan or casserole dish. Pour in batter. Stir in fruit and juice. Bake 35–40 minutes at 350° until brown.

NOTE: The girls' dad used to make this cobbler. Don't stir too much after adding fruit, especially berries, or it turns into a haunting purple concoction.

MAKING A PERFECT MERINGUE

- Do not allow even one speck of yolk to get into the egg whites. It will keep the meringue from making.
- Eggs at room temperature make a fluffier meringue and more of it.
- Use only clean beaters and a glass bowl with a narrow bottom and tall sides for the best results. Any fat or film or a plastic bowl will keep the meringue from making. The narrow-deep bowl will allow the beaters to get into more egg whites and the result will be fluffier meringue.
- Beat the egg whites until white in color before adding sugar.
- Cream of tartar keeps the meringue from *weeping*–tiny brown droplets that form on the surface of the meringue.
- When putting the meringue on top of the custard, make sure the meringue touches the pie crust all the way around—this will keep it from shrinking away from the edge.
- Make soft mounds and swirls in the top of the meringue. Little peaks will burn before the meringue browns properly.
- If garnishing the meringue with coconut, lightly press it down so it does not burn. Watch closely when baking meringue.
- Soft peaks are formed when the meringue makes a soft mound with the top slightly folded over when the beaters are lifted from it.
- Stiff peaks are formed by beating longer. When the beater is raised, a stiff point will form.

"Housework is a breeze. Cooking is a pleasant diversion. Putting up a retaining wall is a lark. But teaching is like climbing a mountain."
– Fawn M. Brodie

Coconut Cream Pie

My Mama

¼ c. flour
1½ c. milk
½ c. sugar
¼ tsp. salt
1 c. coconut
1 T. butter
4 egg yolks, beaten
1 tsp. vanilla
1 pie shell (9 inch), baked
Meringue

Combine flour, sugar, and salt in saucepan. Add milk; cook over low heat until thick, stirring constantly. Gradually pour half of the mixture into the beaten egg yolks, stirring constantly. Pour this egg mixture back into the saucepan and cook 2 minutes more. Add coconut, butter, and vanilla; stir. Set aside to cool.

Meringue

4 egg whites
Pinch of salt
6 T. sugar

Beat egg whites until soft peaks form. Slowly add sugar and salt. Beat until medium peaks form. Fold half of the meringue into the custard mixture; pour into the baked pie shell and cover with the remainder of the meringue. Sprinkle with a little more coconut. Brown in 350° oven for about 12 minutes.

Aunt Vera and Aunt Louise always brought coconut pies to gatherings–no matter which side of the family was gathering, we had coconut pie. I would always hide a piece to eat later. One time I hid it behind a candle-cup centerpiece on the counter and when I went to retrieve it, the glass candle cup broke and my pie was history. I guess some would say it serves me right. The best coconut pie story hails from my Daddy's 80th birthday celebration. We all spent the week in Fulton Beach in separate little cottages right on the bay. Shrimp boil, music, beer, spa, and pool–a great and happy time for all. The men and boys went fishing in the bay and Daddy caught the biggest red fish. The girls made not one, not two, not three, but four coconut cream pies for the fish fry-birthday party. I still remember Daddy's huge smile. We took a family photo of everyone and it evokes a favorite memory for us all.

Daddy's favorite pie was coconut, so we made four of Mama's Coconut Cream Pies for his 80th birthday party. There was so much pie, no one had to hide a slice. We had a grand celebration!

French Apple Pie

Julie

4–5 lg. Granny Smith apples
2 T. flour
¾ c. sugar
½ tsp. salt
½ c. cream
½ c. butter
2 sheets pie crust

Line 9 or 10-inch pie pan with single crust. Combine flour, sugar, and salt; sprinkle half on crust. Add apples, peeled and sliced. Sprinkle remaining flour, sugar, and salt on apples. Add cream and place pats of butter on apples. Put pastry strips on top, making a lattice. Flute edges. Place pie plate on baking sheet to catch any over run. Bake at 400° for 5 minutes and 350° for 60 minutes.

NOTE: Julie adds, "This is the best apple pie ever. It looks and tastes like it took hours, but is really so simple. I love that it is not too sweet and is super creamy. Thanks so much to my funny friend, Cynthia the Great."

AVERAGE FRESH FRUIT YIELD

From My High School Homemaking Class

1 lb. apples = 3 medium apples; 2¾ cups slices
1 lb. apricots = 8–12 apricots; 5 servings
1 lb. avocado = 2 avocados; 4 servings
1 lb. bananas = 2¼ cups, sliced; 3–4 med. bananas; 2 cups mashed
1 qt. blueberries = 6 servings
1 qt. cherries = 2 cups pitted cherries
1 lb. cranberries = 4 cups
1 grapefruit = 2 servings
1 lb. Concord grapes = 1 quart or 4 servings
1 doz. lemons (medium) = 2 cups juice
1 doz. oranges (medium) = 4 cups juice; 3 qt. slices
1 lb. peaches = 4 servings or 4 medium peaches; 2¾–3 cups slices
1 lb. pears = 4 servings or 4 medium pears; about 3 cups slices
1 pineapple = 6 servings or 3 cups
1 lb. plums = 4 servings
1 lb. rhubarb = 2 cups cooked; 4–8 stalks
1 qt. strawberries = 4 servings; 3 cups sliced; 3¾ cups whole

TIPS FOR A PERFECT PIE CRUST

- ✦ The action of cutting in the shortening is what makes the pastry flaky. Use a pastry blender or two knives to cut-in. Over-handling the dough will cause the crust to be tough and doughy.
- ✦ Use ice cold water and the crust will not be as sticky to handle.
- ✦ When putting the crust into the pie pan, lift and scooch it down into the pan, filling the curved bottom of the pan. If stretched up the sides to fit, it will just shrink back into its original shape when baked.
- ✦ Allow a 1-inch overhang when making a pie crust. Trim off excess if necessary.
- ✦ For a single-crust pie, fold under the excess crust and build an even rim all the way around. Using your thumb and forefinger along with your other thumb, create the fluted edge.
- ✦ For a double-crust pie, allow the bottom to overhang and trim to ½–1 inch. Fill pie and moisten edges of crust with water using your fingertips. Top with the second crust or lattice top, build the rim–joining both crusts, and flute.
- ✦ When baking a single crust without any filling, poke holes all over the bottom and sides of the pie crust with a fork. This will prevent the crust from bubbling up during baking.
- ✦ When baking fruit pies and others that require a longer baking time, covering the fluted edge of the crust with strips of aluminum foil will prevent burning before the pie is done. Tear several strips about 3 inches in width; join by folding pieces together on the short ends. Fold in half and tent over the outside edge of the crust, overlapping when they meet.
- ✦ Always place pie pans on a baking sheet when baking, especially when using aluminum pie pans. Once, when taking a meringue pie from the oven, it doubled up and fell up-side-down on the kitchen floor–learned that lesson real well. Also, the baking sheet keeps the pot holder from getting into the food.
- ✦ For a special treat, roll out the excess pie dough, cut into pieces, and sprinkle with cinnamon-sugar mixture. Bake.
- ✦ Brush the top crust with beaten egg whites before baking for a finished shine.

Never Fail Pastry

Mom

3 c. flour
1¼ c. Crisco
1 egg, beaten
5 T. water
1 T. vinegar
Pinch of salt

Cut the shortening into the flour until mixture resembles small peas. Combine the egg, water, vinegar, and salt. Add to flour mixture and stir around the bowl just until it leaves the sides of the bowl. Divide in half. Roll between two sheets of wax paper until crust is 1-inch larger than the inverted pie pan. Peel off the top wax paper and replace. Turn over and peel off the bottom wax paper. Remove top wax paper and invert into pie pan.
Yield: 2 single crusts

NOTE: Bake a single, empty pie crust at 450° for 10–12 minutes. Be sure to poke holes all around the sides and all over the bottom before baking.

Grandma's Fresh Strawberry Pie

Julie

3 T. strawberry Jello, dry
3 T. cornstarch
1 c. sugar
1 c. water
1 pkg. (8 oz.) Cool Whip
1 pt. fresh strawberries, sliced
1 pie crust, baked

Cook sugar, water, cornstarch, and Jello over medium heat until mixture comes to a boil and thickens. May add red food coloring for color. Remove from heat and cool. Add fresh strawberries, sliced. Pour into baked pie crust and chill. Top pie with Cool Whip and keep refrigerated.

NOTE: My girls' Grandma, Mom, used to make this pie all the time. When we had family get-togethers, she made several. It's light and delicious. Julie and Jennie always loved it and now Lydia is asking for strawberry pie. I'm so glad we were able to locate this recipe and continue to make memories with it.

Key Lime Pie

1 chocolate wafer crumb crust
1 can (14 oz.) sweetened condensed milk
½ c. Key lime juice
4 egg yolks
½ tsp. vanilla extract
1 c. whipping cream
3 T. sugar
Key lime zest

Preheat oven to 375°. Combine the sweetened condensed milk, key lime juice, egg yolks, and vanilla in a mixing bowl and mix until smooth. Spoon into the crumb crust and bake for 8 minutes. Cool on a wire rack. Beat the whipping cream in a mixing bowl until frothy. Add the sugar gradually, beating constantly until soft peaks form. Spoon over the top of the pie. Chill until serving time. Garnish with lime zest. (I use Cool Whip instead of whipped cream if I am traveling with this pie or just serving a few pieces at a time.) Yield: 6–8 servings

NOTE: For those who have never squeezed Key limes: get ready. Key limes are small and don't produce a whole lot of juice. Don't substitute regular limes though–the flavor is just not the same. Green key limes are immature fruits, prized for their acidity. As they ripen to a yellow color, the acid content diminishes greatly, resulting in a sweeter fruit. Most Key limes today are from Mexico, but they got their name from the Florida Keys where they were grown in the early 1900s.

Light Key Lime Pie

Make the following substitutions for a lighter version.

- ✦ Fat-free sweetened condensed milk for sweetened condensed milk
- ✦ ¾ c. egg substitute for egg yolks
- ✦ Reduced-fat, ready-made graham cracker crust for chocolate crust
- ✦ Fat-free frozen whipped topping for whipped cream and sugar

"Tis an ill cook that cannot lick his own fingers." – William Shakespeare

Lemon Meringue Pie

1 c. sugar
3 T. cornstarch
1½ c. cold water
3 egg yolks, slightly beaten
Grated rind of 1 lemon
¼ c. lemon juice
1 T. butter or margarine
1 baked pie shell

MERINGUE
3 egg whites
⅓ c. sugar

In 2-quart saucepan, stir together sugar and cornstarch; add water and egg yolks. Bring to boil over medium heat. Remove from heat and add lemon rind, lemon juice, and butter. Cool. Beat egg whites until white in color; continue beating at high speed and gradually add sugar. Beat until soft peaks form. Pour pudding in baked pie shell and top with meringue. Bake at 350° for 12–15 minutes. Watch closely.

Mrs. Kellogg's Pecan Pie

(a.k.a. The Best Pecan Pie I Have Ever Made)

3 eggs
1 c. white Karo syrup
½ c. sugar
1 T. butter
Dash of salt
1 tsp. vanilla
1½ c. pecans
1 unbaked pie shell

Beat eggs; add Karo syrup, sugar, butter, vanilla, and salt. Beat well. Add pecans. Bake in uncooked pie shell for 10 minutes at 400°; then 40–45 minutes at 350°. If crust starts to brown, fold 3-inch-wide strips of foil over it for the remainder of the baking.

SOURCE: This recipe is from our church cookbook. Mrs. Kellogg was a tiny woman who loved to laugh and have a good time. Her son was in my confirmation class way back in the 60s. Time flies when you are having fun–watch out or it will be Thanksgiving or Christmas and time to bake pies again.

Old-Fashioned Dewberry Pie

Dewberries
1 unbaked pie shell
2 eggs, well-beaten
½ c. flour
1½ c. sugar
½ c. heavy cream

CRUMB TOPPING
8 T. flour
4 T. butter
8 T. sugar

Into the unbaked pie shell, place enough fresh or frozen berries to fill level with the top. Then mix together the eggs, ½ cup flour, and 1½ cups sugar. Add the cream and pour this over the berries and allow to settle to bottom. Then mix the remaining flour, butter, and sugar until crumbly; spread over top of pie. Bake at 325° for 45 minutes.

NOTE: Julie makes this pie with the dewberries that grow along their back fence. It's delicious. Evaporated milk can be used in place of the heavy cream.

Dewberries remind me of a scary childhood memory. We called them blackberries back then and my two sisters and I were picking them along the side of the road. We got about a quarter of a mile from home and Debbie, who was about two then, started yelling, "Nake, Nake, Nake!" crying, and holding her ankle. We looked and saw two marks on her leg, so Elaine and I took turns carrying her while running home as fast as we could. We just knew she was going to die from a snake bite. Well, when we got home, Mama looked at it and pulled out two tiny stickers from the berry vine. I don't remember what happened to the berries we had picked, but I don't remember having pie or cobbler that night either. Debbie, however, cried "wolf" many times thereafter.

"Life is short, and it's up to you to make it sweet." – Sadie Delany

Pineapple Chess Pie

Granee J

1½ c. sugar
2 T. flour
3 eggs, well beaten
¼ c. margarine or butter, room temperature
1 sm. (8.25 oz.) can crushed pineapple, drained
1 tsp. vanilla
Pinch salt
9 in. pie pastry

Mix all the pie ingredients together well. Pour into unbaked pie shell and bake at 400° for 10 minutes and turn down the oven to 350° and bake for about 50 minutes or until golden brown. Coconut flakes can be added, if desired.

NOTE: My sister-in-law got this recipe in her first cooking class with Mrs. Donley in Marlin, Texas. With permission, I have copied it from one of my sister Debbie's cookbooks. She says, "This recipe is so special because Mrs. Donley was like a mother to me after my mama died. She couldn't have been a more truly loving person." This recipe so fits the theme: God bless those who teach–one and all!

Pumpkin Chiffon Pie

Jennie

1 box (5.1 oz.) vanilla instant pudding mix
1 jar (11 oz.) New Canaan Farms Pumpkin Butter
1 pt. heavy cream
1 ready-made graham cracker or chocolate pie crust

In a large bowl, combine pudding mix, pumpkin butter, and heavy cream. Beat on medium speed until fluffy. Spoon mixture into pie crust and refrigerate. Top with toasted pecans and nutmeg, if desired.

*Comparable brand of pumpkin butter or apple butter can be substituted in this recipe.

COOKIES, BARS & CANDY

BAKING COOKIES

- Use three cookie sheets for maximum speed when baking cookies. Fill the first sheet and place on the bottom rack of the oven. Set the timer for half the baking time. Fill the second sheet. When the timer dings, move the first sheet of cookies to the top rack, place the second sheet on the bottom rack, and set the timer for half the baking time. Fill the third sheet. When the timer dings, take out the top sheet, move the bottom sheet up, and place the third sheet on the bottom. Continue filling and rotating until all cookies are done. (When using two sheets in the oven, they must be rotated even if this method isn't used. Otherwise, one pan will have cookies too brown on top and the other pan will have cookies too brown on bottom.)
- A cookie sheet does not have connected sides, just a slightly turned up edge. Use cookie sheets for cookies and the other pans (ones with 1-inch sides–known as a jelly roll pan) for bars and jelly rolls. The 1-inch sides of the jelly roll pan will keep the cookies on the edge from baking evenly. Turn the jelly roll pan upside-down and use it for cookies, or just place the cookies 2 inches from the sides of the pan to allow even browning.

Baking Cookies, continued

- ✦ Use two teaspoons to drop cookies; scoop dough into one and use the back of the other to push dough onto the cookie sheet. If a little too much dough is on the spoon, use the second spoon to scrape off just the right amount.
- ✦ Cookies dropped on a sheet together should all be the same size so they bake evenly and all get done at the same time.
- ✦ It is not necessary to wash the cookie sheet before refilling it. Just brush off any crumbs.
- ✦ The cookie sheet should be cool enough to touch with your hand before refilling.
- ✦ Remove cookies from the oven just before they are done. The heat from the pan will continue baking the cookies and they can burn after taking them out of the oven.
- ✦ Remove cookies from the baking sheet when they come out of the oven unless the recipe instructs differently.
- ✦ Cool cookies on a rack and allow to cool completely before stacking or they will stick together.
- ✦ Store soft cookies in a container with a tight-fitting lid. Store hard cookies in a container with a loose-fitting lid.
- ✦ Allow cookie sheets and all baking pans to cool completely before putting in water. Hot pans placed in water will warp. Sometimes baking pans will make a popping sound in the oven when they get hot and the opposite corners of the sheet pop up. This is a result of putting hot pans in water. The same thing happens to your skillets and griddles, so let them cool before washing, too. If used on an electric range, especially a flat-surface one, these warped pans will not cook very well, if at all.

NOTE: The Swedish are credited with the creation of cookies. Way back in the 1500s, they placed small dollops of cake dough on a pan and baked them to test the temperature for baking their cakes.

Amazing Peanut Butter Cookies

1 c. peanut butter
1½ c. sugar
1 egg
1 tsp. vanilla

Combine all ingredients, shape into balls, and roll in additional sugar. Press a crisscross pattern on cookies using a fork. Bake 12 minutes at 350°.

Apricot Bars

Julie

1½ c. sifted flour
1 tsp. baking powder
1 c. brown sugar
1½ c. quick cooking oats
¾ c. butter or margarine, melted
1 jar (16 oz.) apricot jam

Mix flour, baking powder, brown sugar, and oats. Combine with melted butter. Pat ⅔ of mixture into a 9 x 13 x 2-inch pan. Spread with jam. Cover with remaining crumb mixture. Bake at 350° for 35 minutes. Cool and cut.

Butterscotch Treats

Donna

1 pkg. (12 oz.) butterscotch morsels (chips)
2 T. peanut butter
1 can (12 oz.) unsalted peanuts
½ c. pecans, chopped
1 can shoestring potatoes

Melt peanut butter and morsels in double boiler. Add all other ingredients. Drop from spoon onto wax paper. Place in refrigerator to cool.

NOTE: Donna says, "My daughter loved these and couldn't wait to get to Granny's. As Grannies do, these treats were always waiting for her. Now Sara makes them in the fall for her friends. I don't think she knows what a double boiler is. She uses the microwave."

Chess Cake Squares

Estelle

CRUST
1 pkg. Duncan Hines Butter-Flavor Cake Mix
1 egg, beaten slightly
½ c. butter, soft

FILLING
3 eggs, beaten slightly
1 tsp. vanilla
8 oz. cream cheese
1 lb. (3¾ c.) sifted powdered sugar

Mix the crust ingredients and pat evenly in a greased 13 x 9 x 2-inch pan. Mix the filling ingredients until smooth and pour over cake mix in pan. Bake at 350° for 10 minutes. Reduce to 325° and bake for 30 minutes. (May have to bake longer; just bake until done.)

NOTE: Estelle, the source of these delicious squares, also bakes wedding and special occasion cakes that are absolutely the best!

Chewy Squares

½ lb. margarine
1 box brown sugar
2 eggs
2 tsp. baking powder
2 c. flour
1 tsp. vanilla
1½ c. pecans

Mix all ingredients and bake on greased jelly roll pan. Bake at 350° for 20–25 minutes. Cool and cut into squares.

SOURCE: These bars are chewy, delicious, and bring back memories of my church youth group. I am on my way to the store to buy brown sugar right now. That's the neat thing about my goal of writing a cookbook–I have to test the recipes.

Chocolate Chip Cookies

Classroom Standard

2¼ c. all purpose flour
1 tsp. baking soda
1 tsp. salt
1 c. butter, softened
¾ c. sugar
¾ c. brown sugar, firmly packed
1 tsp. vanilla
2 eggs
1 pkg. (12 oz. or 2 c.) semisweet real chocolate chips
1 c. chopped nuts, optional

Preheat oven to 375°. In small bowl, combine flour, baking soda, and salt; set aside. In large bowl, combine butter, sugar, brown sugar, and vanilla; beat until creamy. Beat in eggs. Gradually add flour mixture; mix well. Stir in chocolate chips and nuts. Drop by rounded teaspoonfuls onto ungreased cookie sheets. Bake at 375° for 8–10 minutes. Yield: 60 cookies, 2-inches diameter

Pan Cookie

Spread the cookie dough into greased 15 x 10 x 1-inch baking pan. Bake at 375° for 20 minutes. Cool; cut into 35 squares, 2 x 2-inches.

It was my first year teaching and Rebecca was a special needs student. She could barely talk, lived in poverty, hung on my every word. I was helping her group determine if their chocolate chip cookies were ready to come out of the oven or not. As I bent over the open oven door, Rebecca planted a very juicy kiss on my forehead. I will never forget that moment. It spoke volumes to me about all kinds of things. Never, ever take anyone for-granted. Know that, while we think others do not appreciate us, there is always someone who does. Do not underestimate the value of your health and well-being. Treat others, no matter their station in life, with respect. I could go on and on. Just know that Rebecca's kiss helped me form a foundation of love and understanding as a teacher and as an individual. That kiss, while startling and a little uncomfortable, was a defining moment in my life.

Drop Cookies

2 c. sifted flour
2 tsp. baking powder
½ tsp. salt
½ c. butter or margarine
1 c. sugar
½ tsp. vanilla
1 egg
¼ c. milk
½ c. chopped nuts, or dried or candied fruit or coconut

Mix and sift flour, salt, and baking powder. Cream fat until soft. Add sugar gradually and cream. Add vanilla. Beat the egg; add to the sugar mixture. Beat until smooth. Then add a small amount of milk to this mixture and beat until smooth. Continue this process, adding flour and milk alternately and ending with an addition of flour. Add nuts or fruits. Drop from teaspoon on greased baking sheet. Drop far enough apart that cookies will not touch when baking. Bake in moderate oven 375°–400° for 8–12 minutes. Remove from baking sheet and place on rack or paper towels to cool. Yield: 60 cookies.

NOTE: This recipe card is stained and yellowed. I bet I made a hundred batches of this cookie when I was in school. The original recipe came from a 4-H pamphlet, so that means I probably started baking these cookies when I was about nine. Enjoy!

"A balanced diet is a cookie in each hand." – Author Unknown

Divinity–NOT!

I haven't tried to make divinity since the time Mama and I attempted it in the kitchen of our big house years ago. Somehow or another, all I remember is that we had this beige mess that stuck to a Jewel Tea dinner plate so bad, we wound up throwing the plate away. I was new to cooking and I don't remember anything about a thermometer being used. Maybe it was raining that day. My hat's off to candy makers. Since that catastrophe, Mama and I stick to buying orange slices.

Fruit Cookies

½ c. butter
1½ c. brown sugar
4 eggs, unbeaten one at a time
1 c. whiskey
3 T. milk
3 c. flour
2 lb. candied pineapple, cut fine
2 lb. candied cherries, cut fine
6 c. pecans, chopped
1 tsp. soda
1 tsp. cinnamon
1 tsp. nutmeg
1 tsp. allspice
1 tsp. cloves

Drop on cookie sheet and bake at 250° for 30 minutes. Makes enough for the town. (Can buy cut pineapple.)

NOTE: This recipe is from my coordinating teacher back when I did my student teaching. She gave no instructions except for the egg thing. I guess, as a fellow homemaking teacher, she thought I didn't need any. These cookies are a great holiday substitute for fruit cake–the whiskey provides an added kick sometimes needed to get through the days before Christmas vacation arrived. By the way, it really does make enough cookies for the town–great for a cookie swap.

INSTRUCTIONS: Cream butter and sugar together. Add eggs (unbeaten) one at a time and cream. Add milk; blend. Sift together the flour, soda, and spices. Use a little of this mixture to coat the chopped fruit. Add whiskey and flour alternately, ending with an addition of flour. Stir in fruit and nuts. Drop on greased cookie sheets and bake as instructed.

Grandmother Craig's Oatmeal Cookies

Classroom Standard

¾ c. soft shortening
1 c. brown sugar
½ c. sugar
1 egg
¼ c. water
1 tsp. vanilla
1 c. sifted flour
1 tsp. salt
½ tsp. soda
3 c. old-fashioned oatmeal, uncooked
½ c. nuts, chopped

Place shortening, sugars, egg, water, and vanilla in mixing bowl; beat thoroughly. Sift together flour, salt, and soda. Add to shortening mixture, mixing well. Blend in oats and nuts. Drop by teaspoon on greased cookie sheet. Bake in moderate oven at 350° for 12–15 minutes. Allow to cool on pan 3–4 minutes; then place on racks to cool.

Raisin-Spice Oatmeal Cookies

Add 1 teaspoon cinnamon, ¼ teaspoon nutmeg, and 1 cup raisins when adding the oats and nuts.

Fudgie Scotch Ring

(a.k.a. Traditional Christmas Candy)

Rosemary

6 oz. semi-sweet chocolate morsels
6 oz. butterscotch morsels
1 can sweetened condensed milk
1 c. walnuts, chopped, plus extra for lining pan
½ tsp. vanilla

Cut parchment paper to fit a 9-inch round cake pan. Place something in the middle (glass, candle cup, etc.) of the pan to form the center of the wreath; lightly grease it so it comes out easily. Line the ring with walnuts. Using a double boiler or microwave, melt the 2 types of morsels and milk together. Add vanilla and nuts. Cool and spoon mixture into outer circle of pan. To serve, remove from pan and decorate as desired.

"Forget love; I'd rather fall in chocolate." – Unknown

Julie's Hello Dolly Bars

(a.k.a. Hello Daddy Bars)

Julie

1 c. pecans, chopped
½ c. butter
1½ c. graham cracker crumbs
2 T. brown sugar
1 can Eagle Brand sweetened condensed milk
2 c. semisweet chocolate chips
1⅓ c. flaked coconut

Toast nuts in heavy pan, stirring often. Preheat oven to 350°, 325° for glass dish. In 9 x 13 x 2-inch baking pan, melt butter in oven. Combine graham cracker crumbs and brown sugar; sprinkle over melted butter. Mix and press firmly into pan with a fork. Pour milk over crumbs evenly. Top with other ingredients. Press firmly with a fork, until milk comes through. Bake 25–30 minutes until browned. Cool. Cut into small bars. Store covered at room temperature.

NOTE: Julie adapted the traditional recipe especially for her husband who loves her version. Julie says, "These are so delicious and it doesn't take long for them to disappear. Sometimes I add chopped pecans to the crust."

Lemon Bars

Frances & Teacher Bake-Off

CRUST
2 c. sifted flour
½ c. sifted powdered sugar
1 c. margarine

FILLING
4 eggs, beaten
2 c. sugar
⅓ c. lemon juice
¼ c. flour
½ tsp. baking powder

Sift flour and sugar together; cut in margarine and mix until mixture clings together. Press into a 13 x 9 x 2-inch pan. Bake in a 350° oven for 20 minutes. To prepare filling, beat together eggs, sugar, and lemon juice. Sift in dry ingredients, stir into the egg mixture, and pour over baked crust. Bake at 350° for 25 minutes. Cool and cut into squares.

NOTE: We all loved it when our business teacher Frances, brought these to a dinner or to the teacher bake-off. They are absolutely delicious. Frances retired before I did and it's been a very, very long time since I had a lemon bar. It seems I remember that the tops of her bars were dusted with powdered sugar.

Microwave Peanut Brittle

From the Food Lab

1 c. sugar
1 c. raw peanuts
⅛ tsp. salt
½ c. white corn syrup
1 tsp. butter
1 tsp. vanilla
1 tsp. soda

Stir together the sugar, peanuts, salt, and corn syrup in a 4 cup Pyrex measuring cup. Microwave on high for 4 minutes. Stir well. Microwave another 3½ minutes on high. Stir well and mix in vanilla and butter. Cook 2 minutes longer on high. Remove from microwave and add 1 teaspoon soda; lightly stir until light and foamy. Pour onto buttered cookie sheet. Cool and break into small pieces. Store in airtight container. Makes about 1 pound of candy.

> My students used to make tons of this around the Christmas holidays and deliver it to their teachers just before their final tests. They were pretty smart, huh? Come to think of it, they probably ate their peanut brittle themselves. I was so naive.

Microwave Peanut Patty

Rosemary

2 c. sugar
½ c. water
½ c. light corn syrup
2 c. raw peanuts
½ c. butter
1 tsp. vanilla
5 drops red food coloring

Stir together sugar, water, and syrup. Cook in microwave for 8 minutes. Add peanuts; stir and cook for 4½ minutes. Stir and cook for another 4½ minutes. Add butter, vanilla, and food coloring. Stir until texture starts to change. Quickly pour in pan (or spoon into patties); break apart when cool.

"No man in the world has more courage than the man who can stop after eating one peanut." – Channing Pollack

No Bake Cookies

2 c. sugar
½ c. cocoa
½ c. milk
½ c. margarine
1 T. vanilla
3 c. three-minute oats

Stir sugar and cocoa together; add milk and bring to a boil. Add margarine, vanilla, and oats. Drop by spoonful on waxed paper.

These were the girls favorite growing up–they were one of the first things they learned to make. "Train up a child in the way he should go: and when he is old, he will not depart from it." Proverbs 22:6. Scripture just doesn't make mistakes. My girls are both excellent cooks and my grandchildren are not far behind.

Speaking of girls, here we are: Jenn, Jules, Lyd, and me.
It's my birthday–everyone smile...1...(snap)...2...3.

Oatmeal Chocolate Chip Cookies

Janis

¾ c. vegetable shortening
1 egg
1 c. brown sugar, firmly packed
½ c. sugar
¼ c. water
1 tsp. vanilla
1 c. flour
1 tsp. salt
½ tsp. baking soda
3 c. uncooked oatmeal
1 c. chocolate chips
1 c. coconut

Cream together shortening, egg, brown sugar, sugar, water, and vanilla. In a separate bowl, combine flour, salt, baking soda, and oatmeal. Add dry ingredients to creamed ingredients; stir until blended. Mix in chocolate chips and coconut. Drop by rounded spoonfuls on cookie sheet and bake for 12 to 15 minutes at 350°.

NOTE: For chocolate lover's: omit coconut and use two cups chocolate chips instead of one. Janis says, "When I lived in Nebraska around 1980, a friend gave us some of these cookies to take camping with us. They were so delicious with coffee on a rainy afternoon in the camper."

Orange Slice Cookies

Mom

4 eggs, beaten lightly
2 c. brown sugar
2 c. flour
1 c. nuts, chopped
1 tsp. vanilla
¼ tsp. soda
1 T. water
1 c. orange slices, chopped

Dissolve soda in water. Mix all ingredients together and bake in a greased jelly roll pan at 350° until brown on top. Cut into small squares and roll in powdered sugar.

Orange slices are such a part of my heritage. They were even the preferred candy of Mama and Daddy's little Dachshund, Sammy, who lived to the ripe old human age of 91. He could hear the lid of the candy bowl moving, even if you are were so careful, and he immediately started to bark, sat up on his haunches, and begged until he got a piece of orange slice, too. Daddy used to sneak Sam bites of food under the table. Sam was a much loved, lucky dog and we all miss him so much.

Our Christmas Sugar Cookies

⅓ c. margarine or butter
⅓ c. shortening
2 c. all purpose flour
1 egg
¾ c. sugar
1 T. milk
1 tsp. baking powder
1 tsp. vanilla
Dash salt
Powdered Sugar Icing

Beat margarine and shortening with mixer on med-high speed for 30 seconds. Add half of the flour, egg, sugar, milk, baking powder, vanilla, and salt. Beat until thoroughly combined. Beat in remaining flour. Divide dough in half, cover and chill for 3 hours. On lightly floured surface, roll out one-half dough at a time to ⅛-inch thick. Cut with 2½-inch cutters. On an ungreased cookie sheet, bake at 375° for 8–9 minutes, until edges are firm. Rotate from top to bottom rack halfway through. Cool on wire rack. Ice and decorate. Yield: 36–48 cookies

Powdered Sugar Icing

1 c. sifted powder sugar
¼ tsp. vanilla
Milk

Mix sugar and vanilla. Add milk 1 teaspoon at a time until of spreading consistency.

JULIE'S NOTE: "We have a lovely time making and decorating 4–6 batches of these yummy cookies every year. I make the dough the night before and start the baking early in the morning. It is always a good time, even if we sometimes eat only cookie dough and chips and dip."

"C is for cookie, it's good enough for me;
oh cookie cookie cookie starts with C."
– Cookie Monster, Sesame Street

Family traditions are so powerful. Making sugar cookies and gingerbread boys and girls is a family affair and Christmas tradition we all treasure.

Our Gingerbread Cookies

½ c. shortening
2½ c. all purpose flour
½ c. sugar
½ c. molasses (Grandma's is best)
1 egg
1 T. vinegar
1 tsp. baking powder
1 tsp. ground ginger
½ tsp. baking soda
½ tsp. ground cinnamon
½ tsp. ground cloves
Thin Icing

Beat shortening on med-high speed for 30 seconds. Add half of the flour, sugar, molasses, egg, vinegar, baking powder, ginger, baking soda, cinnamon, and cloves. Beat until combined. Beat in remaining flour. Divide in half, cover and chill 3 hours. On lightly floured surface, roll out half of the dough at a time to ⅛-inch thick. Cut with 2½-inch cutters. Place 1 inch apart on greased cookie sheet. Bake at 375° for 5–6 minutes until edges are lightly browned. Cool on cookie sheet 1 minute then cool on wire rack. Dip in thin powdered sugar icing. Yield: 36-48 cookies

NOTE: "These are soft gingerbread cookies and entirely addictive, even to non-gingerbread fans. We're usually so tired after decorating 4-6 batches of sugar cookies to do these cute little cookies justice." Julie

Thin Icing

Sifted powdered sugar
¼ tsp. vanilla
Milk

Mix sugar and vanilla. Add milk 1 teaspoon at a time until very thin. Place in a flat bowl and carefully dip the top surface of each gingerbread boy and girl into the icing. Place on rack to dry.

NOTE: A few years back, we started doing this fast-frosting technique because we were too tired to go any further. We just added more milk to the frosting left from the sugar cookies and started dipping. Now, this has become a tradition and the preferred way.

Peanut Butter Haystacks

Project Show

1 pkg. (6 oz.) butterscotch chips
½ c. peanut butter
½ c. salted peanuts
2 c. Chow Mien noodles

Place chips and peanut butter in a 2-quart pan. Melt until chips are slimy and soft. Blend well. Stir in peanuts and Chow Mien noodles. Drop by forkfuls onto wax paper. Cool until noodles remain set. Yield: about 2½ dozen

SOURCE: Quick and easy, plus delicious, these haystacks were entered in the project show–a blue ribbon winner in my opinion.

Haystacks bring back a precious memory. During my senior year in high school I won several awards, one of which was presented at a luncheon on a Saturday. Mama had to work that day so Daddy went with me on this occasion. I think I have mentioned the fact that he was a fairly picky eater, so I was horrified when our plates were brought out. What looked to be a bird's nest, covered with some sort of chicken a la king looking stuff, was the main attraction. A few skimpy vegetables lay idly beside this sad and scary looking concoction. I just knew Daddy would have a fit, but he ate it all without saying a word. I love and miss him so much and I thank God for the time I spent with him after retiring. Some things just can't be replaced.

Peanut Butter-Chocolate Kiss Cookies

1 can (14 oz.) sweetened condensed milk
¾ c. peanut butter
2 c. baking mix
1 tsp. vanilla
¼ c. sugar
1 pkg. (13 oz.) Hershey's Kisses

Beat milk and peanut butter on medium speed until creamy. Add baking mix and vanilla, beating at low speed until blended. Shape into balls 1-inch in diameter. Roll in sugar. Place on lightly greased baking sheet. Bake at 350° for 11 minutes. Remove from oven; place a kiss in the center of each cookie. Remove to rack to cool.

Skillet Cookies

(a.k.a. Rice Krispies Cookies)

Mom

½ c. margarine
¾ c. sugar
2 egg yolks
½ lb. dates, chopped
1 tsp. vanilla
1 c. nuts
2 c. Rice Krispies
1 c. coconut

Combine margarine, sugar, dates, and egg yolks in cast iron skillet; cook about 10 minutes, stirring and mashing dates to make a paste. Turn off heat and add vanilla, nuts, and Rice Krispies. Mix well. When it cools, shape into small balls and roll in coconut.

Ranger Cookies

My Mama

1 c. shortening
1 c. brown sugar
1 c. sugar
2 eggs
2 c. flour
1 tsp. baking powder
2 tsp. soda
½ tsp. salt
2 c. crushed corn flakes
(Mama uses Rice Krispies)
2 c. quick-cooking oatmeal
1 c. pecans
1 c. coconut
1 tsp. vanilla

Cream shortening and sugars until smooth. Add eggs and beat until smooth. Sift flour, soda, baking powder, and salt together and add to the creamed mixture. Then add cereal, oatmeal, pecans, and coconut. Mix until all is combined together. Drop by teaspoon on ungreased cookie sheet and bake 12–15 minutes in a 350° oven. Yield: about 5 dozen

NOTE: Mama told me she might try Cheerios the next time she makes these cookies. Sometimes she puts chocolate chips in them. I have seen this recipe in so many cookbooks–the ingredients might be a little different, but they are all basically the same. Mom says these were her children's favorite, but she called them ranch cookies. Ranger cookies are so popular around here, it would be hard to believe there's anyone around who hasn't had one. If you've never baked these, give this recipe a try–they just might become your favorite.

I remember Mom always had gorgeous trays of desserts at Christmas. I am so glad I have found recipes for my favorites. To think, all the time they were in the St. Paul church cookbook she gave me years ago. Guess I was too busy being a mother to spend time with it.

Lydia carries on the family tradition of baking. It just has to involve tasting the dough!

Recipe for Chocolate Chip Chews

Project Show—In Memory of My Student, Jerry Lyon

2 c. brown sugar
⅔ c. shortening
3 eggs
1 tsp. vanilla
2 c. flour
½ tsp. salt
1 tsp. baking powder
1 pkg. (6 oz.) chocolate chips
1 c. nuts, chopped

Beat together the brown sugar and shortening. Add remaining ingredients and mix well. Pour into well-greased 9 x 13 x 2-inch pan. Bake at 350° for 30–35 minutes.

Every year we had a project show and students were required to enter a baked product. Jerry was from Boys Country, a home for children from families in crisis. The judges were so impressed with Jerry's bars they rated them first place and he received a blue ribbon. For some reason, Jerry made a lasting impression on me. He tried so hard and seemed to have a bright future ahead of him. Jerry was killed in a single-person vehicle accident just after his graduation. The location of his accident has become a fairly dangerous stretch of road and several crosses are present on the right-of-way. Even before any crosses were placed, I always thought of Jerry when I drove by...and I still think of him. I wonder if someone placed one of those crosses there in his memory?

Soft Peanut Butter Cookies

Julie

½ c. margarine or butter
½ c. peanut butter
1¼ c. all purpose flour
½ c. brown sugar or ¼ c. honey
1 egg
½ c. sugar
½ tsp. baking soda
½ tsp. baking powder
½ tsp. vanilla
Sugar

Beat peanut butter and butter on medium-high speed for 30 seconds. Add ½ cup of flour, the sugars, egg, baking soda, baking powder, and vanilla. Beat in remaining flour. Cover and chill until dough is easy to handle. Shape into 1 inch balls; roll in sugar. Place 2 inches apart on ungreased cookie sheet. Flatten by crisscrossing with tines of a fork. Bake at 375° for 7–9 minutes until bottoms lightly brown. Cool on wire racks. Yield: 3 dozen

NOTE: According to Julie, "The honey is the secret to these super soft peanut butter cookies."

Spotted Brownies

1 pkg. brownie mix (9 x 13 size)
½ c. vegetable oil
2 eggs
½ tsp. coconut extract
1 pkg. (8 oz.) cream cheese, softened
2 eggs
1 tsp. coconut extract
1 tsp. vanilla extract
3¾ c. powdered sugar
1 c. flaked coconut

In a large mixing bowl, beat the brownie mix, oil, eggs, and extract on medium speed until blended–it will be stiff. Reserve 1 cup of this batter for topping. Spread the remaining batter into a greased 13 x 9 x 2-inch baking pan. Bake at 350° for 10–15 minutes or until edges crack. To prepare the filling, put the cream cheese, eggs, extracts, and powdered sugar in a mixing bowl; beat until smooth and creamy. Fold in coconut. Spread over the brownies being careful not to mess up the baked brownie. Drop the reserved batter over filling like dropping cookies. Bake for 45–50 minutes. Use a toothpick test to determine doneness. Cool on a wire rack. Refrigerate. Yield: 3 dozen

Sweet Pretzel Rods

1 pkg. (10 oz.) pretzel rods
1 pkg. (14 oz.) caramels
1 T. evaporated milk
1¼ c. miniature semisweet chocolate chips
1 c. plus 2 T. butterscotch chips
⅔ c. milk chocolate toffee bits
¼ c. walnuts, chopped & toasted

Cut the pretzels in half using a sharp knife. Place caramels and milk in a heavy saucepan and cook over low heat until melted. Meanwhile, combine the chips, toffee bits, and walnuts in a shallow bowl. Pour melted caramel mixture into a 2-cup glass measuring cup. Dip the cut end of each pretzel piece about ⅔ of the way into caramel mixture. Let extra caramel drip off, then roll the pretzels in the chip & nut mixture. (Reheat caramel in microwave if it gets too thick.) Place on waxed paper. Store in an airtight container when completely set. Yield: about 4 dozen

The Best Cookies in the World

Estelle

1 c. butter
1 c. sugar
1 c. brown sugar
1 egg
3½ c. flour
1 tsp. soda
1 tsp. salt
1 c. salad oil (Mazola)
1 c. uncooked Quaker Oats
1 c. corn flakes, crushed
½ c. pecans
½ c. coconut
1 tsp. vanilla

Cream butter, add egg and sugars and mix well. Combine flour, soda, and salt. Add alternately with salad oil, then add rest of ingredients. Drop by teaspoonfuls onto greased cookie sheet. Dip fork in ½ cup water and press down on each cookie. Bake at 325° for 10–12 minutes or until brown. Put on paper towels to drain.

SOURCE: A lifelong family friend, Estelle is renowned for her baking expertise, so be sure to try her recipes. By the way, when a cook specifies a specific ingredient, I always use that because I want my foods to turn out just as good as theirs.

Pecan Sandies

Cheryl

1 c. margarine, softened
1 c. vegetable oil
1 c. sugar
1 c. powdered sugar, sifted
2 eggs
1 tsp. vanilla extract
4 c. all purpose flour
1 tsp. baking soda
1 tsp. cream of tartar
1 tsp. salt
2 c. pecans, chopped
½ c. sugar for decoration

Preheat oven to 375°. In a large bowl, cream together the margarine, vegetable oil, 1 cup sugar, and powdered sugar until smooth. Beat in the eggs one at a time, then stir in the vanilla. Combine the flour, baking soda, cream of tartar, and salt; stir into the creamed mixture. Mix in the pecans. Roll dough into 1 inch balls and roll each ball in remaining sugar. Place the cookies 2 inches apart onto ungreased cookie sheets. Bake for 10–12 minutes in the preheated oven, or until the edges are golden. Remove from cookie sheets to cool on wire racks. Ready in 30 minutes.
Yield: 96 servings

NOTE: Cheryl, a past student of mine who comes from renowned cooking roots and has published a cookbook for her family, says, "I made this recipe for the first time about three years ago for the family cookie bake. It has become one of the most popular cookies there. I also make an almond sandie, substituting almond flavoring for the vanilla and almonds for the pecans. Finally, could I please get a passing grade rather than the 'I' that I received in Home Ec when you taught me?" It's been a long, long time since Cheryl was in my class–but since she quickly responded to my email, listed the recipe ingredients in proper order, and even included preparation time, I am bequeathing her a 95. She obviously paid attention to something I taught!

Walk to School Cookies

Waller ISD Cafeteria, Reprinted from Cheryl's Cookbook with Permission

1 lb. butter
1 c. sugar
4⅞ c. flour
¼ tsp. salt
½ tsp. vanilla
¾ c. pecans, chopped

Cream butter and sugar; add flour and salt. Mix well. Stir in vanilla and pecans. Drop by teaspoonfuls onto ungreased cookie sheet. Bake at 350° for 10–12 minutes.

Cafeteria Quantity (serves 225)

5 lb. butter
5 c. sugar
6 lb. flour
1¼ tsp. salt
2½ tsp. vanilla
3¾ c. pecans, chopped

Follow directions above. The cafeteria ladies dropped these cookies using a scoop so they were always rounded with little pieces hanging on the edges.

I always took my lunch to school except on special occasions–like when they had Walk to School Cookies on the menu. I ate these cookies in the same cafeteria for 38 years, first as a student and then as a teacher. Smelling these delicious cookies baking right across the hall from my classroom always made my stomach growl.

Whisky Balls

Mom

6 c. vanilla wafers, finely crushed
2 c. powdered sugar
6 T. light or dark syrup
3 T. cocoa
4 jiggers whiskey
Powdered sugar

Mix well and make into balls; then roll in powdered sugar.

NOTE: I think I'm going to use the food processor to crush the vanilla wafers. It will be interesting to see if 6 cups equals one box. These are so easy to make and I remember that, while delicious, they packed a punch. I wonder if Grandma and Grandpa ever had these whiskey balls along with their margaritas?

Wreath Delights

1 lg. bag miniature pretzels, heart shaped
1 pkg. almond bark
Nonpareils
Assorted sugar candies

Place almond bark in heavy saucepan or top of double boiler and melt or follow package instructions for melting in the microwave. For each wreath, dip rounded bottoms of 5 miniature pretzels, one at a time, into bark; let excess drip off. Lay pretzels onto wax or parchment paper, forming a circle. Allow sides to touch and point the rounded bottoms toward center. Repeat with 5 more pretzels, placing on top of first circle staggering top pretzels so each covers half of two pretzels on the bottom layer. Decorate with nonpareils and colored sugar. Let stand until set. Store at room temperature in an airtight container up to 1 week.

My granddaughter had a ball making these with me. I didn't realize she loved pretzels so much–she must have eaten at least a 100 while we were working. She's already quite the cook. The last time we made sugar cookies, she filled her cookie sheet right along with me. For six hours, she worked just as hard as the adults and probably had more fun. That's what it's all about. Remember, she already plans to become a teacher. That's all we play now, but at least I get to be the student. She told me the other day that her class (imaginary) was really improving at self-discipline and manners. Where was she when I struggled with those high school kids? I could have used her help!

BATTERS, SAUCES & MORE

Al's Shrimp Batter

Al

1 c. sifted flour
½ tsp. sugar
½ tsp. salt
1 egg, slightly beaten
1 c. ice water or buttermilk
2 T. salad oil

Combine all ingredients. Dip shrimp into batter and fry. The best yet!

Basic White Sauces & Gravies

From the Food Lab

Butter
Flour
1 c. milk
Salt & pepper to taste

First select thickness desired and type of sauce from below. Then melt butter in a saucepan and stir in flour. Cook and stir about 2 minutes. Add the milk all at one time. Cook and stir until mixture comes to a boil and thickens. Lower heat and stir every couple of minutes to keep a skin from forming on top. If mixture forms lumps, use a wire whisk to beat them away or pour through a strainer, catching the lumps. Be sure to lower the heat and stir constantly next time.

NOTE: Once the basic white sauce technique is mastered, it can be used to make gravy, too.

Thin White Sauce

Use 1 tablespoon butter and 1 tablespoon flour, following recipe otherwise.

Medium White Sauce

Use 2 tablespoons butter and 2 tablespoons flour, following recipe otherwise.

Thick White Sauce

Use 3 tablespoons butter and 3 tablespoons flour, following recipe otherwise.

Cream Sauce

Substitute heavy cream for half of the milk.

Cream Gravy for Chicken Fried Steak

Make the Medium White Sauce, using pan drippings in place of the butter. Double or triple recipe as needed.

Brown Gravy

Using pan drippings and Medium White Sauce proportions, allow the flour to brown (stirring constantly) before adding liquid. Water can be used in place of the milk for a browner gravy. The browner the flour, the less its thickening power.

Cheese Sauce

Classroom Standard

Add ¼ teaspoon dry mustard in with the melted butter and flour of the Medium White Sauce. Add 1 cup shredded cheese just after the milk has been stirred in. Do not bring to a boil, but cook over low heat, stirring constantly until the cheese melts. Use Velveeta or processed cheese to insure smooth melting. High or too much heat will cause natural cheese to curdle. Add ½ teaspoon additional dry mustard and 5 drops red pepper sauce for zesty version.

I told a woman at church that I was writing a book and, courteously, she asked what it was about. Well, this lead to a brief discourse of my life history and she got so excited. She told me, "The one thing I remember about home economics class is how to make a white sauce. For some reason the one tablespoon butter–one tablespoon flour just stayed in my head. I can't tell you how much I have used the two tablespoon sauce! It took me a little practice to make gravy because I never measured the grease left in the pan. I had just watched my mother make gravy. Eventually I got to where I could make a gravy that wasn't so thick I had to add all the milk in the refrigerator to thin it enough." I am so proud of her teacher and since I already had this recipe in my cookbook, I nearly broke my arm patting myself on the back later. Ahh...the priceless value of recipes and experience.

Beer Batter for Frying

1 c. beer
1 c. flour
Salt & pepper to taste

Mix all ingredients and let set for 15–20 minutes. Leisurely sip the remaining beer, if desired. Dip dry food (shrimp, zucchini, onion rings) into batter and cook in at least 3 inches of hot oil. Food will float when done.

NOTE: When using oil for the first time, foods will not be as golden brown. Oil can be used 2 or 3 times. Strain it if necessary and store in the refrigerator to maintain freshness. I keep my Fry Grandaddy in the fridge in the garage with the beer. Don't forget to remove that plastic cover before reheating the oil. I say that from experience.

Caramelized Onions

2 med. onions
1 T. oil
1½ tsp. sugar
2 T. balsamic vinaigrette dressing

Peel onions, cut into ¼-inch thick slices. There should be about 2 cups of onion slices. Heat the oil in a large, heavy skillet on medium heat. Add onions; cook 20–25 minutes or until lightly browned, stirring occasionally. Stir in sugar and cook 5 minutes longer or until golden brown, stirring occasionally. Drizzle with dressing just before serving. Yield: 4 servings, ¼ cup each

NOTE: For plain grilled onions, omit sugar and dressing. Can be stored in an airtight container for several days. Try these serving ideas:

- ✦ Top bruschetta, focaccia bread, or salads.
- ✦ Use as a topping on pizza.
- ✦ Serve on the side with roast or steak.
- ✦ Dollop onto grilled burgers, steak, chicken, or baked potatoes.
- ✦ Add to scrambled eggs, omelets, quiches, and frittatas for incredible flavor.

Caramel Sauce

½ c. butter
1 c. sugar
1 tsp. lemon juice
½ c. whipping cream

Melt butter in a 1½-quart heavy saucepan over medium heat; add sugar and lemon juice and cook, stirring constantly with a long-handled wooden spoon for 8–10 minutes or until mixture turns light golden brown. Gradually add cream and cook, stirring constantly, 1–2 minutes or until smooth. Mixture will bubble and spatter when adding cream. Remove from heat and cool 30 minutes.

NOTE: Don't be tempted to skip the lemon juice: It doesn't affect the flavor, but it does prevent the sugar from crystallizing.

"Hunger is the best sauce in the world." – Cervantes

Chinese Sauce

1 can (14 oz.) chicken broth
Juice from 4 oz. can mushrooms
2½ T. cornstarch
3 T. soy sauce

Combine ingredients, stirring well to mix in cornstarch. Cook over low heat until thickened. Serve with stir-fried anything.

NOTE: Beef broth or water with bouillon cubes of either flavor can be substituted for the chicken broth. Use low sodium broth or bouillon and soy sauce to reduce the sodium content. Use the drained mushrooms in your Chinese dish or add to sauce–it's your choice.

Chocolate Syrup

2 c. boiling water
2 c. sugar
⅛ tsp. salt
6 oz. unsweetened chocolate or 1 c. cocoa
1 tsp. vanilla

Cook and stir water, sugar, salt, and chocolate over moderate heat until smooth. Cool. Add vanilla. Store in a covered jar. Yield: 3 cups

Christmas Ornaments

4 c. flour
1 c. salt
1½ c. water

Combine ingredients and keep mixing until dough is pliable enough to handle. Place dough on floured surface and knead like yeast bread. Knead a full 5 minutes. If dough is too dry, add a bit more water. If too sticky, add more flour. Flour the rolling pin and roll out like pie crust to ¼-inch thickness. Cut out figures or roll into balls and make head, body, etc., for ornaments. Attach hooks for hanging. Bake at 275° for 1 hour and at 325° for 30 more minutes. Cool. Paint with acrylic paint.

NOTE: Use this dough for making bread baskets and other accessories, too. Cut into strips and weave over an up-side-down ovenproof dish–like maybe a loaf pan. Fashion a top edge and bake. It will take longer to bake these if the dough is thicker. Applying polyurethane after cooling makes creations shine and last. Experiment and have fun.

Cooked Play Dough

From the Food Lab

1 c. flour
½ c. salt
1 tsp. cream of tartar
Food coloring
1 c. water
1 T. oil

Mix together over warm heat until thick. Knead with hands until smooth. If the cream of tartar is added while kneading, play dough will have a marbled look.

While this is not food, we made it in class along with the creative clay and finger paints. When I was a student and during the first few years of my teaching career, we hosted a play school for preschool children during our regular class periods. Occasionally, someone will come up to me and ask if I remember them. They will let me off the hook by saying, "I was in your preschool. Don't you remember me?" Times used to be a lot simpler–and I think maybe even a lot more fun–although the thought of hosting a preschool now is daunting. I can barely keep up with my grandchildren.

Creative Clay

From the Food Lab

1 c. cornstarch
2 c. baking soda (1 lb. pkg.)
1¼ c. cold water

Stir starch and soda together. Mix in cold water and cook over medium heat, stirring constantly, until mixture has consistency of mashed potatoes. Turn onto a plate and cover with a damp cloth until cool enough to handle. Then knead. Use immediately or store in airtight container.

NOTE: Clay can be modeled or rolled thin and cut with cookie cutters. Clay creations will dry at room temperature in 3 days or can be dried in a 200° oven.

Finger Paints

From the Food Lab

2 T. cornstarch **1 c. cold water**

Mix to smooth consistency. Cook until clear and of pudding thickness. Add poster paint or other coloring while warm. Works best on freezer wrap, on the wax-coated side.

David's Cooking at Home

As Told by My Brother David

1 can Ranch-Style Beans **Salt & pepper**

Hurry home from working hard. Open the beans, pour into pot and boil 30 seconds. Pour on a plate, add salt and pepper. Eat. Put your plate and the pot in the sink for your sisters to wash later.

I love my brother to death! He is a survivor and has never met a stranger. His early eating habits mirrored Daddy's very closely–that is to say, he was a picky eater. He was skinny as a rail, with a white curly head of hair. As he approached his teens, the hair got longer and longer. He was the only white boy at Waller High School with an Afro. For his 40th birthday party, I made all the girls a wig (really it was more like a shower cap) from imitation sheepskin. We looked like wooly boogers dancing around our embarrassed brother. Tables were decorated in style with black table cloths and Ranch-Style Bean cans artistically placed. Oh, I almost forgot, of course we served barbecue and Ranch-Style Beans!

David's School Lunch

2 slices white bread
Peanut butter
Grape jelly

Spread the peanut butter and jelly on a piece of bread; top with the other piece of bread. Wrap.

NOTE: I don't know if David cut his sandwich in half or not. We sister's were always jealous: David didn't have to do dishes–he got to take the trash out, burn it, play with fire, mow the grass on a riding lawnmower, and drive the tractor.

I remember when we were much younger, David lived in California. When he came home, as usual, music was a part of our gathering. David has played guitar and been a part of a band of some sort or another most of his life. He is really good and has two CDs of which to boast. Now he is building a DJ business so he can retire in style; he even owns his own tuxedos. I digress...when he and his family came home, it was always an occasion, and on this occasion, he asked, "Verna, what did you do with the money Mama gave you?" Remember, music was abounding and I was singing along. Gullible as I am, I asked, "What money?" He replied, "The money Mama gave you for singing lessons." I let him live–David is a survivor! I still wish those big boys hadn't broken my drumsticks. I am so glad I have a brother.

Family is what counts. Here we are, four siblings all squeezed into a tiny photo for a pocket watch we gave Daddy on his 80th birthday.

Flavored Butters

School Dinner Recipe

Lemon Butter

Melt ¼ cup butter. Add 1 to 2 tablespoons lemon juice, 2 tablespoons snipped parsley, ½ teaspoon salt, and a dash pepper. Heat and serve over fresh steamed veggies or any type of seafood.

Garlic Butter

Whip ½ cup softened butter until fluffy. Stir in 1 tablespoon snipped parsley and 1 clove crushed garlic. I like to use a garlic press; the Pampered Chef one works great. Spoon into serving dish and refrigerate the butter; allow to come to room temperature before serving.

Orange Butter

Whip ½ cup softened butter with 2 teaspoons grated orange peel.

Honey Butter

In a small mixing bowl, whip ½ cup soft butter with ½ cup honey until fluffy. For sweeter flavor, add 2 tablespoons of brown sugar before whipping.

I mentioned that we often found something we had forgotten to serve in the refrigerator after a school dinner was over; often times it was bowls of these beautiful and tasty whipped butters. Speaking of butter, I am not that old, but I remember we had a cow that Mama milked when I was a little girl. We had fresh milk and churned butter. We would put the butterfat (cream skimmed off the top of milk) in an antique butter churn and turn the handle until the fat turned to butter. The liquid left was the original buttermilk. Buttermilk today is a cultured product and quite different. I have my grandma's big metal spoon that she used to skim the butterfat off of the top of milk. I even have her big pottery bowl that the milk was kept it, but I don't have a churn or a cow! Butter could be made today using whipped cream and a blender or electric mixer, but why bother?

Fresh Ricotta

Cheesecloth*
8 c. whole milk
1 tsp. salt
3 T. fresh lemon juice

Line large strainer with 4 layers of cheesecloth and set over a large bowl; set aside. In heavy 4-quart saucepan, heat milk and salt to boiling over low heat, stirring to prevent milk from scorching. Watch closely. Stir in lemon juice; cover and remove from heat. Let stand 5 minutes. With slotted spoon, gently transfer curds from saucepan to lined strainer. Drain 3 minutes. Discard whey in bowl. Transfer ricotta to clean bowl; cover, and refrigerate up to 1 week.

*Cheesecloth can be found in the kitchen supply aisle of most supermarkets.

Reduced-Fat Ricotta

Substitute 4 cups reduced-fat (2%) milk for 4 cups whole milk.
Yield: 15 ounces or about 2 cups

WHAT WAS LITTLE MISS MUFFETT EATING?

By the way, milk contains two parts: the curd and the whey. The curd is the part that *curdles* when sour and is used in cheese-making. Whey is the liquid part, and also the part that used to be left over from churning milk into butter. The fat solidified and the whey, or *buttermilk*, was left. So now you know what Little Miss Muffett was really eating when that spider sat down beside her!

Indian-Style Cashews

In a hot skillet, toss cashews with a bit of safflower oil, garam marsala and salt until coated. Transfer to a bowl and add dried apricots.

NOTE: I had never used garam marsala until I discovered that I am allergic to about 28 foods and went on a mission to find ingredients I could eat. Garam marsala adds tasty variety to regular foods.

Goat Cheese Marinara

Jennie

½ white onion
2 cloves fresh garlic
Jar of chunky spaghetti sauce
Basil
Garlic
Oregano
Pepper
Balsamic vinegar
Sugar
4 T. basil pesto sauce
¼ log goat cheese, cut into 4 pats
Fresh mushrooms (if desired)

Chop half of a white onion, mince some fresh garlic and sauté in a cast iron skillet with a splash of olive oil. If using mushrooms, slice and add with the onion and garlic. Add fresh cracked pepper to the mixture. Once the onions are translucent, add the jar of spaghetti sauce. Season with pepper, basil, garlic, and oregano to taste; add a couple dashes of balsamic vinegar and a dash of red wine, if there happens to be some open. Add a tiny bit of sugar, just a pinch. Let this simmer. Taste for perfection. Add dollops of basil pesto sauce. Once this has thoroughly cooked, add chunks of goat cheese and let melt a bit.

NOTE: According to Jennie: "This is my rendition of a treat from an airport pub–turned out to be the best thing about a layover in Denver and is a guaranteed crowd-pleaser every time. This can be served as an appetizer in a cast iron skillet with toasted French bread or bagel chips or used as a sauce with meatballs over pasta."

Grandma Werner's Cinnamon Pecans

Nurse Werner

1 c. sugar
1 tsp. vanilla
1 tsp. cinnamon
⅓ c. canned milk
3 c. pecans

Combine sugar, cinnamon, and milk in a saucepan and boil until mixture reaches soft-boil stage. Remove from stove and add pecans. Spread on waxed paper separating pecans with fingers.

NOTE: These are so delicious–I found at least 4 copies of this recipe in my collection. I must have asked for the recipe every time Nurse Werner brought them to school. I know she must have thought I was senile asking for the recipe so many times. Maybe now all my recipes will be organized–for a while at least.

Koch Kase

(a.k.a. Cooked Cheese)

24 oz. cottage cheese, small curd, not drained
2 tsp. baking soda
5 T. flour
1 c. margarine
Caraway seeds

Mix the cottage cheese and baking soda in a bowl and let stand for at least 30 minutes. Stir the flour into the cheese mixture. In a large nonstick fry pan melt the margarine. (Do not use diet margarine.) Add cheese mixture to melted margarine and cook until creamy, slightly thickened, and cottage cheese is melted. Stir in caraway seeds to taste. Spread on fresh baked bread or crackers. Store in refrigerator and it will thicken.

> Mama tells me about the Koch Kase her mother made when she was growing up. That's cooked cheese and they had it between two slices of fresh-baked bread. Mama doesn't remember how it was made, just eating it when they had little else; she says it was the best thing she has ever eaten. I found a recipe, made a few adaptations, and Mama says, "It's close, very close. Grandma didn't put caraway seeds though."

No-Salt Substitute

5 tsp. onion powder
1 T. garlic powder
1 T. paprika
1 T. dry mustard
1 tsp. thyme
½ tsp. white pepper
½ tsp. celery seeds, crushed

Mix all ingredients and store in a tightly covered container in a cool, dark place. Never store spices near the stove—they lose their zip.

"To the old saying that man built the house but woman made of it a 'home" might be added the modern supplement that woman accepted cooking as a chore but man has made of it a recreation." – Emily Post

Spicy Ketchup

My Grandson, Peyton

1 c. ketchup
1 tsp. Cajun seasoning
½ tsp. Tabasco sauce

Mix everything together real good. Refrigerate for at least 20 minutes. Serve with anything you would normally eat ketchup with: chicken nuggets, french fries, or fish.

NOTE: Peyton told this recipe to me when he found out I was writing a cookbook. Later, he came over one weekend and I asked him to get out the measuring cups so I could make sure he had the correct amounts. He told me, "We don't have to do that because I used Mom's measuring stuff like she showed me." Never underestimate the power of example.

My grandson is creative in the kitchen and loves to cook. I am thrilled that he shares his cooking experiences with me.

Shrimp Batter

Rosemary

1 egg
1 c. ice water
1 c. flour
1 tsp. salt
1 tsp. sugar
Pepper to taste
1½ c. flour
1½ c. cornmeal

Beat the egg and mix together with water, 1 cup flour, salt, sugar, and pepper. Combine 1½ cups of flour and cornmeal together with a little more salt and pepper in a Ziploc bag. Dip shrimp in batter, then shake in dry mixture. Fry.

NOTE: With so many shrimp recipes, there has to be more than one opinion about the best batter for frying those Gulf Coast delicacies.

Sweetened Condensed Milk

1 c. non-fat dry milk
⅔ c. sugar
⅓ c. boiling water
3 T. butter

Place all ingredients in blender and mix well. Use in all recipes that call for "Eagle Brand" milk.

All Purpose Crepe Batter

Janis

4 eggs
¼ tsp. salt
2 c. unbleached flour
2¼ c. milk
¼ c. butter, melted

In medium bowl, combine eggs and salt. Gradually add flour alternately with milk, whisking constantly until smooth. Whisk in melted butter. Refrigerate batter for at least one hour. Cook on upside-down crepe griddle or in traditional crepe pan. May be covered and refrigerated 2–3 days. Return to room temperature or warm before filling. Yield: about 32 crepes

NOTE: Fill these crepes following Chicken Crepes recipe, page 155, or turn into a luscious dessert using the Chocolate Éclair Crepes recipe, page 256. A long time ago Janis owned a tea room and she says, "Customers all loved these crepes. My family really likes them, too."

Texas Trash

This recipe is an old one...might even be the original Texas Trash

1 med. box (5–6 c.) Cheerios
1 med. box (5–6 c.) Rice Chex
1 med. box (5–6 c.) Corn Chex
2 c. mixed nuts or peanuts
1 pkg. (3 c.) thin pretzel sticks
1 c. oleo (margarine)

SEASONINGS
1 T. Worcestershire sauce
2 T. garlic powder
2 T. season salt
2–2½ tsp. crushed red pepper
½ c. bacon drippings

Put together cereals, nuts, and pretzel sticks. Melt oleo and put seasonings in with it. Once all the cereals are together, place them in electric roaster. Need not spray this pan at all. Once these are placed in this pan, pour oleo mixture on top of cereal mixture. Mix well and bake at 325° for 10 minutes, then 200° to 225° for 50 to 60 minutes. Stir often and well. Take mixture and place in quart jars and seal. Be sure and seal mixture while hot. This makes the flavor stay.

NOTE: When stirring all ingredients, try and be gentle with spoon, so it won't crush mixture.

Mama would keep a jar of this between her and Daddy's recliners for an afternoon or late night snack. One year, she finally shared the recipe with everyone by giving us each a jar of our own Texas Trash along with the recipe glued onto green construction paper–both cut out with pinking shears, tied on with a ribbon. How special that was.

Notes

CANNING

Apple Butter

Donna's Granny

4 lb. tart apples
2 c. cider
3 c. sugar
¼ tsp. salt
1 tsp. ground cinnamon
¼ tsp. ground cloves
2 T. lemon peel, grated
2 T. lemon juice

Sterilize 5 (8 oz.) jelly glasses. Wash apples; remove stem and blossom ends; cut up; do not pare or core. In large saucepan, combine apples and cider. Bring to boiling; reduce heat and cook until soft-about 15 minutes. Press mixture through strainer or mill. Measure pulp; there should be about 7 cups. Preheat oven to 300°. Combine apple pulp with rest of ingredients; mix well. Divide evenly into two 13 x 9 x 2-inch baking dishes. Bake uncovered 2 hours, stirring occasionally. Pour immediately into jars or glasses. Cover at once with ⅛-inch hot melted paraffin. (see note) Yield: 2½ pints

NOTE: When melting paraffin, it is best to cut up wax and place in a container in a pan of boiling water to melt. Never melt it over direct heat as it may catch on fire. About this recipe Donna says, "Wish I had some apples! This apple butter is so good. We always made it with a whole bushel of Colorado apples Mama and Daddy brought back from deer hunting."

Grape Jelly

My Mama

3 c. Welch's Grape Juice
1 c. water
4½ c. sugar
1 pkg. Sure-Jell

Follow instructions on Sure-Jell package exactly. Don't deviate from them or you won't have good jelly.

Bread & Butter Pickles

Circa: May 29, 1972

2 qt. cucumbers
4 lg. onions
1 green pepper
¼ c. coarse salt
2½ c. sugar
¾ tsp. turmeric
¼ tsp. powdered cloves
1 T. mustard seed (white)
½ tsp. celery seed
1 tsp. ginger
3½ c. vinegar

Slice onions and cucumbers into thin pieces. Cut pepper into narrow strips. Combine and sprinkle with salt; let stand 3 hours. Rinse off salt with cold water and drain. Combine remaining ingredients and heat to scalding. Add drained vegetables and heat just to boiling. Pack and seal at once in sterilized jars.

NOTE: We had a small pot of water held at a simmer on the stove and placed the jar lid and ring sets in there to sterilize. Just use a pair of tongs to get each set out and place on top of clean jar rim. Tighten. While the bread and butter pickles were soaking in the salt, undoubtedly, we had dill pickles, tomato relish, and who-knows-what-else going on. We definitely had the multitasking down to a fine art.

Jalapeño Jelly

Mom

3 jalapeño peppers
4 bell peppers
1 c. white vinegar
5 c. sugar
1 bottle liquid pectin

Cut peppers in half. Remove seeds and stems. Run peppers through food grinder, using fine blade. Use all the juice. Slowly boil first four ingredients for 10 minutes. Remove from heat. Add liquid pectin and boil hard 1 minute. Pour into sterilized half-pint jars, to within ½-inch of top. Put on cap. Screw band firmly tight. Process in boiling water bath 5 minutes or seal with paraffin. Yield: 5 half-pint jars. Instead of processing in boiling water bath, place jar caps in boiling water and seal with bands. Make sure the top rim of jar is clean.

NOTE: Wear gloves when handling the jalapeño peppers or don't get your hands near your eyes for a long time. Those little babies pack a burning punch. I like to serve this jelly over a square of cream cheese with crackers. This makes great teacher gifts, too.

My Mama and Daddy

Jello Fig & Berry Preserves

My Mama

3 c. mashed figs (about 1 lb.)
1 lg. (8 serving-size) pkg. strawberry flavored gelatin
2½ c. sugar
Squeeze of fresh lemon juice

Thoroughly mix figs, gelatin, sugar, and lemon juice in a large, heavy saucepan. Bring to a boil over medium heat; continue boiling 30 minutes, stirring occasionally. Pour quickly into sterilized canning jars, wipe tops with a clean cloth, carefully run a knife blade around edge to release bubbles, and seal at once with a sterilized lid and ring. Yield: 5–6 (6-ounce) canning jars

NOTE: Growing up, we had two huge, I mean really huge, fig trees in the pasture with the cows. Mama made a ton of pint jars full of fig preserves and she and Daddy were the only ones who ate them. For fig preserves, she cut figs in half, added a little water and sugar and cooked like above until they were done, making sure they were sweet enough. She started making strawberry-fig preserves when she found this recipe in the newspaper and fooled us for a while. They really do taste like strawberries.

SAFETY: Home canning is not safe unless proper procedures are followed, so make sure you have studied up on the subject–preferably seek tutoring from an experienced German lady.

Grandma Wernecke's Dill Pickles

Julie, Following Grams' Recipe

1 qt. vinegar
2 qt. water
¾ scant c. pickling salt
Dill
Cucumbers
Jalapeños, fresh
Powdered alum

- To make brine, mix vinegar, water, and salt. Bring to boil. Keep hot while you're canning.
- Sterilize jars and lids in boiling water (or really hot dishwasher cycle).
- Wash pickles and dill. Slice jalapeños.
- Place dill in the bottom of the jar (enough to cover the bottom, but not too deep).
- Add jalapeños if you're using them (more than 3, less than a handful).
- Pack cucumbers tight in the jar. You should really have to push them in so that they stay tight and don't float.
- Add a little more dill to the top of the jar. Add a dash of alum.
- Pour hot brine in jar and seal with a new, hot lid. Rings should be tight, but with a little room to tighten up when you take them out of the water bath. You can reuse the rings, but the lids are best fresh so they seal well.
- Put in water bath until bright green turns to dull green–5 minutes, but check them. I usually take them out before they're totally dull green. (Don't tell the FDA…)
- Carefully place on towels to dry. You should hear the lids start to pop as they seal.
- Let them cool. Wipe jars to remove dried salt. Check lids for seal (shouldn't pop when you push the top) and tighten the rings. If any jars don't seal, just put in the fridge.
- If you have brine left over store it in the fridge for the next batch.

Pickled Okra

Use this recipe for pickled okra, substituting fresh okra for the pickles.

NOTE: When Mom and I were the Forrest Gump of the garden, we followed these directions. I see that my daughter learned by watching. Our adapted ingredients follow in Mom and Verna's Dill & Hot Garlic Pickles. We always processed packed jars for 20 minutes in the hot water bath. That was a standard for safety. Notice, we did not use alum. We had an abundance of fresh dill from Norman's garden, so we hardly ever used the seed heads. Much better flavor comes from the fronds and stems of fresh, young dill.

Just got back from my daughter Julie's house and she gave me a quart of dill pickles. Like mother, like daughter! A few days later Lydia called and, as usual, she was multitasking. There was a long pause and then she said, "Just a second, Grams. I have to go wipe the pickle juice off my arm. Mom's pickles are so good. Have you ever had one?" Some things never change. And now I am the Grams.

Mama's Dill Pickles

My Mama

½ gal. water
⅔ c. pickling salt
3 c. vinegar, 5% acidity—Heinz preferred
Pinch of alum in each jar
Fresh pickles, scrubbed to remove all the pricklies
Fresh dill

Pack about 1 inch of dill fronds and small stems into bottom of sterilized wide-mouth quart jars. Pack larger pickles tightly and top with smaller pickles. Bring water, salt, and vinegar, to a boil and ladle over pickles. Add pinch of alum (provides crispness). Wipe rim and seal with sterilized jar lids and rims. Fill canning pot with rack about ½–⅔ full of hot water. Heat to boiling. (Do this early on so it's ready when jars are.) Place sealed jars in canning pot and add more water, if needed, to cover. Process for 20 minutes. Remove from water bath and listen for the tops to seal. Jars that do not seal must be processed again or kept in refrigerator. It takes about 6 weeks before pickles are ready to eat.

NOTE: Mama only canned little to medium-size pickles. She filled the top of the jar with the tiniest pickles of all. Pickles grow exceptionally fast, hiding under the leaves and becoming a cucumber before you know it!

We always had a garden: a very large garden with lots of watermelons, cantaloupes, and fresh sweet corn, plus tomatoes, squash, black eyed peas, okra, and green beans. When it came to pickles, Daddy always picked the smallest ones–he loved those little bitty ones and would pick the pickles every morning to snag them. He would save a few cucumber size for Mama to make her cucumber salad and throw the rest over the fence to the cows. I remember one year Mama had so many pickles to can she tried cleaning them in the washing machine on the wash cycle. I don't think she put it through the spin cycle though. It worked!

Mom & Verna's Dill & Hot Garlic Dill Pickles

½ gal. water
¾ c. salt
3 c. vinegar with 5% acidity
Fresh pickles, sm. to med. size
Fresh dill

FOR HOT GARLIC DILL
3–4 garlic cloves, peeled
3–4 jalapeños, whole

Follow instructions for Grandma Wernecke's Pickles, but process for a full 20 minutes.

FROM "MY MEMORIES OF MOM": "Canning and preserving the world. Perfecting recipes and never having to open a store-bought jar or can for years: dill pickles, hot-garlic dill pickles, bread-and-butter pickles, squash pickles, ketchup, tomato relish, tomato sauce, canned tomatoes, picante sauce, green beans, corn, pinto beans, black-eyed peas, okra; fig, strawberry, strawberry-fig, peach, and plum jelly and preserves–your carport and garage were a food processing factory every summer. We were the Forrest Gump of the garden. At one time I counted over 18 dozen pints, 16 half-gallons, and who knows how many quarts of food–those were just my portion of the goods. Let's not forget the foods put-up in the freezer. One summer we thought we burned that old freezer out, but it just couldn't keep up with us! Then there were the fresh vegetables–eggplant fritters and your amazing fried chicken; squash, cantaloupe, and watermelon." My mother-in-law was a special person and very much a mother to me. I miss her dearly. This is an excerpt from my writings after her death.

"When one has tasted watermelon he knows what the angels eat."
– Mark Twain

Hot Tomato Relish

Grandma Wernecke

1 gal. tomatoes
3 c. sugar
3 lg. onions
1 c. vinegar
1 tsp. cinnamon
1 tsp. salt
1 tsp. black pepper
1 green hot pepper

Crush tomatoes and dice hot pepper. Then combine all ingredients in large, heavy pot. Boil until thickened, stirring often. This usually takes at least 30 minutes. Pack in hot sterilized jars leaving ½-inch head space; clean rim and seal with hot lids and rings.

Picante Sauce, Circa 1980

Mom & Verna

1 gal. + 1 qt. tomatoes, cut into sm. pieces
3 lg. onions, chopped
1½ c. sugar
4 jalapeño peppers, chopped
2 cloves garlic, minced
1 T. salt
1 tsp. cumin
1 tsp. basil, crushed
½ tsp. cayenne pepper
1 c. vinegar

Cook until thick, about an hour or so. Ladle into sterilized pint jars, wipe top edge clean, and seal with sterilized lids and rings.

NOTE: When Mom and I started canning, circa 1980, we adapted Grandma Wernecke's recipe for hot tomato relish, which was actually sweet. It had 3 cups sugar and only one green hot pepper. We adapted that recipe a little more with every batch we made until we derived our refined version of picante sauce on the next page. It took a few years, but we finally got it right. Pace can be thankful we never marketed it–yes, it was that good. Try any of these three recipes for a great tasting treat.

"In the childhood memories of every good cook there's a large kitchen, a warm stove, a simmering pot, and a mom." – Barbara Costikyan

Refined Picante Sauce

Mom & Verna

1 gal. tomatoes, cut in sm. pieces
3 lg. onions, chopped
1 T. sugar
2 jalapeño peppers, chopped
3 long green peppers, chopped
2 cloves garlic, minced
2 T. + 1 tsp. salt
2 tsp. cumin
1 T. cayenne pepper
¼ c. vinegar
1 tsp. coriander

Cook until thick, about an hour or so. Ladle into sterilized pint jars, wipe top edge clean, and seal with sterilized lids and rings.

Spiced Tomato Sauce

Mom & Verna

13 c. pureed, cooked tomatoes
2 tsp. oregano
1 tsp. basil
1 tsp. onion powder
1 tsp. garlic powder
1 tsp. marjoram
1 tsp. red peppers, dried

Cook 15 minutes. Put in hot sterilized jars and seal. Process in hot water bath 20 minutes.

Squash Pickles

Mom & Verna

8 c. sm. to med. yellow squash, sliced ¼-inch thick
2 c. white onion, sliced
2 c. green pepper, chopped

Soak these ingredients in ¾ cup salt and 3 quarts ice and water. Drain.

2 c. vinegar
3 c. sugar
2 T. mustard seed
2 tsp. celery seed

Bring these ingredients to a boil. Add vegetables and bring to a simmer. Pack in sterilized jars and seal. Yield: 3 pints

NOTE: Sometimes we tied the mustard and celery seed in cheesecloth and removed after cooking. Every year we made slight adaptations to the recipes we used. We also pickled zucchini using this recipe.

Sweet Jalapeño Pickles

Julie

1 gal. sliced hamburger dill pickles, drained
1 bag (4 lb.) sugar
1 pt. pickled jalapeño slices

Drain pickles. Mix ingredients together and return to gallon jar. Refrigerate. Stir once a day for seven days. Place in quart or pint jars and keep refrigerated. Share with friends.

NOTE: Use 1 quart of jalapeños for hotter pickles. Seal jars in hot water bath if desired. Julie just keeps hers in the refrigerator.

JULIE WRITES: "Mom, you should be proud, the pickles and salsa were a huge hit at the races! The Front Row Motorsports racing team loved them. I can't even remember how many I promised okra in November. You and Grandma taught me everything I know about canning and Jason and I just applied the knowledge. Thank you."

Notes

RECIPE INDEX

ENTRÉES: PORK, 183

ENTRÉES: SEAFOOD, 201

PIES, 279

SALADS, 69

SALADS, 69

SOUPS, 53

VEGETABLES & SIDE DISHES, 93

LESSONS

BASIC SKILLS

RECIPE SOURCES

TEACHER BAKE-OFF & PROJECT SHOW